ISRAEL/PALESTINE —————

D0859246

Hot Spots series

ISRAEL/PALESTINE ──────

Alan Dowty

Fourth Edition

polity

Copyright © Alan Dowty 2017

The right of Alan Dowty to be identified as Author of this Work has been asserted in accordance with the UK Copyright, Designs and Patents Act 1988.

First edition published in 2005 by Polity Press
This fourth edition first published in 2017 by Polity Press
Reprinted: 2019, 2020

Polity Press
65 Bridge Street
Cambridge CB2 1UR, UK

Polity Press
350 Main Street
Malden, MA 02148, USA

All rights reserved. Except for the quotation of short passages for the purpose of criticism and review, no part of this publication may be reproduced, stored in a retrieval system or transmitted, in any form or by any means, electronic, mechanical, photocopying, recording or otherwise, without the prior permission of the publisher.

ISBN-13: 978-1-5095-2077-0 (hardback)
ISBN-13: 978-1-5095-2078-7 (paperback)

ALibrary of Congress Cataloging-in-Publication Data

Names: Dowty, Alan, 1940- author.
Title: Israel/Palestine / Alan Dowty.
Other titles: Hot spots in global politics.
Description: 4th edition. | Cambridge, UK : Polity Press, 2017. | Series: Hot
   spots in global politics | Includes bibliographical references and index.
Identifiers: LCCN 2017001650 (print) | LCCN 2017007937 (ebook) | ISBN
   9781509520770 (hardback) | ISBN 9781509520787 (pbk.) | ISBN 9781509520800
   (Mobi) | ISBN 9781509520817 (Epub)
Subjects: LCSH: Arab-Israeli conflict--History. | Jewish-Arab
   relations--History. | Palestinian Arabs. | Israel--Politics and
   government. | Palestine--Politics and government. | West Bank--Politics
   and government. | Gaza Strip--Politics and government. |
   Jerusalem--Politics and government. | Zionism--History.
Classification: LCC DS119.76 .D69 2017 (print) | LCC DS119.76 (ebook) | DDC
   956.04--dc23
LC record available at https://lccn.loc.gov/2017001650

Typeset in 10.5 on 12pt Sabon by
Servis Filmsetting Ltd, Stockport, Cheshire
Printed and bound in the United States by LSC Communications

The publisher has used its best endeavors to ensure that the URLs for external websites referred to in this book are correct and active at the time of going to press. However, the publisher has no responsibility for the websites and can make no guarantee that a site will remain live or that the content is or will remain appropriate.

Every effort has been made to trace all copyright holders, but if any have been inadvertently overlooked the publisher will be pleased to include any necessary credits in any subsequent reprint or edition.

For further information on Polity, visit our website:
politybooks.com

This book is dedicated to

SANDRA WINICUR

Strength and honor are her clothing, and she shall rejoice in time to come. She opens her mouth with wisdom, and in her tongue is the law of kindness.

Proverbs 31: 25-6

Contents ────────────────────────

Preface ─────────────────────────────────

Can an introduction to the highly charged Arab–Israel conflict be "objective" and yet communicate the depth of emotions and humanity on both sides? Perhaps the goal is hopelessly naive, as modern theories of knowledge have repeatedly claimed; indeed, the very concept of objectivity has in recent decades been subjected to relentless attack. Yet it is precisely in the discussion of hotly contested issues, where it is hardest to achieve, that the subject refuses to go away. Perhaps it is an unachievable goal, but in my view that does not relieve us as scholars from the responsibility of trying to approach it as much as we possibly can.

The approach I have followed in this introduction to the clash between Israelis and Palestinians is to present the opposed perspectives in their full intensity, leaving readers to think through the claims and counterclaims for themselves. The analysis follows a conceptual framework that emphasizes the various approaches to resolution of the conflict.

The book assumes no previous knowledge on the part of the reader. It covers the basic features of the confrontation with a strong historical emphasis, since the very vocabulary of the conflict requires historical knowledge. (The text is followed by a chronology, as well as suggestions for further reading and Internet links.) But within this framework, it focuses on larger developments such as changing public attitudes on both sides, rather than the details of forgotten diplomatic episodes.

The original purpose in offering this account, as stated at the outset, was "to chart the origins and evolution of the conflict, to explore the different motivations and claims of those groups involved, and to discuss the prospects for resolution."

I am grateful to Louise Knight and her fellow editors at Polity for their confidence and support at all stages, and to Susan Beer for her superb copy-editing. Since this book draws on the accumulated wisdom, such as it is, of over forty years of academic and personal involvement in the conflict, it would be pointlessly tedious to try to mention everyone who has had some influence, direct or indirect, on the content of these pages. I will simply mention those who read all or part of the manuscript and made useful suggestions, which I probably should have used more extensively: Sandra Winicur (as usual, my closest reader), Phil Mikesell, David Freeman.

Gail, my life's partner, who was an extraordinary source of support through the first three editions of this book, is no longer with me for the fourth. But her presence is on every page.

Maps, Figures, and Tables ———————

Maps

Figures

Tables

| 1 | Introduction: Two Worlds Collide |

However, if the time comes when the life of our people in Eretz Israel develops to the point of encroaching upon the native population, they will not easily yield their place ...

Zionist leader Ahad Ha'am (Ginzberg 1891: 162)

Dispelling Myths

The conflict over Israel/Palestine may be the quintessential "hot spot" on today's globe. Even the label attached to it is contentious. If we call it a conflict over "Israel," Palestinian or Arab observers would consider that a Zionist or pro-Israel framework. By the same token, calling it a conflict over "Palestine" favors the definition and terminology of anti-Zionist critics of Israel. I will, therefore, use both labels, depending on whose viewpoint is on stage, and also employ the somewhat awkward compromise of "Israel/Palestine."

There is another problem with the label. Although the clash between Israelis and Palestinian Arabs is the core of the conflict, the involvement of neighboring Arab states after the emergence of Israel in 1948 expanded the confrontation into an "Arab–Israeli" conflict. Before then, Jews (they were not yet Israelis) contended with Arabs within British-ruled Palestine, a Mandate of the League of Nations, and Arab states played secondary roles. The label "Arab–Israeli conflict" is still more common, even though Palestinians have reclaimed their previous position as Israel's major antagonists, and Arab states have to some extent disengaged (Egypt and Jordan have signed peace treaties with Israel). Given this re-emergence of the core conflict and the Palestinians as core actors, we will focus on "Israel/Palestine," while not overlooking the historical importance and current role of Arab nations.

By any label, the Arab–Israeli conflict (or Israel's fight for existence, or the Palestine question) is often described as the bloodiest, or one of the bloodiest, battlegrounds in today's world. Pundits speak about "age-old ethnic hatreds" between Arabs and Jews going back "thousands of years," about the "clash of religions" between Islam and Judaism that lies at the center of these hatreds, and about the "unceasing cycle of violence" that fuels the hatreds and intensifies the conflict, making it an "unending and insoluble" dilemma. There is a major problem with these characterizations. They are all myths.

- This is not an "age-old" conflict. Its origins lie in the 1880s, when Jewish immigrants from Eastern Europe began settling in the historical Land of Israel (*Eretz Yisrael*), then a part of the Turkish Ottoman Empire, in order to re-establish a Jewish presence there. The broader Arab–Israeli dimension came into full existence only with the 1947–9 war.
- This is not a conflict caused by ethnic hatreds. For one thing, the ethnic identity of the existing population in *Eretz Yisrael/Filastin* as Arabs or as Palestinians was only beginning to emerge in the late nineteenth and early twentieth centuries, and the assertion of this identity came more in reaction to conflict with Jewish settlers than as a cause of it. For that matter, the assertion that Jews constitute an ethnic group as well as a religion – an assertion that was necessary in order to stake out a territorial claim in the "national homeland" – was a relatively new, and not yet universally accepted, idea among Jews. Clearly mutual hatred between Jews and Arabs has grown apace over the

course of the conflict, and it has much in common with patterns of ethnic conflict elsewhere (I will return to this issue). But historically, Jewish minorities generally fared better among Arab populations than in most European states.

- This is not a conflict rooted in a "clash of religions." To be sure, as the conflict developed, it created religious issues, and the religious dimension has become increasingly important. But Judaism is a non-proselytizing religion that accepts Islam as a legitimate monotheistic faith, while Islam regards Jews and Christians as "People of the Book" or *dhimmi* (protected people) who, while not having equal status with Muslims, are regarded as part of a common tradition and are given freedom to practice their own religions. Again, the position of Jews in Muslim (including Arab) societies was generally better than their position in Christian states; they were subject to certain restrictions, but within this framework were generally secure from arbitrary persecution (Lewis 1984). The same could not be said in Europe, at least during the more turbulent periods. If Jews fleeing the pogroms (racial massacres) of late nineteenth-century Tsarist Russia had entered the Ottoman Empire seeking no more than the right to live as a minority practicing its own religion, there would have been no Arab–Israeli conflict.

- Finally – though this is more arguable – this is not a conflict of unceasing violence, nor are there compelling grounds for pronouncing it "insoluble." During the century and a quarter of its existence, the struggle between Jews/Israelis and Arabs/Palestinians has undergone several key transformations in intensity and scope. Along with periods of dramatic and explosive violence, there have been periods of relative stability and quiet. There has been continued economic interaction. In terms of loss of human life, the Arab–Israel conflict is far from the "bloodiest" conflict of the last century; it is dwarfed not only by general wars such as the two world wars, but also by other ethnic conflicts that have involved the slaughter of entire populations.

Seeing the conflict in this long-range perspective also provides the best evidence that it is not, in fact, insoluble. We see that the violence is not constant; there must be, therefore, some conditions under which the two sides exercise restraint. This is not simply an irrational eruption of hatred and hostility. In fact, contrary to the popular image, the gap between mainstream opinion on the two sides has actually narrowed over time. To show this, we must look at the broad historical picture, which will follow this introduction.

Defining the Conflict

The Israel/Palestine issue is not, then, age-old; it is not a result of long-standing antipathies between Arab and Jew, is not (at least originally) about religious differences, and is less unremittingly and hopelessly violent than its public image would indicate. This clears away some common misunderstandings. But how, then, do we define and characterize this dramatic clash that has seized the world's attention?

The core of the Israeli–Palestinian conflict is the claim of two peoples to the same piece of land. Stripped of other layers and dimensions added over the years, it was and is a clash between a Jewish national movement (Zionism) seeking to establish a Jewish state in *Eretz Yisrael* – the historic Land of Israel – and an Arab/Palestinian national movement defining the same territory as *Filastin* (Palestine) and regarding it as an integral part of the Arab world. Supporters of Israel would prefer to define the core issue in somewhat different language; they argue that the basic cause of the conflict is the refusal of Palestinians and other Arabs to acknowledge the existence and legitimacy of a Jewish state in the historic Jewish homeland. Arabs define the core issue as the violation of the natural right of the Palestinian people to self-determination in its ancestral homeland. But these two opposed formulations both actually confirm the basic definition above; stripped of the advocacy of their own answers, both agree that this is a question of conflicting claims to the same territory.

This hardly makes Israel/Palestine a unique case. Nations and groups within nations fight over territory as often as anything. But in contrast to most other territorial conflicts, the claims overlap totally in this case. By most definitions *Eretz Yisrael* and *Filastin* are the same exact piece of land, delineated conveniently (if fairly recently) by the borders set for the British Mandate of Palestine after World War I. So long as both sides claim all of it, the loser faces the threat of being left stateless. Just as two objects cannot occupy the same space at the same time, so two sovereign states cannot govern the same territory at the same time. Without territorial compromise, this becomes what game theorists call a zero-sum game: whatever one side gains comes at the expense of the other (gains and losses thus total zero). There is no potential "win–win" outcome where both sides gain. It is a situation of total conflict, with no incentives for cooperation or negotiation.

A fight over territory is a "real" conflict, in the sense that it is not simply a result of emotions, misunderstandings, misperceptions, and other human imperfections. Even if all hostile thoughts and emotions could be eliminated, the question would remain: Who gets what? This brings us to a basic distinction that is critical in analyzing international conflicts. Objective sources of conflict, like territory, can be thought of as "givens": they exist independently of our thoughts and feelings, and by their very existence they create differences of interest among us. Not only land, but all forms of wealth and material resources raise the issue of "who gets what." The same is true of intangible assets such as political power and national security; just as there is not enough wealth to satisfy everyone's potential demands, so the ability of some to determine public policy means that those with conflicting policy goals will be dissatisfied. Land, wealth, and power are all "scarce goods"; a conflict of interest exists because it is impossible to meet all demands, and we need a political process to decide who gets what. Among states, the issue of security plays out in a similar way, since measures that make one state feel more secure (arms buildups, territorial gains, alliances, intervention) makes other states feel less secure.

This is known as the security dilemma, and it explains why frictions and conflict among states are not necessarily a sign that their leaders are simply being obtuse and unreasonable. Emphasis on objective sources of conflict is characteristic of those who stress rational behavior and focus on "interests" in the analysis of politics, domestic or international, such as the "realist" school of thought. When different interests are created by the fact that not all demands can be met, pursuit of one's own interest is hardly irrational. It is no more remarkable than the expectation that, in the marketplace, sellers will press for the highest price and buyers will look for the lowest. Of course the assumption of rationality as a guideline does not mean that all conflict is, in fact, over such "real" issues; nor does it eliminate the possibility that human beings, even when they are trying to do the "rational" thing, do not often make horrendous mistakes and miscalculations. Nevertheless, and despite such reservations, to the extent that conflicts are "objective" there are certain expectations about the behavior of the parties involved. In the first place, there should be less expectation that the conflict can be eliminated completely, since no amount of goodwill can offset the fact that something real is at stake and that each side will emerge with either less or more of it. On the other hand, since the two parties are presumably acting on the basis of interest rather than emotion or doctrine, there is greater hope for a cooperative or compromise solution – especially since, in the real world, conflicts are rarely "zero-sum," and a "win–win" outcome is often possible.

This is important in the Israeli/Palestinian case. The core issue – land – is a real issue in which a rational negotiated solution, such as partition, is theoretically possible. Chapter 4 will take up this thread of thought. But in the meantime we need to look at other, non-objective, conflict patterns, which may not have been critical in the origins of this conflict but which have clearly developed over time as a result of it. What is not objective is, by definition, *subjective*: produced by the mind, feelings, or temperament of the subject. This includes ideas and ideologies, perceptions and misperceptions, cultural and societal biases, emotions and passions – in short, the whole spectrum of mental activity. Theoretically, conflicts rooted in subjective thoughts and feelings should be more soluble, since they do not necessarily correspond to a "real" conflict of interest. Misunderstandings, passions, and distrust are in a sense artificial; since they are creations of our minds, our minds can also erase them. But, by the same token, they may be less responsive to a self-interested bar-gaining process, since they are not the result of a "rational" process. Are "irrational" hatreds or distrusts necessarily easier to resolve than conflicts of interest? It seems that aggressive ideas or emotions, or even simple distrust, can sometimes drive combatants into a "lose–lose" outcome, damaging their presumed interests.

Subjective sources of conflict are a natural focus for behavioral scientists who study the psychological, cultural, and societal aspects of human behavior. Scholars and practitioners in the field of conflict resolution, and "normative" or "idealist" theorists who advocate the strengthening of international law and morality, also tend to emphasize subjective factors such as misunderstanding or misperception, since they reject the idea that conflict is natural and inevitable, and since these flaws are in theory correctable. Questions from this perspective include such issues as: What is the image of "the enemy"? What is the perception of the other side's aims and methods? How do fear and insecurity influence attitudes and behavior? Do participants understand the impact of their own actions on the other side? As we shall see, these questions are all relevant to the Israeli/Palestinian impasse. Thus, while we begin with an objective core issue (land), we will also pay close attention to the ways in which Israelis and Palestinians perceive and express their respective positions, beginning with the Jewish and Arab backgrounds in chapters 2 and 3 respectively.

This is important because, while Israelis and Palestinians have a territorial conflict, it is not a run-of-the-mill territorial conflict, and it is not only a territorial conflict. Jewish and Arab national movements emerged in the context of late nineteenth- and early twentieth-century nationalism. In recent years nationalism and nationalist conflicts are usually subsumed in the broader category of ethnicity and ethnic conflict, given the flood of ethnic quarrels that broke out following the end of the Cold War.

Ethnic groups, in Max Weber's classic definition, are those human groups that share "a subjective belief in their common descent . . . whether or not an objective blood relationship exists" (Weber 1968: 389). In other words, what is important is self-identification as members of a particular group, whatever the historical basis for that identification (this is particularly important in the Israeli/Palestinian case, where identities have changed over time and have often been challenged by the other side as lacking a historical foundation). In more recent work the definition of an "ethnic group" has been understood broadly to include groups differentiated by color, language, religion, nationality, shared culture or history, or simply a shared consciousness (Horowitz 1985: 53; Stavenhagen 1996: 4–5).

By such standards both Jews and Arabs qualify as "ethnic groups," and their conflict can be categorized as an "ethnic conflict." But the vast majority of ethnic conflicts in the world today take place within nation-states, not between them, and they center on questions of minority rights, civic equality, power sharing, and autonomy. There are aspects of the Arab–Israeli conflict that fit this pattern: the problem of Arab citizens of Israel (about 20 percent of the Israeli population) and the fate of remaining Jewish minorities in some Arab states. Israel's clash with Palestinians in the West Bank and the Gaza Strip (Palestinian areas that Israel has occupied since 1967) does not fit this pattern, since Israel has not annexed these areas. Legally the West Bank and Gaza fall under the international law of wartime occupation, and thus somewhere between an internal and an interstate conflict. In addition, during long periods of time (especially 1948–67) the interstate dimensions of the conflict (Israel versus Egypt, Syria, Jordan, Lebanon) dominated the Israeli/Palestinian core.

It makes better sense, then, to consider this conflict as a "nationalist" conflict within the broader ethnic conflict spectrum, and to look back to the context of emerging nationalism in which its origins lie. "National" conflicts might be defined as clashes involving groups that claim not only an ethnic identity but also the collective political right of national self-determination in their own independent sovereign state. In the second half of the nineteenth century the idea of national self-determination and the nation-state as the basic unit of world politics swept over Europe as group after group discovered, or rediscovered, its identity as a "nation" entitled to statehood. In some cases (Germany, Italy) this led to unification of existing states, while in others (Greece, Serbia, Romania, Bulgaria) it sparked movements for secession from existing multinational empires.

The nationalist spirit of the times made its mark on both Jews and Arabs. A vast majority of the world's Jews lived in Europe at this time, over half of them in Tsarist Russia (which then included most of Poland). The idea of a Jewish nation-state had tremendous positive appeal, given the long Jewish history of statelessness. But Jews were also pushed toward this option by two seemingly contradictory threats. The first, felt more in Western Europe, was the fear that liberalization and extension of civic equality to Jews would lead to massive assimilation and threaten Jewish survival. The second, stronger in Eastern Europe, was that nationalism actually made life more precarious for remaining minorities; emerging nationalist governments celebrated their newly affirmed identities by tyrannizing those who did not share it. The last two decades of the 1800s were scarred by waves of anti-Jewish persecution that threatened simple physical survival. These pressures on the Jewish community will be explored more fully in chapter 2.

Arab populations in the Middle East were also becoming aware of the new winds blowing out of Europe. Most lived in the Ottoman Empire, which had for two centuries been vainly resisting the loss of territory to European powers and the expansion of European influence within its borders. During the nineteenth century the Christian provinces of the Ottoman Empire in the Balkans, one by one, liberated themselves from Turkish rule and proclaimed their own nation-states: Greece, Serbia, Bulgaria, Romania. Arab intellectuals grasped the potential power of nationalism as a mobilizing and unifying force that could restore the Arab world to its grandeur of past centuries, countering both the stagnation of the Ottoman Empire and the threat from European states that seemed to believe that self-determination applied only in Europe. These currents in the Arab world, and in Palestine in particular, will be traced more fully in chapter 3.

Out of this emerged both Jewish and Arab national movements. In an age when others were rediscovering or inventing their own national identities, nationalist Jews (Zionists) felt that by virtue of their 3,500-year history as a people with a distinct identity, culture, religion, history, and language, their claim to national rights was as solid as any. In fact Jews possessed many of the attributes of a "nation," in the modern sense, long before modern nationalism came onto the scene. Yet in one respect Jews were certainly not like other "nations" in nineteenth-century Europe: they lacked a defined territorial base. They were a minority in every European nation, and no state or region on that continent could be claimed as an ancestral homeland. This claim could only be on another continent and across two millennia of history.

Palestinian/Arab nationalism was also anomalous in one important respect. Was it Palestinian nationalism or Arab nationalism, or both? The answer has implications for the response to Zionism. Was Jewish immigration into Palestine the major issue, or was it merely one problem among many? In the early days there was even talk of Arab nationalist–Zionist cooperation against European imperialism: Arabs would concede one corner of their vast domain to the Zionists in return for Jewish support for liberation of the rest. The first Arab nationalists, who appeared in Beirut and Damascus around the turn of the twentieth century, had a pan-Arab focus, calling for the unification of all Arabic-speaking peoples. But in the first decade of the new century the word *Filastin* also made its appearance as a political, and not just a geographic, term within what was to become the Palestinian Arab community. In the decades to come, the pendulum was to swing back and forth between the two poles of identity, depending on the situation in Palestine and, even more, on trends in the broader Arab world.

Yet while Jewish and Palestinian/Arab nationalism both had unusual features, they also had striking parallels to each other. Both involved a Semitic people with roots in antiquity and a long history as a coherent political community. Both peoples looked back to a "golden age" that inspired efforts to restore the position they had once enjoyed. Both felt challenged in one way or another by European modernization and penetration, viewing it as a threat to their identity, and both reacted by turning to an idea that, although itself European in origin, could be turned to their own defense: the idea of national self-determination (Tessler 1994: 2–4).

So far we have seen that Israel/Palestine is a territorial conflict, though one with some unique features. It is also a nationalist conflict, or a conflict between two national movements, though once again one with unique features. There is a third category that is often seen as relevant, and once again the case at hand is not typical of conflicts in that category. This is the category of *colonialist* conflicts, involving the establishment of settlements in foreign lands with the intent of expanding one's own culture and influence. A recent variant is Thomas G. Mitchell's characterization of Israel/Palestine as a "settler conflict," defined as "conflict between a settler population, which was part of a colonization effort, and a native population, which was resisting the colonizing enterprise" (Mitchell 2000: 1). Many elements of this picture fit: Jewish settlers from Europe did enter Palestine in order to establish a new community not based on the existing culture there, and – living in an age when few questioned the superiority of European culture – they believed that their presence would bring the benefits of a more advanced civilization to the native population. From the Palestinian perspective, the uninvited intrusion of European Jewish settlers is part and parcel of the overall penetration of European influence and culture into the Middle East, and cannot be understood outside that context. The Jewish settlers even referred to themselves as "colonists."

However, there was no home country whose interests or specific culture was tied to the enterprise; the settlers received some help from particular powers, but never saw themselves as agents of those powers. In their minds they were reestablishing a Jewish homeland that would, above all, be independent; that was a core element of Zionist thinking. They did not even come from a single home country, but from many; in addition, before 1948 they had no control over the territory in which they settled, and made no effort to rule over the native population (Penslar 2003: 84–98). In sum, since they were not acting on behalf of any colonial power, it is more accurate to characterize their settlement as "colonization" rather than "colonialism."

The Setting: Ottoman Palestine

There was another sense in which the Jewish settlers in late nineteenth-century Ottoman Palestine were not typical colonizers: the land of their dreams was anything but prime colonial territory. Apart from the hostility they faced from both government and populace, the Palestinian provinces of the Ottoman Empire were poor in resources, economic potential, and strategic importance. It would have been hard to locate a more unpromising focus for colonial ambitions. *Eretz Yisrael/Filastin* was rich only in history, as the birthplace of monotheism and the three monotheistic world faiths of Judaism, Christianity, and Islam.

For the Hebrew tribes who spent forty years in the wastes of the Sinai desert, the biblical Land of Israel may have seemed to be "flowing with milk and honey." Visitors to the same area in the 1800s came away with a different impression. Arid, bleak, and uninviting, the landscape is described as a desolate backwater within a larger stagnant Ottoman state and society. Visiting in 1867, Mark Twain exclaimed: "Of all the lands there are for dismal scenery, I think Palestine must be the prince ... It is a hopeless, dreary, heart-broken land" (Twain 1974: 606). The southern half of what became Palestine was the Negev Desert, essentially a continuation of the Sinai Desert. The northern half was divided geographically into three north-to-south zones: a coastal plain, much of it marshy and malarial, which was considered unhealthy and had a sparse population; a central hilly region that, despite its arid and stony appearance, contained most of the cultivable land and most of the population, and the Jordan valley from the ridge of the hills to the river, which received almost no rainfall and thus had few settlements apart from an occasional oasis such as Jericho. Splitting through the central hilly range in the north was the Jezre'el Valley, connecting the coastal plain to the Sea of Galilee, with hot and often marshy conditions similar to both of those areas. The Jordan River, the conventional modern eastern border of *Eretz Yisrael/ Filastin*, is already below sea level where it enters and leaves the Sea of Galilee; by the time it reaches the Dead Sea in the south, it marks the lowest spot on earth and one of the most desolate.

The three Ottoman districts corresponding to modern Palestine had, according to adjusted Ottoman records, a total population of 462,465 in 1881–2, on the eve of the first new wave of Jewish immigration. Of this number, 403,795 (87 percent) were Muslim, 43,659 (10 percent) were Christian, and 15,011 (3 percent) were Jews (McCarthy 1990: 10). Nearly all the Muslims, and the vast majority of the Christians, were Arab in language and culture. Since many Jewish residents were not Ottoman citizens, other scholars put the Jewish total at 20,000–25,000 (Ben-Aryeh 1989–90: 78). But whatever the total number, Jews still constituted a small percentage of the population at this time. The Jewish population was almost totally urban, concentrated in the holy cities of Jerusalem, Hebron, Safed, and Tiberias, and very religiously traditional in its way of life.

As a whole, however, the population was still largely rural and agrarian; in 1890, it is estimated, the population of the three provinces was 67 percent rural (though only six percent of Jews lived in rural areas) (Bachi 1974: 32).

The picture of stagnation in Ottoman Palestine needs to be qualified. The nineteenth century was a period of dramatic change in the Middle East, and the Ottoman government was reacting to enormous internal and external challenges with serious efforts of reform and renewal. In the middle of the century it embarked on a broad program of reform – the

Tanzimat – designed to strengthen its own authority through-out the Empire. In Palestinian areas this brought about greater security in the countryside, better transport and communica-tion, and increased attention to maintaining the loyalty of the Arab population to Constantinople (Divine 1994: 107–35). While the 1881–2 population may still have been fewer than half a million, this was almost double the population of 275,000 in 1800 (Bachi 1974: 32). While the region may have appeared technologically backward to European eyes, significant changes were taking place.

The "Holy Land," that area made familiar to Western civili-zation by the Christian Bible, had, except during the Crusades, been under Muslim rule since 638 CE. The Ottomans, a Turkish dynasty founded by the first Sultan, Osman, at the end of the thirteenth century, conquered the area along with Syria and Egypt in 1516–17. Based in Western Anatolia, the Ottomans had conquered Constantinople (today's Istanbul) in 1453 and made it their capital, and embarked on cam-paigns of expansion that brought most of the Muslim world, and many other areas, under their control.

The Turks came from Central Asia, speaking a language unrelated to either Indo-European tongues (such as Persian) or Semitic languages (such as Arabic and Hebrew). When the early Arab conquests brought Islam within reach, they (like the Persians) became Muslims, adopted the Arabic alphabet for their own language, and became a part of the extensive multicultural World of Islam (*dar al-islam*). The Turks were known as formidable warriors, which led Arab Muslim rulers, beginning in the ninth century, to begin importing Turkish slaves for service as soldiers. The "slaves" soon became a privileged military caste, and within two centuries translated their military command into a political domination that lasted for almost 1,000 years. The Ottomans were preceded by other Turkish dynasties – the Seljuks, the Mamluks – and over time, the division of labor between Turks, as command-ers and rulers, and Arabs, as religious and cultural leaders, became the standard pattern (Lewis 1963).

At its peak, in the seventeenth century, Ottoman rule stretched from the borders of Morocco in the west, across

North Africa and the Arabian peninsula, to the Caspian Sea and the Persian Gulf in the east, and in the north included most of southeastern Europe and the north shore of the Black Sea. Twice (in 1529 and 1683) Ottoman armies laid siege to Vienna. The Ottoman ruler was not only Sultan of the Empire, but was also generally recognized as Caliph (*khalifa*), successor to Muhammad as leader of all Muslims, which translated into influence beyond Ottoman borders. For two centuries the military might of "the terrible Turk" was the nightmare of Europe, while the Ottoman regime was also known for "its thriving economy, its meticulous government, and its rich and brilliant culture" (Lewis 1963: 33).

But the legendary grandeur of the first two centuries was matched by an equally legendary decline during the two centuries that followed. In the words of Bernard Lewis, "if the first ten Sultans of the house of Osman astonish us with the spectacle of a series of able and intelligent men rare if not unique in the annals of dynastic succession, the remainder of the rulers of that line provides an even more astonishing series of incompetents, degenerates, and misfits" (Lewis 1968: 22–3). Prior to the second attack on Vienna, the Sultan's forces had seldom suffered defeat; from that time forward, they seldom tasted victory. By the time Zionism appeared on the scene, the Ottoman Empire had lost half its territory to a combination of Western imperialism and nationalist unrest. War with Russia was almost constant; by 1917 the two autocratic empires had fought over a dozen times, with the Russians seizing all Ottoman territories north and east of the Black Sea. North African territories, ruled by Constantinople through local dynasties, were lost in the course of the nineteenth century, with France claiming Algeria (1830) and Tunisia (1881) and Great Britain occupying Egypt in 1882 (in 1912 Italy completed the sweep by annexing Tripoli and Benghazi, present-day Libya). The British, who had earlier protected the Ottomans against other European powers, also established a dominant presence in Aden (present-day Yemen) and the Persian Gulf.

Finally, the Ottoman Empire lost most of its European territories. Austria took Hungary, Croatia, and Transylvania in the eighteenth century. In the century that followed, the non-Muslim nationalities in the Balkans managed to win their independence from "the yoke of the Turk": Greece in 1830, Serbia and Romania in 1878, Bulgaria in 1905. In the Balkan Wars of 1911–12, even Muslim Albania emerged as a new nation, and the Ottomans were left with a bare toehold in Europe, around Constantinople itself.

But the loss of territory is not the entire story. The declining Ottoman regime, no longer a match for European armies that had surpassed it technologically, was also threatened by broader Western economic, cultural, and political penetration. In 1798 Napoleon invaded Egypt as part of France's war with Great Britain, advancing as far as Acre on the "Palestinian" coast. His campaign was not only a military embarrassment for the Ottoman defenders, but also brought with it an influx of Western economic, scientific, and political influences that, within a few years, made deep inroads in Egypt and elsewhere (providing the basis for a regime in Cairo, under one Muhammad Ali, that later threatened Constantinople itself).

The decline of the Ottoman Empire was part of a broader development that changed the shape of human history: the rise of Europe relative to other parts of the globe and the spread of European ("Western") imperial control into all other regions. This transformation included Europeanization of the entire Western hemisphere, domination over equally venerable civilizations in Asia, and subjugation of Africa. In this light the question might be: How did the Middle East, located on the borders of Europe, resist these pressures as long as it did? The answer, in part, was the existence of the Ottoman Empire, which up to the end of the seventeenth century still threatened Europe more than *vice versa*, and even thereafter constituted a leaky but still substantial shield against the West. And in large part it was because, before the twentieth century, European powers blocked each other.

The United States was still a minor player in this drama: studiously neutral in the European power game, but by no means "isolated" from the Old World, as later mythology would have it. During the Crimean War, for example, while

Britain and France defended the Ottomans against Russia, US policy tilted toward Russia as a means of putting pressure on the British to make concessions on outstanding issues elsewhere (Dowty 1971). In its stance toward the Middle East, including Palestine, the United States was torn between its identity as part of the West and its ideology as the champion of freedom and democracy. As part of the West, the new American nation made war on the Barbary pirates, maintained a naval presence in the Mediterranean throughout the nineteenth century, and was active – privately, not governmentally – in the "civilizing mission" through a missionary/ educational/philanthropic nexus. As champions of a new world order, the United States spoke up for human rights in locations from Morocco to Bulgaria, and on occasion Middle Eastern regimes appealed to American anti-colonialism as a possible counterweight to European pressures.

One trend in US thinking that united both Western identity and ideology was a religious movement known as "Restorationism": a Christian doctrine promoting the restoration of the Jews to their historic homeland. The idea attracted wide support from such figures as former President John Adams, who envisioned "a hundred thousand Israelites" conquering Palestine (Oren 2007:90). This was well before the advent of Zionism among Jews, but it fostered several attempts to found American Christian colonies in the Holy Land dedicated to the revival (and conversion) of Jews.

Western penetration took many forms, but one that Ottoman authorities found particularly humiliating was the practice of "Capitulations" under which European nations exercised judicial powers in the heart of Ottoman territory. The Capitulations were actually introduced as a result of one of the more tolerant aspects of Ottoman (and earlier Muslim) tradition, under which recognized non-Muslim minorities (Christians and Jews) were allowed to settle disputes within their own communities according to their own religious traditions. The Ottoman government had willingly agreed, for example, to allow French representatives to handle legal issues among French Catholics within the Empire's borders. But as Ottoman power declined, the demands of European states grew more intrusive, with competing powers using these extra-territorial rights to increase their own influence and block their rivals inside Ottoman territory. France sought the right to protect all Catholics, and Russia posed as guardian of all Orthodox Christians, while Britain and Prussia (later Germany) competed for the Protestants. Russia's claim of the right to intervene on behalf of all Orthodox Christians, Russian or not, throughout Ottoman territory, was a major cause of the 1853–6 Crimean War, when Britain and France defended the Turks against overbearing Russian demands (Isaiah Friedman 1986: 280–93). By this time, of course, Ottoman authorities were determined to eliminate the Capitulations entirely.

The issue was especially sensitive in the "Palestinian" provinces. Since the Crusades, Jerusalem had been closed to European diplomats, and foreign non-Muslims had no right of permanent residence there. Only when Muhammad Ali of Egypt controlled the city were the first European consuls allowed in Jerusalem, beginning with Britain in 1838, and the hostility to Europeans was still such that at first the consuls moved about the city only with an armed escort, and no open display of Christian or Jewish symbols was allowed. After the Crimean War the Ottoman government, having been rescued by Britain and France, was compelled to issue an edict extending legal equality and non-discrimination to non-Muslims throughout the Empire. This of course strengthened the hand of foreign consuls acting on behalf of those whom they protected.

In this context, Ottoman authorities were hardly likely to welcome the immigration of European Jews able to claim the protection of the country of origin. Ironically, the Ottoman Empire had traditionally been open to Jewish refugees; it took pride in having offered a haven to those expelled from Spain in 1492. But earlier refugees had settled throughout the Empire, and those who did choose the Palestinian provinces did so as individuals, not as an organized movement; they also assimilated into Arab culture and became Ottoman citizens. The Muslim tradition of religious tolerance accommodated this easily. European Jewish immigrants in the nineteenth century were another matter. Even before the rise of Zionism, Ottoman officials had developed an aversion to European Jews who clung to their foreign citizenship, invoked the protection of their consul, and showed no inclination to assimilate. Furthermore, foreign consuls were actually competing for the right to represent Jewish immigrants; for a time Great Britain claimed the right to protect Russian Jews, since the Russian government had hardly bothered to protect them even when they were still in Russia.

As indicated, while there was no territorial unit within the Ottoman Empire corresponding to historical *Eretz Yisrael/Filastin*, there was a particular sensitivity with regard to Jerusalem and the areas associated with it historically. The Ottoman administrative borders went through many changes; in 1864–71 the area corresponding to historic Palestine was made part of a province (*vilayet*) ruled from Damascus, consistent with a tendency to designate the entire region as part of Syria. But after the first wave of Jewish immigration had sensitized Constantinople, in 1888 the Jerusalem area (corresponding to the southern half of Palestine) was constituted as an independent district (*sanjak*) under direct rule from Constantinople. The northern half of present-day Palestine was divided into two *sanjaks*, centered in Nablus (Shechem) and Acre, both of which were part of the Beirut *vilayet* (see map 1.1).

In short, the Ottoman government, in these final decades of its existence, was fighting a rearguard action against foreign penetration and internal disintegration. It feared the European powers that had reduced its power both externally and internally; only by exploiting the splits among these powers had the Ottomans managed to survive such crises as the challenge from Muhammad Ali's Egypt and the Crimean War during the tumultuous nineteenth century. The creation of a new, Western-oriented, non-Muslim minority in the Ottoman heartland, and precisely in an area of particular sensitivity in the long struggle between Islam and the West going back to the Crusades, was simply out of the question. With the loss of its European possessions, the Arabs were – apart from the Turks themselves – the last remaining

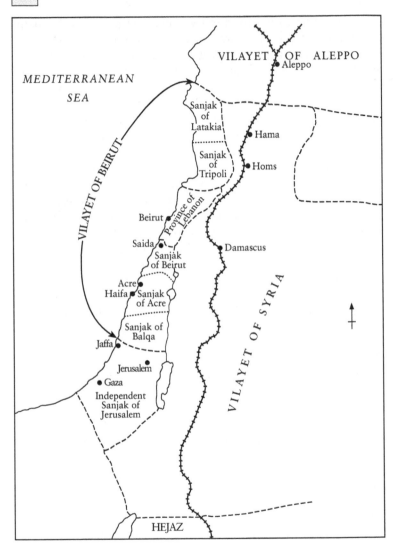

Map 1.1 Ottoman Palestine 1888–1918.

bastion of the Empire. Ottoman authorities could not fail to be solicitous toward the concerns of their fellow Muslims.

But would Arabs also be infected by the nationalist fever emanating from the West? This had not been an issue in the past; the dominant identities within the Empire were religion, clan, tribe, and family. Only toward the end of the nineteenth century were voices heard calling for Arab liberation from Turkish rule, on the basis of a rediscovered identity as members of an Arab-speaking nation stretching from Morocco to Iraq. The first glimmers came in the late 1870s, when a secret society (with 22 members) in Beirut, Damascus, Tripoli, and Sidon (in present-day Lebanon and Syria) posted placards denouncing the evils of Turkish rule and calling for an Arab uprising against it (Antonius 1946: 79–80).

However, before these ideas reached the Palestinian areas of the Ottoman Empire, they had already reached the Jews of Tsarist Russia and had evoked a thunderous echo.

The Jewish Story ————————

As long as in the inner heart a Jewish soul still beats,
and an eye still searches for Zion in the East,
our hope is not lost; the hope of two thousand years,
to be a free people in our own land, the land of Zion and
Jerusalem.

> Hatikvah (The Hope) – Israeli national anthem
> (Naftali Herz Imber, 1878)

A Fossilized Relic?

Both Jews and Arabs have long and proud histories. The
conflict between them may be comparatively recent, but to
understand it, we must consider each side's historical traditions and memories. This chapter traces the Jewish historical
experience, in its full intensity, and then takes a closer look
at Jewish perspectives and prospects during the early period
of Zionist settlement. Chapter 3 will provide a parallel narrative showing the great importance of Arab history in shaping
Arab views and actions during this same period.

Jewish history, according to the Jewish Bible (the Old
Testament of the Christian Bible), began almost 4,000 years
ago with the patriarch Abraham, traditional forefather of
both Jews and Arabs. Apart from its religious importance,
the Bible is a remarkable historical document for the detail

it offers regarding the chronicles of the Hebrew people, centuries before any such accounts existed elsewhere, and for its focus on defeats and tragedies as well as victories and glory (it is, after all, a morality tale). The first non-biblical mention of the Jewish people is an Egyptian inscription, the Merneptah Stele, dated c. 1220 BCE, in which the Egyptian ruler boasts that "Israel is laid waste and his seed is not" (Malamat 1976: 42). This corresponds roughly to the period of the Israelite conquest of Canaan following the Exodus from Egypt, as recorded in the Bible. Many of the conquered peoples were related Semitic groups, some of which apparently assimilated to the Israelite tradition while others remained separate during and after the biblical period. Other archeological and historical records of biblical people and events begin appearing around the time of Kings David and Solomon and the building of the First Temple in Jerusalem, roughly 1000 BCE, and they multiply over the following centuries.

Jews therefore have one of the longest histories – if not the longest – as a distinct people with a continuous identity expressed in language, culture, genealogy, and religious practice. Furthermore, this identity endured despite geographic dispersion and the lack of a physical homeland. The survival of the Jews as a distinct people is often regarded as one of history's greatest puzzles. The eminent historian Arnold Toynbee, who constructed an elegant intellectual edifice of world history built on the rhythmic rise and fall of successive civilizations, classified the Jews of today as one of a handful of "fossilized relics of societies now extinct" (Toynbee 1955: 51). How could the Hebrews or Israelites of antiquity have survived when other peoples of the Bible – Canaanites, Jebusites, Philistines, Hittites, Babylonians, Moabites, etc. – had long since vanished from the stage of history?

The answer to this question clearly relates in some way to the key contribution that Judaism made to human history: Jews introduced monotheism to the world. From this small patch of arid land came the stunning insight that revolutionized religious belief and practice everywhere. In the words of Israel's 1948 Proclamation of Independence, "The Land of

Israel was the birthplace of the Jewish people . . . Here they achieved independence and created a culture of national and universal significance. Here they wrote and gave the Bible to the world." The monotheistic revelation was not just a theological event; it also introduced an entirely new way of looking at the world. Thomas Cahill, in *The Gifts of the Jews* (1998), sums it up in the book's subtitle: *How a Tribe of Desert Nomads Changed the Way Everyone Thinks and Feels*. The belief in one God moved people from a cyclical view of history, in which change is illusory, to a linear view that lays the foundation for ethical responsibility. In Cahill's words, "the Jews were able to give us the Great Whole, a unified universe that makes sense and that, because of its evident superiority as a worldview, completely overwhelms the warring and contradictory phenomena of polytheism" (Cahill 1998: 240).

Out of this tradition came three monotheistic world religions: Judaism, Christianity, and Islam. Toynbee himself connected Jewish survival to its relationship with Christianity and Islam: "The Jews' present-day importance, celebrity, and discomfort all derive from the historic fact that they have involuntarily begotten two Judaic world-religions whose millions of adherents make the preposterous but redoubtable claim to have superseded the Jews" (Toynbee 1961: 479). Though often at war with each other (and within themselves), the three faiths constitute an "Abrahamic" family of religions, and in more reflective moments they recognize their mutual kinship. As Pope Pius XI declared, "we are spiritual progeny of Abraham. Spiritually, we are all Semites" (Martin 1983: 18).

But while Christianity and Islam claim universal validity, and have sought converts among all nations and peoples, Judaism has retained a sense of peoplehood. Being Jewish is not a matter of professed belief, but of sharing a common heritage; one may be Jewish without being religious. From one perspective, this makes Judaism more limited and parochial, with an emphasis on the "particularism" of one ethnic group rather than on a universalist message that (at least in theory) is addressed to all races and cultures. However, by the same token there is a fundamental tolerance for other traditions and religions, since there is no impulse to make all non-Jews into Jews.

The particularism of Judaism is a matter not only of shared ancestry and history as a people, but also of attachment to a particular place. The geography of *Eretz Yisrael* is interwoven into Jewish scripture, litany, ritual, and tradition. Jews may have a portable package of religious practices that they can carry with them to any place, but there is never any doubt that *Eretz Yisrael* remains the eternal spiritual center. Religious Jews pray three times a day for the return to Jerusalem. As long ago as the Babylonian exile (fifth–sixth centuries BCE), the yearning to return was expressed lyrically in Psalm 137:

> By the rivers of Babylon, there we sat,
> And we wept, as we remembered Zion.
> On the willows there we hung up our harps,
> For our captors there asked us for songs,
> Our tormentors, for amusement,
> "Sing us one of the songs of Zion."
> How can we sing the Lord's song in a strange land?
> If I forget thee, O Jerusalem,
> Let my right hand forget her cunning;
> If I do not remember thee,
> Let my tongue cleave to the roof of my mouth,
> If I prefer not Jerusalem above my chief joy.

The theme of exile and return is a central motif in Jewish tradition that, given the biblical tales of Joseph (exile to Egypt) and Moses (exodus from Egypt), predates the Babylonian captivity by several centuries. After the return from Babylon, and the building of the Second Temple, came exile at the hands of the Romans, in the first and second centuries CE, following the crushing of two Jewish revolts against Roman rule. In the traditional structure of a morality tale, exile is punishment by God for the collective failings of the Jewish people, while return signifies divine mercy as the sinners are given another chance to redeem themselves. The idea of Return to Zion also came to be associated with messianism, the belief in the promised appearance of the messiah (the "anointed one") who would not only lead Jews back to Zion (emblem of the Holy Land), but would also bring about the final redemption of Jews and, ultimately, of all mankind.

Palestine, like most areas of the Roman Empire, was gradually Christianized in the early centuries of the Christian era. After the Arab conquest of 636–40, immigration and conversion created an Islamic and Arab majority, though Christian and Jewish minorities remained. From the third to the tenth centuries the center of Jewish life passed to Babylonia, where – despite the return from the earlier exile, recorded in the biblical chronicles of Ezra and Nehemiah – a significant Jewish population had remained. It was during this period that the Talmud, the great repository of Jewish law, was compiled, with the Babylonian rendition as the dominant version.

As a protected minority under Islam, from the ninth to the thirteenth centuries Jews also became active participants in a vibrant Muslim culture centered in Spain. This period is considered a "golden age" in both traditions. Spain replaced Babylonia as the center of Jewish culture and creativity, producing many of the most illustrious names in Jewish history: among them the great philosopher-theologian-scientist Maimonides (Moses ben Maimon). Eventually, however, religious zeal and intolerance undermined the creative interaction of the three traditions that had sustained this cultural flowering. The Christian reconquest of Spain, completed by King Ferdinand and Queen Isabella in 1492, brought with it a surge in Christian zealotry. For the century before this, Jews had been under enormous pressure to convert; those who did were then subjected to the Inquisition, established in 1483 to determine whether their new Christianity was genuine. Finally – and also, strikingly, in 1492 – the remaining Jews were given the choice of conversion or expulsion.

The Spanish expulsion of 1492 was a major watershed in Jewish history. It ended a remarkable chapter of collaborative creativity and achievement, and produced a flood of refugees (known as *Sephardim*: "Spaniards" in Hebrew) who came to constitute a major recognized group within the Jewish world. Many found their way into the rising Ottoman Empire, whose ruler (Sultan Bajazet) reputedly exclaimed, "What! Call ye this Ferdinand 'wise' – he who depopulates his own dominions in order to enrich mine?" (Roth 1961: 252). Some even settled in *Eretz Yisrael,* where they were prominent in the emergence of Safed (in the Galilee) as a center of Jewish law and religious mysticism.

Throughout Jewish history, and especially in turbulent times, the idea of Return to Zion remained an important fixture in Jewish thought. Many individuals did manage to return, often toward the end of their lives so that they might at least be buried in holy ground. Though still more of a religious yearning than a political program, the vision of a collective return of Jews to Zion was never far from the surface, as evidenced in the excitement raised by a series of "false messiahs" who stirred the Jewish world over succeeding centuries: Solomon Molcho (in sixteenth-century Italy), Shabbetai Zevi (in the seventeenth-century Ottoman Empire), and Jacob Frank (in eighteenth-century Poland and Ukraine).

From the fifteenth century the center of Jewish life shifted to Eastern Europe. Persecutions and expulsions in Western Europe, beginning with the First Crusade in the late eleventh century, had forced many Jews to flee. At the same time, some rulers in Eastern Europe were welcoming Jewish refugees, who brought Western commercial and artisanal skills. In 1264 the Polish Duke Boleslaw issued the Statute of Kalisz, granting Jews rights of residence and protection. This began a tradition of Polish and other rulers granting autonomy to Jewish communities, which developed into flourishing and largely self-governing entities. Since most of the refugees came from Germany, they brought with them a mixture of medieval German dialects that evolved into Yiddish, a Germanic language written in Hebrew characters. From the Hebrew word for Germany, *Ashkenaz,* came the designation of this community, and most European Jews, as *Ashkenazim.*

Beginning in the 1700s these communities experienced an astounding population growth – a "demographic miracle" – as the mortality rate dropped sharply with improved health and living conditions. The estimated world Jewish population in 1700 was about one million, which was about what it had been 1,200 years earlier (after peaking in the first century at about 4.5 million). Two centuries later, in 1900, there were an estimated 10.6 million Jews in the world, with Eastern Europe accounting for about 90 percent of this total (Barnavi 1992: xii–xiii; Ettinger 1976: 790–3). By this time, following the partition of Poland at the end of the eighteenth century, about half of the world's Jews were living in territory annexed by Tsarist Russia, a state that had traditionally tried to forbid Jewish residence on its soil.

The Theme of Persecution

As this brief overview of Jewish history indicates, the central thread of Jewish history, as seen by most Jews, is the omnipresent threat of persecution. Persecution lies behind Jewish population movements, demography, and geography. Persecution is the recurrent theme that connects Jewish life in widely separated times and places.

What explains the persistence and virulence of anti-Semitism? (The term itself was invented by the anti-Semites to make hatred of Jews sound more clinical (Wistrich 1991: 252).) But perhaps the question should be: What explains the persecution of any minority? There is no reason to think that hostility to Jews differs essentially from persecution of other minorities; what is different is that, historically, Jews have found themselves more often in an exposed, isolated, and vulnerable situation. All too often Jews have been the most distinctly different minority, or the only minority in critical respects – for example, the major visible non-Christian group in times and places when militant Christianity was on the march. In addition, the organic link with Christianity (and Islam to a lesser extent) was a curse rather than a blessing, since it led both faiths, at certain times, to consign Jews to a theological role as villains.

Persecution of Jews began before the rise of Christianity. In the biblical book of Esther, set in Persia five centuries before the Christian era, King Ahasuerus (Xerxes) is told by his counselor Haman that "there is a certain people scattered abroad and dispersed among the people in all the provinces of thy kingdom; and their laws are diverse from all people; neither keep they the king's laws: therefore it is not for the king's profit to suffer them" (Esther 3:8). This certainly demonstrates classic suspicion of a minority, but with the rise of Christianity it acquires a religious basis, as early Christians sought to distinguish their religion from, and to discredit, the Judaism of the day. Likewise, in the *Qur'an* (the holy scripture of Islam) Muhammad's anger at the Jews for rejecting his message is reflected in negative passages about Jews, though Jews as People of the Book are also given the right to practice their own religion.

The Jewish *Haggadah* telling the story of Passover, which was compiled during the centuries of exile, declares that "it was not one enemy alone who rose up against us to destroy us; in every generation there are those who rise up against us and seek to destroy us." By this time the recurrence of persecution was already deeply embedded in Jewish consciousness. But the worst was yet to come. The First Crusade, launched to rescue the Holy Land from Muslim "infidels," began in 1096 with orgiastic massacres of the enemies of Christ – the Jews – in Europe. It is estimated that one-quarter to one third of the Jews in Germany and northern France were murdered. In the climate of religious fervor that prevailed in the following centuries, religious figures and rulers condemned Jews, as a people, to perpetual servitude, and the infamous blood libel – the fantasy that Jews murdered Christian children and used their blood to make Passover matza – became the trigger for savage massacres (Wistrich 1991; Barnavi 1992).

Jews were expelled from England in 1290, from France in 1306 and 1394, from most German states in the fifteenth century, from Provence in 1500–1, from Saxony, Sicily, and Sardinia in 1536, from Tuscany in 1571, from Milan in 1597, and from most other Western European areas at one time or another (including, of course, Spain in 1492). The Spanish Inquisition, which targeted Jews who had converted to Christianity, was the first eerie premonition of "modern" anti-Semitism based on race rather than religion; in the late nineteenth century its full-blown emergence would be a key factor in persuading many Jews that Zionism – a Jewish state – was the only answer.

Flight from West to East was the immediate Jewish response, and one which fitted the pattern of Jewish history. Fortunately there was usually a haven: Poland during the late Middle Ages, the Ottoman Empire after the expulsion from Spain, the New World more recently. But by the seventeenth century the Eastern European haven was also shaken by violent outbursts of anti-Semitic assaults. In 1648–9 a massive Cossack and peasant uprising led by a minor Ukrainian noble, Bogdan Chmielnicki, focused with particular intensity on the massacre of Jews, who were caught between Polish landlords and Ukrainian peasants. Subsequent attacks on Jews in Poland took place in 1680, 1687, 1734, 1750, and 1768. Annexation of Ukraine and much of Poland by the notoriously anti-Semitic Tsarist regime promised no relief.

By this time the Enlightenment and the spread of liberal institutions in Western Europe had created a new situation. Jews had returned to Western Europe and were building strong communities, and in some cases were being granted total civil equality. By the late nineteenth century they were leaving Russia and other Eastern European nations in large numbers for Western destinations, including the New World, where new societies were being built and prejudice was much less institutionalized. In view of this progress and this promising situation, why should this period, of all periods in Jewish history, produce the first serious organized movement for a return to *Eretz Yisrael*? Just when it appeared that liberalization might succeed in resolving the age-old problem of Jewish persecution, why should a significant proportion of the Jewish community decisively reject assimilation?

Part of the answer is that assimilation was not without costs or problems. To more traditional elements it was seen as a critical threat; as in other modernizing societies, more strictly religious Jews reacted by separating themselves, as much as possible, from modern secular influences, and "returning to their roots." This characterizes the *hasidic* movement (founded in the eighteenth century) and more recent "fundamentalist" groups, collectively known today as *haredim* (literally, "those who tremble [before God]"). But even less traditional, more secularized Jews did not want an integration that meant loss of Jewish identity. In many cases it appeared that Jews were being offered the chance to integrate only as individuals and not as a group, and only if they did not insist on remaining Jewish in any meaningful sense. One could become French, but only if it was a total conversion. In some ways life had been simpler before; Jews were confined by their group identity, but at least they knew who they were.

A second problem was that the new nationalism in Europe was less welcoming than it appeared. As the stress on common ethnicity grew, the question arose: Could a Jew truly become a Frenchman or a German? One could convert to another religion, but not to another ancestry. The dilemma was strikingly represented in the experience of Theodor Herzl, the founder of modern political Zionism. In 1881 Herzl, as a "good German," joined a German nationalist fraternity at his university; but within two years he was forced to resign when it became clear that Jews were not being accepted as Germans. By the end of the century a new and more vicious anti-Semitism, based on race rather than religion, had emerged. The 1894–5 Dreyfus trial in France, where a totally assimilated French Jewish army officer was deliberately framed for treason, shocked and disillusioned the Jewish world, and those who had been the most eager to assimilate now became the most disillusioned. These were people known as *maskilim* – proponents of the Jewish enlightenment (*haskala*) and of integration into modern Western liberal society – who felt betrayed and began to look for new, and radical, answers to the problem they had thought was on its way to resolution.

The surest way to foment revolution, it has been claimed, is to extend real hope of a better future and then snatch it away. This was about to be tested in Tsarist Russia, "prison house of nations," where half the world's Jews were living as the decade of the 1880s began.

"Come, Let Us Go"

On March 1, 1881, Tsar Alexander II was assassinated. Alexander II's reign (1855–81) was the period of "Great Reforms" in Russia: the serfs were liberated, and other far-reaching measures were decreed to pull Russia out of its backward ways. This included vast changes in the status of Jews: residence restrictions were loosened, opportunities in higher education and government service were expanded, and integration into Russian society was encouraged. With doors open as never before, many Jews – especially the *maskilim* – made great strides during these decades.

But the new Tsar, Alexander III, was dominated by conservative advisors who feared and detested Western liberal ideas. Signals from the top were picked up quickly; within weeks a wave of violent attacks on Jewish communities began to sweep the country (the Russian word "*pogrom*," or devastation, came into use during this period). By the year's end an estimated 250 pogroms had devastated Jewish communities across Russia, all with little or no interference by the police or the army. Instead, the new Russian regime, calculating that anti-Semitism was a useful tool for diverting popular discontent, blamed the Jews for having roused "the anger of the people," and used the situation to justify the reimposition of extensive restrictions on Jews (Ettinger 1976: 881–8).

Thus began a dark period in Russian Jewish history that led to the massive flight of four million refugees over the next four decades. Following the historical pattern, most moved to new places of refuge, this time in Western Europe and the Americas. But a small trickle, fewer than two percent of them, chose instead to enact a Return to Zion (Zion, a hill in Jerusalem, had since biblical days served as a poetic reference to the Land of Israel). Why return to Zion at this time? Anti-Semitism was persistent in Jewish history, but it had never sparked a significant movement to Eretz Yisrael. Zion had always seemed an unpromising and inhospitable alternative, and this was certainly no less true in the declining years of Turkish rule there.

But this time there were important differences. In the first place, as the various nations of Europe discovered and reaffirmed their own claims to nationhood and national self-determination, Jews were also drawn to the model of the nation-state. The Return to Zion, previously a religious aspiration, became a political program. Were the Jews less entitled to national sovereignty than the Serbs or the Albanians? Secondly, as the ugly side of the new nationalism began to show itself, the possibility of successful assimilation into someone else's nation-state appeared increasingly a delusion. The new wave of anti-Semitism, not just in Russia but also elsewhere in Eastern Europe (Romania in particular), Germany, Austria-Hungary, and even liberal, progressive France, led to one conclusion: anti-Semitism was incurable. The assimilation experiment had been tried, and had failed. Why repeat the mistake?

Again, only about two percent of the Jewish refugees, at the time, found this argument compelling enough to take on the rigors and challenges of *Eretz Yisrael*. Who were these brave – or foolhardy – pioneers? They were not the elderly, who had previously traveled to the Holy Land in order to be buried there, nor were they among the devoutly religious who were drawn to Zion out of religious obligation. They were overwhelmingly young, relatively well educated, and from the ranks of the *maskilim*. They were precisely those who had tried to assimilate, and were now bitterly disillusioned. They came to *Eretz Yisrael* not in order to find personal salvation, but in order to further an entirely new solution to the age-old "Jewish problem." The mood of the times is recorded in the 1881 diary of one pioneer:

With my own eyes I saw the terrible tragedy in one of the more beautiful and enlightened cities, in which important people were joining in. If they did not actually do the beating, they were stirring the fire and adding fuel to the flames. When I saw all this something in me snapped . . . In one flash all my illusions were revealed, and all the beautiful pictures of the future, that I and my friends painted for ourselves, dissipated like smoke.

> And I, a law student, a member of a cosmopolitan intellectual society, devoted to progress – I felt suddenly my unique Jewish soul, and with all my might I felt that these unfortunate people, heartbroken and at wit's end, are my brothers and with them I am in distress from now and evermore . . .
>
> There is a source of hope. *Eretz Yisrael* must become our future land. Only there will our people find rest and relief. Only there will it find a place to bring its old, dry bones to life. It only needs a beginning. (Druyanov 1933)

The writer of these lines was one of about 500 young people in the Kharkov area, many of them university students, who came together to form the *Bilu* society. The name was taken from Isaiah 2: 5: "*Beit Ya'akov, l'chu v'nelcha* [House of Jacob, come, let us go]." As an early manifesto declared, Jews needed to awaken from "the false dream of assimilation." The goal of the movement was defined as "a home in our country," which the *Biluim* proposed to beg of the Sultan himself. Recognizing implicitly that the Sultan might not be so generous, they proposed asking for at least "a state within a larger state" that would govern itself domestically but act with the Turkish Empire in foreign affairs "so as to help our brother Ishmael in the time of his need" (Laqueur and Schueftan 2016: 3–4).

The *Biluim* were insignificant numerically; only fourteen managed to enter Eretz Yisrael during the first year, and altogether only about sixty actually settled there, and many of those did not remain. Their significance was that of an intellectual vanguard that first declared the explicit goal of statehood, which only a few Jewish intellectuals were ready to support openly (one of these was Leon Pinsker, whose 1882 pamphlet *Self-Emancipation* was the first Zionist scripture, though at the time it was little noted outside Russian Jewish circles).

At this point, in fact, these early tentative movements were hardly known even in Jewish communities elsewhere. Theodor Herzl in Vienna, who later founded the World Zionist Organization, heard only then of Pinsker and his pamphlet. Groups similar to Bilu were, however, springing up in Jewish communities across Russia. By the mid-1880s they had become loosely linked together as *Hovevei Tsion* (Lovers of Zion) movement, soon to be known simply as "Zionists." *Hovevei Tsion* focused on settlement in *Eretz Yisrael* and the rebuilding of Jewish life there, sending several thousand settlers during the 1880s and a total of somewhere between 20,000 and 30,000 by 1903 (Bachi 1974: 79). Since immigration to *Eretz Yisrael* is extolled in Hebrew as *aliyah* (ascent), this wave of settlers is known as the first *aliyah*. These newcomers founded ten new settlements during the 1880s and another seven in the 1890s, while many others settled in existing cities. The new settlements were concentrated in low-lying, often marshy areas that were relatively sparsely populated: the coastal plain, the Jezre'el Valley between the coast and the Sea of Galilee, and the Jordan Valley around and north of the Sea of Galilee. This was because only in these areas were significant plots of potential agricultural land available for purchase.

There was a strong agrarian thrust to this settlement effort, reflecting a deep-seated yearning for a return to the soil as part of the return to life as a "normal" nation. Because of their all-Jewish character and their ideological virtues, the rural settlements have received most of the attention in Zionist history, even though there were always more Jews in the cities (which included not only many in the "new" *yishuv*, or community, but also all of the "old" *yishuv*, the more traditional Jewish community that had existed before Zionism and was largely hostile to the newcomers). The new rural settlements faced monumental obstacles and hardships, not least the total lack of agricultural experience or knowledge among the young intellectuals who founded them. Most of them survived only through the generous support of "the well-known benefactor," Baron Edmund de Rothschild from the French branch of the illustrious family.

Nevertheless, despite the hardships, and despite hostility from the old *yishuv* and open opposition from Turkish authorities and Arab neighbors, the new *yishuv* slowly gained ground. By 1903 there were about 50,000 Jews in the areas that later became the Palestine Mandate. The new *yishuv* was dedicated to the aim of building a self-reliant and prosperous Jewish society and culture; one of its triumphs was the rebirth of Hebrew as a spoken language after two millennia of confinement to written and liturgical use only. The explanation for this feat lies not only in the ideological fervor of the advocates, but also in the fact that nearly all educated Jews had some knowledge of the language, and in the reality that there was no other common tongue with which European Jews and non-European Jews could communicate with each other.

Nevertheless, the achievements of the first two decades of Jewish settlement were not impressive. Jews still constituted less than ten percent of the population, and of this number only a few thousand were in the new "Zionist" settlements, and their presence was little noted. The first *aliyah*, in and of itself, failed to put the Return to Zion on the world's agenda. This was achieved, however, at the end of the century, by an entirely unexpected and dramatic development from a different quarter.

Herzl and the Second *Aliyah*

The unlikely figure who put Zionism on the world map was a 35-year-old assimilated Viennese Jewish journalist and some-time playwright who knew little about Judaism or the first *aliyah*. Theodor Herzl was representative of Jews in Western Europe who, like those in Russia, had put their confidence in assimilation into modernizing European societies, only to be stunned by the new nationalist and racial anti-Semitism of the 1890s. Herzl covered the 1894–5 conviction and degradation of French army officer Alfred Dreyfus for Vienna's leading newspaper, the *Neue Freie Presse*; he was even more appalled by the rising tide of Jew-hatred in his own Vienna, where the rabidly anti-Semitic Karl Lueger won a smashing victory in municipal elections in September 1895 (Kornberg 1993). Three months earlier Herzl had spent a feverish two weeks composing a "new solution" to the Jewish problem; now he reworked this material into a pamphlet, *The Jews' State: An Attempt at a Modern Solution to the Issue of the Jews*, and published it in February 1896.

Though Herzl was unaware of the earlier Zionists and their ideas, his argument brought these ideas together in dramatic style and took them one step further. Herzl argued that:

1 Anti-Semitism is inevitable, even in supposedly enlightened countries.
2 Assimilation is therefore doomed to failure, and Jewish life will remain deformed.
3 The only logical solution is a Jewish state; even anti-Semites should support the idea.
4 For this to happen, there must be broad international support (Herzl was not impressed by the small-scale "infiltration" into Ottoman Palestine).
5 The "present possessors" of territory set aside as a Jewish state would benefit from its development into a modern society. (Herzl 1997)

In essence, Herzl was arguing for the integration of Jews into world history – but as a nation, not as individuals. Jews would achieve a normal existence only when they enjoyed equality with other nations that had achieved independent statehood. Other key points worth noting are that the project is conceived as a rescue from persecution more than an assertion of Jewish identity, that it in fact contains little "Jewish" content in Herzl's formulation, and that it does not recognize any serious conflict of interests with other parties (existing states, native populations, and even anti-Semites will all gain from the venture).

Herzl's little pamphlet was one of those landmark historical documents whose impact derives not from their content but from their success in striking the right chord at the right moment. *The Jews' State* was rapidly translated into numerous languages, and had an explosive impact on both Jewish and non-Jewish worlds. This was the breakthrough that brought Zionism to the world's attention. Herzl exploited the momentum created to organize the World Zionist Organization (WZO) at a conference in Basel, Switzerland, in August 1897, bringing together most of the disparate groups loosely organized previously into *Hovevei Tsion.* The aim of the movement was defined as "to create for the Jewish people a home in Palestine secured by public law." The emphasis on "public law" reflected Herzl's insistence on working openly within the existing state system; the designation of "Palestine" reflected the fact that the bulk of Herzl's clientele came from Eastern Europe and, unlike Herzl, could not conceive of a Jewish state anywhere but in the ancestral homeland. The specification of "home" rather than "state" reflected sensitivity to the fact that Palestine was already part of a state (the Ottoman Empire) whose government was unlikely to welcome yet another secessionist threat in its heartland.

Herzl wanted a "charter" from the Ottoman Sultan that would permit Jewish settlement in Palestine. When his attempts to approach the Ottoman government directly led nowhere, he turned to European governments with influence in Constantinople. In an age when European expansion was at its peak, this was not an idle hope. The Ottoman Empire, reduced to half of its dominions of two centuries earlier, clung to its reduced core only thanks to the splits and rivalries among encroaching European states. The main threat, Russia, had been contained in mid-century by the British and the French in the 1853–56 Crimean War. Later, the French and eventually the British came into alliance with Russia as Europe began to coalesce into the two warring camps that would eventually face off in World War I; the Ottoman Turks therefore turned to the new empire of Kaiser Wilhelm's Germany for needed support. And meanwhile, all the European powers competed to gain footholds within the Ottoman Empire, and in particular in the Holy Land, through constant pressure and exploitation of the "Capitulations" that gave them standing to intervene on behalf of designated groups within Ottoman territory (see chapter 1).

From Herzl's perspective, this meant that any of the Great Powers might prove a valuable ally in achieving his charter, Germany by virtue of Ottoman dependence and the others by virtue of Ottoman vulnerability to their demands. Exploiting the attention gained by the new WZO, in the following years Herzl conducted a frenzied diplomacy trying to bring the

German, British, and French governments, the Pope, and
many others, even including the Russian Tsar, to support
the project and use their influence in Constantinople. Only
once, in 1901, was Herzl himself granted an audience with
the Sultan – and this was on condition that he not raise the
subject of Zionism! Burned out within a few years by his
frenetic pace, Herzl died in 1904 at the age of 44, without
having achieved his charter or having significantly advanced
actual Jewish settlement in Palestine. He left behind, however,
a mass movement that had galvanized the hopes and dreams
of Jews everywhere, but especially the increasingly desperate
masses in Eastern Europe. He also left behind an organizational framework ready to respond to the next emergency in
Jewish life anywhere.

This next emergency was already looming. As before and
since, the Zionist movement was revived by another wave
of savage persecution and another wave of embittered refugees. It began with a bloody pogrom in the Russian city of
Kishinev in 1903, an atrocity that led to a classic statement
of helplessness and rage by the emerging Hebrew national
poet Haim Nahman Bialik, in "On the Slaughter" (Carmi
1998: 152–3):

> You, executioner! Here's my neck – go
> to it, slaughter me! Behead me like a
> dog, yours is the mighty arm and the
> axe, and the whole earth is my scaffold
> and we, we are the few . . .
> And cursed be the man who says:
> Avenge! No such revenge – revenge for
> the blood of a little child – has yet
> been devised by Satan.

As the Russian regime continued to allow Jews to serve as
a convenient target in diverting popular discontent, the first
Russian Revolution of 1905 triggered a massive repetition
of what had begun at Kishinev. The resulting exodus from
Russia brought about 34,000 Jewish settlers to Ottoman
Palestine in the decade before World War I, a wave of newcomers known as the second *aliyah* (Bachi 1974: 79). This,

rather than the first *aliyah*, was the group that produced most of the leaders and set the ideological tone for the *yishuv* until well after Israel became a state (until 1977, in fact). Second *aliyah* pioneers, imbued with the Russian revolutionary spirit, combined Zionism not just with an agrarian ethos, but also with a socialist and proletarian ideology that made all manual labor an object of worship. The emphasis on reforming and rebuilding the basic structure of Jewish life, and not just saving Jewish lives, became an integral and central pillar of the enterprise. First *aliyah* settlers were denounced for employing Arabs in their villages, on the grounds that this undercut the aim of self-reliance, duplicated colonial patterns of exploitation of native labor, and would not contribute to the rehabilitation of Jewish life and the Jewish occupational structure. On the other hand, some of the veterans defended the practice on the grounds that it created a moderating mutual dependence and brought benefits to the Arabs that would soften their opposition to Zionism.

The doctrine of manual labor as a form of secular redemption was represented in its purest form by Aaron David Gordon, who came to Palestine in 1904, at the unusually advanced age of 47, to work as an agricultural laborer. His writings on self-realization through physical labor were a strong influence in the emergence of the *kibbutz* (communal settlement) as the second *aliyah*'s iconic contribution to the developing *yishuv*. In Gordon's words,

> We were defeated through lack of labor . . . Work will heal us. In the center of all our hopes we must place work; our entire structure must be founded on labor. If only we set up work itself as the ideal – rather, if only we bring into the open the ideal of labor, shall we be cured of the disease which attacked us. We shall then sew together the rents by which we were torn from nature. (Gordon 1938: 56)

With ideological primacy assigned to physical labor and a return to the soil, it is easy to lose perspective on the actual structure of Jewish life in Ottoman Palestine. In 1880 the existing Jewish population (the old *yishuv*) was 99.3

percent urban; by 1914 the total Jewish population was still 87.1 percent urban (Bachi 1974: 6). Much of the new *yishuv* settled in existing cities such as Jerusalem, Jaffa, and Haifa. Furthermore, many of the early rural settlements (Rishon Letsion, Petah Tikva, Hadera, Rehovot, Gedera) evolved into substantial cities in the course of time. The urban proclivity of most newcomers was also expressed in the founding, in 1909, of the first all-new all-Hebrew city, Tel Aviv, and by its rapid growth in the following decades.

This brings us, however, to a pivotal question. When Jews motivated by the Zionist vision entered Palestinian areas of the Ottoman Empire during the last decades of its existence, they encountered a population already in place. Only those imagining Palestine from afar could describe it as an "empty" land, and such fantasies did not survive actual settlement experience. What notice did the first "Zionist" settlers take of the population that they encountered, and what did they make of it? Above all, did they see it as a problem?

First Encounters

In fact, Zionist settlers did not see the presence of Arabs in *Eretz Yisrael/Filastin* as a problem. They certainly noted the presence of an indigenous population, but they rejected the notion that their new Zion would replicate the Diaspora pattern of an insecure Jewish minority contending with a hostile majority. In the first place, as they saw it, Jewish religious and historical ties to the Holy Land were undeniable and incontestable. The world seemed to recognize this link beyond any doubt; despite their sometimes hostile attitudes, both Christianity and Islam recorded a Jewish history in Palestine as part of their own scriptures. Furthermore, the world certainly did not seem inclined to welcome a Jewish homeland anywhere else on the globe.

As for the existing residents of Palestine, they would be treated fairly and would share in the benefits of the developing homeland. In the spirit of the times, the introduction of a modernizing population would raise the level of the entire country, bringing the blessings of modern (read: Western) civilization to all its inhabitants. It was sufficient, in this view, to better the welfare of non-Jewish residents as *individuals*, since they had not (yet) laid claim to a national identity, and *collective* rights, as a people (see chapter 3). One early Zionist leader, Israel Zangwill, used the phrase "a land without a people for a people without a land," by which he meant that Palestine was a land not identified with a specific nation (other than Jews), not that it was uninhabited (Garfinkle 1991).

Thus the early Zionists saw no necessary, objective conflict between the rebuilding of a Jewish homeland in *Eretz Yisrael* and respect for the rights of the non-Jewish population – so long as these rights were considered on the individual level. As individuals, Arab inhabitants would prosper and would enjoy the freedoms of liberal societies: religious freedom, civil and political rights, equality before the law. The process by which the first settlers concluded that this was not a "real" problem is strikingly condensed in a few pages of the diary of Eliezer Ben-Yehuda, considered the key mover in the revival of Hebrew as a spoken language, who arrived in 1881. Ben-Yehuda's encounter with demographic reality when he landed in Jaffa was disconcerting:

> I must confess that this, my first meeting with our cousins Ishmael, was not a joyous meeting for me. A depressing feeling of fear, as though before a fortified wall, suddenly filled my soul. I felt that they see themselves as citizens of the land that was the land of my fathers, and that I, the son of these fathers, I come to this land as a stranger, as a foreigner. (Ben-Yehuda 1941: i. 26)

Within a few days, however, Ben-Yehuda is able to record a more reassuring view of this reality:

> However, I also found a little comfort regarding the general position of the Arabs in *Eretz Yisrael*, which I have already managed to observe: that in general it is very lowly, that they are impoverished paupers and total illiterates. This fact . . . was

for me the first ray of light since the moment that my foot trod
on the land of our fathers. (Ben-Yehuda 1941: i. 37)

The lowly position of the Arabs, which Ben-Yehuda exag-
gerates to strengthen his case, becomes justification for the
Jewish role in Palestine. The early Zionists, we should recall,
tended to come from the ranks of the *maskilim* – that is,
from the most Western-oriented sectors of Russian Jewish
society. They saw themselves as "Europeans," a self-reference
that occurs often in their writings, and they were seen as
Europeans by the Arabs. European civilization was, they felt,
more advanced, not only in technology but also in culture,
education, government, law, ethics, and most other spheres of
life. This was an age in which the spread of European ideas
and techniques was not questioned, as the benefits seemed
beyond dispute. In this spirit one of the founders of Rishon
Letsion wrote that "if the colonies are established in bonds of
love and peace, then the holy land will be a land of freedom
and liberty for them; they will not hear the voice of the
gendarme and the taskmaster, and the Arabs who people the
land will submit to them with the attitude of love and respect
they show to all Europeans who work the soil and engage in
commerce here" (Laskov 1982: 190–1).

In this idyllic view, not only is there no objective conflict of
interest between Jews and Arabs in Palestine, but nothing is
required for the future of the relationship beyond the success
of Zionism itself. Achievement of the Zionist program will
assure justice to both sides. Negotiation is not necessary, let
alone any thought of military force. (In fact, the very idea of
military force was ludicrous; Jews had no talent, experience,
or inclination for soldiery!) There is no need to negotiate or
fight, since there is no collective entity on the other side; there
are only individuals to be dealt with on an individual basis.
Negotiation comes into play only on the level of the Turkish
government, which wields real power and can obstruct the
Zionist project (see below).

Ahad Ha'am, Zionism's most vigorous internal critic,
wrote a manifesto entitled "Truth from *Eretz Yisrael*," in
1891, that is widely but inaccurately regarded as the first

serious Zionist recognition of an "Arab problem." He does condemn Jewish conduct toward Arabs: "They walk with the Arabs in hostility and cruelty, unjustly encroaching on them, shamefully beating them for no good reason, and even bragging about what they do." But in fact Ahad Ha'am shared the general view that the success of the Zionist enterprise would in itself resolve any conflict by bringing the blessings of European civilization to the local population, and in the end by simply overwhelming it: "Even if in the course of time jealousy might cause hatred, this is nothing," because "by that time our brothers would be able to secure their position in *Eretz Yisrael* by their large number, their extensive and rich holdings, their unity, and their exemplary way of life" (Ginzberg 1891, tr. Dowty 2000: 175, 178).

Only in 1907 did a Zionist writer finally suggest that the relationship with the Arabs of Palestine was, in fact, "a question that outweighs all the others." Yitzhak Epstein, a teacher who had settled in Rosh Pina in 1886, published an article entitled "A Hidden Question" in *Hashiloah*, the journal founded by Ahad Ha'am (Epstein 1907, tr. Dowty 2001b). Epstein argued for a negotiated solution that would make the Arabs partners and beneficiaries in the Zionist enterprise, though Jews would remain the senior partners. His advocacy of benevolent paternalism had little immediate impact, but did help to frame the debate within the Zionist movement that developed in the following years. Opposed to Epstein's integrative approach appeared separatist or confrontational approaches which argued that Zionism had to maintain its distance from alien cultures, and that in any event a clash with the local population was inevitable (Gorny 1987). Though the positions of all parties have undergone many transformations in the years since, the basic issues and possible solutions remain basically as defined in the early debates.

While it may have taken Jewish settlers some time to recognize the depth and seriousness of Arab opposition, they could hardly ignore the opposition of the Ottoman regime, which opposed them consistently at every turn. In fact, the Ottoman government even banned the entry of Russian Jews before it began, in an 1881 edict. From the Turkish perspective, the ferment in Russia and the gathering flood of refugees could well be a Russian plot to create a base of Russian nationals in Palestine. The Ottoman Empire did not completely abandon its traditional role as a haven for Jewish refugees; Jews were welcome, it announced, anywhere in Ottoman territory *except* for Palestine (meaning primarily the independent *sanjak* of Jerusalem). Also, they could settle only as scattered individuals, not as an organized movement with a geographical concentration, and they must become Ottoman subjects and give up the protection of European consuls.

This remained the basic Ottoman policy until the fall of the empire (Mandel 1976). Some aspects of it were relaxed occasionally under pressure from the European powers, since it conflicted with their use of the Capitulations to further their influence within Ottoman territory. It also conflicted with commitments made by the Ottoman regime, in its 1856 edict, to total non-discrimination on the basis of religion. But, by and large, it is fair to say that the Ottoman government, to the best of its ability, tried to prevent European Jews from establishing a toehold in its Palestinian provinces. In addition to trying to prevent the entry of Jews, it also forbade the sale of land to those who managed to enter anyway, and refused to issue building permits to those who managed to buy land anyway.

In that case, how did the Zionists succeed to the extent that they did? By 1914, there were an estimated 94,000 Jews in what became Mandatory Palestine (Bachi 1974: 5). Of course it is likely that, had the door been open, there would have been many more; the Turkish policies were not totally ineffectual. But Zionists who were really determined found ways around or through the obstructions. One recourse was to enter as religious pilgrims, whom the authorities were obligated to admit. Permits to pilgrims were for a limited period, but enforcement was problematic. Another was to enter through the land frontiers with Egypt or Lebanon, where enforcement was more sporadic than in Jaffa, the main port of entry to the independent *sanjak* of Jerusalem (the northern parts of Eretz Yisrael were, in any event, part of the

Beirut *vilayet*). Apart from sheer inefficiency in the Ottoman bureaucracy, there was also the possibility of bribery (*baksheesh*), though this was more likely to work on the lower levels than with higher officials. Finally, once in Palestine, the new settlers could invoke the protection of their consuls to prevent deportation. In fact, it was the intervention of foreign consuls on behalf of their passport-holders that often proved decisive in gaining entry, in buying land, and in getting the prized building permits.

This, then, is the Jewish story, from its origins through the first phase of the Return to Zion. But there is, of course, another story to be told.

3 | The Arab Story

Two important phenomena, of the same nature yet opposed, which have still not attracted anyone's attention, are emerging at this moment in Asiatic Turkey. These are the awakening of the Arab nation and the quiet effort of the Jews to reconstitute the ancient kingdom of Israel on a very large scale. These two movements are destined to fight each other endlessly until one overcomes the other. The fate of the entire world hinges on the final result of this struggle between these two peoples representing two contrary principles.

Najib Azuri (Azouri 1905: p. v)

The Glory of Islam

The story of the Arabs is closely linked to the surge of Islam across a great part of the globe, but it does not begin there. The first historical mention of Arabs is in an Assyrian inscription of 853 BCE. Assyrian and Babylonian sources mention the Arabs repeatedly in following centuries, referring to nomadic tribes in the neighboring desert regions of the northern Arabian peninsula. Later books of the Bible also contain such references. Greek sources were the first to label the entire peninsula as "Arabia," while use of the term to describe nomads, or what today would be called *Beduin*, spread to the south. Even though both settled and nomadic populations spoke Arabic dialects, the use of the term "Arab" to describe the *Beduin* persisted into modern times (Lewis 1993).

Just as they had avoided direct Roman rule, the tribes in the interior of the Arabian peninsula maintained their independence from contending Byzantine and Persian empires on their periphery. Politically divided into various tribal regimes, they traded with their neighbors and encountered the ideas of Judaism and Christianity. They also possessed a strong tradition of epic poetry, much of which still survives today; the pre-Islamic epic poems testify to the linguistic virtuosity that shaped the poetic Arabic of the *Qur'an*, Islam's holy book.

Which single individual has had the greatest impact on human history? Jesus and Muhammad, the founders of two world religions that grew out of Judaism, both come to mind. Christianity swept the ancient Roman Empire and came to dominate Europe and the Americas; it has more adherents than any other faith. On the other hand, the rise of Christianity stretched over many centuries and was critically dependent on major figures, such as Paul the Apostle, who arose after Jesus' death. Muhammad, however, left at his death a powerful movement whose already-established momentum carried it, within a few decades, to dominion over a vast realm from Spain to India. Drawing again from Arnold Toynbee's sweeping view of world history, "Islam's epiphany was dramatic by comparison to Christianity's." It took 300 years for the impact of Christianity to be felt on a grand scale, while "Islam made a comparable impact during the founder's own lifetime, and its political fortunes were made by the founder himself" (Toynbee 1961: 461).

Nor was this simply a matter of military conquest. The Mongols, after all, conquered an even more extensive territory in an even shorter time. But the Mongols left only a faint imprint on the cultures they conquered, while the Muslim conquerors of the seventh and eighth centuries CE brought with them a system of thought and a way of life that transformed existing cultures forever. Islam triumphed primarily through the force of its ideas, not the military prowess of its leaders. Areas under Islamic rule underwent a process of

Islamization; most of them also adopted the Arabic language, transforming a remote Semitic dialect into one of the world's major tongues. Since the early conquests – and particularly in recent centuries – the spread of Islam has taken place mostly in areas not under Islamic rule, through peaceful conversion.

Muhammad was a middle-aged caravan trader when he began preaching in the city of Mecca in about 610 CE, at the age of forty. Mecca was a commercial center about halfway down the western (Red Sea) coast of the Arabian peninsula, in the area known as Hijaz. By the time of his death 22 years later, Muhammad had unified most of the Arabian peninsula under one political and religious regime, and had set in motion a campaign that, under the rulers who succeeded him (known as Caliphs, from Arabic *khalifa*, or successor), took Islam across North Africa into Europe, greatly reduced the Byzantine Empire, and swept over the Persian Empire and east into present-day India. Most of Iberia (Spain and Portugal) fell under Islamic rule, and Muslims remained there for over 800 years. France was also threatened; only a victory by Charles Martel in 732 at the battle of Tours – only 100 miles from Paris – stemmed the tide.

Palestine was part of the first wave of conquest following Muhammad's death in 632 CE; Jerusalem fell to the Caliph Umar in 638. The indigenous population, descended from Jews, other Semitic groups, and non-Semitic groups such as the Philistines, had been mostly Christianized. Over succeeding centuries it was Islamicized, and Arabic replaced Aramaic (a Semitic tongue closely related to Hebrew) as the dominant language.

Within a century of Muhammad's death Islam had swept across much of the known world; no other historical phenomenon matches it. Nothing in the previous history of the tribes in remote Arabia, or in the character of the arid and barren Hijaz, can explain this stunning explosion of history. It is testimony to the power and attraction of Islam itself. Muhammad was clearly influenced by the messages of Judaism and Christianity, the monotheistic Abrahamic faiths. But acting as the final "messenger" of God, he transmitted a revelation of these messages that achieved breathtaking simplicity, flexibility, and universality. He turned back to pristine monotheism, rejecting the Christian Trinity, and universalized the message across all nations, races, and cultures. All are equal before God and have direct access to God; no mediating clergy is interposed. Islam – which means "submission" – is more than a religion: it is a way of life, with a strong ethical content and a code of law governing all of life. Because of its inclusiveness and simplicity, it is able to accommodate considerable diversity, not only on racial or cultural dimensions, but also in its own laws and practices. To be a Muslim, one need only affirm that "there is no God but God, and Muhammad is the Prophet of God."

The *Qur'an* (literally: Recital) speaks in God's voice, delivered by the angel Gabriel to Muhammad. (Muhammad may have been illiterate, many Muslims point out, and if so it would be further proof that the revelation was miraculous.) The Jewish and Christian Bibles, in comparison, are compilations of both divine and human voices. The *Qur'an* is comparatively brief – 114 chapters – and is written in a clear and poetic Arabic that became the standard for written literary Arabic. Christians and Jews are often surprised by the familiarity of key figures and stories in the *Qur'an*: Adam, Noah, Abraham (father of Arabs as well as Jews), Ishmael, Isaac, Jacob, Joseph, Moses, David, Solomon, and Jesus. The *Qur'an* regards Jesus as one of the prophets, born to the Virgin Mary and with a role in the Last Judgment, but denies his divinity ("God forbid that He Himself should beget a son!" (19: 35–6)).

The best-known words of the *Qur'an* are the first revelation given to Muhammad as he meditated in a cave outside Mecca:

> Recite, in the name of thy Lord, who created,
> Created man from a clot of blood.
> Recite, for thy Lord is the most bounteous,
> Who teacheth by the pen,
> Teacheth man what he did not know. (96: 1–5)

The *Qur'an* regards Jews and Christians as "People of the Book," to whom God's message was given in earlier versions;

they are called upon to accept the final message brought by
Muhammad, but at the same time their role in the process
of revelation is recognized:

> If the People of the Book accept the true faith and keep
> from evil,
> We will pardon them their sins and admit them to the
> gardens of delight.
> If they observe the Torah and the Gospel and what is
> revealed from God,
> They shall be given abundance from above and from
> beneath . . .
> Believers, Jews, Sabaeans, or Christians –
> Whoever believes in God and the Last Day and does what
> is right –
> Shall have nothing to fear or regret. (5: 66, 69)

The first centuries of Islamic rule were a "golden age" in
which the fusion of the new faith with the civilizations it
encountered produced the most impressive flowering of civilization yet seen. From the eighth to the twelfth centuries,
as Europe groped through the Dark Ages, Islamic civilization was "unmatched in its brilliancy and unsurpassed in its
literary, scientific, and philosophic output" (Hitti 1970a: 3).
The shifting center of power reflected the expansion of hori-
zons. The first four Caliphs after Muhammad – the "rightly
guided" Caliphs who still governed an undivided Islamic state
– continued to rule from Mecca. In 661, following a split over
the succession that led to the Sunni–Shi'a division in Islam,
the Umayyad Caliphate ruled from Damascus, and in 750 the
Umayyads were displaced by the Abbasid Caliphate ruling
from Baghdad. Though the Abbasid Caliphate lasted formally
until the Mongol conquest in 1258, it disintegrated politically
well before this, with rival dynasties springing up throughout
the Islamic world. Nevertheless, it was the center of a cultural
flowering that made Baghdad one of the centers of human
civilization at the time, together with a flourishing Islamic
civilization in Spain at the other end of the Arab world.
    Islamic civilization was able to bring together and draw
upon the achievements of Aramaic, Greek, Roman, Byzantine,

Egyptian, Persian, and Indian civilizations. The result was a burst of creativity that made advances in almost every sphere of human endeavor (Hitti 1970a).

- *Language and literature.* The Arabic language came, with the early Muslims, from Hijaz in the north of the Arabian peninsula. Its rapid spread as the language of Islam also made it the primary vehicle of a great civilization. Arabic-speaking areas such as Spain achieved a high level of literacy at a time when only a few of the clergy in medieval Europe could read and write. Books, bookstores, and libraries proliferated in Islamic areas; in particular, the strong Arab tradition in poetry combined with Persian and other models to produce illustrious achievements in literature. Philology, grammar, and lexicography were all highly developed in Arab culture, influencing the development of similar studies in Europe.
- *Education.* Primary education, centered in mosques, was extensive and was supported generously by some of the more enlightened rulers. The first universities in the world, by most accounts, were established in Cordova, Baghdad, and Cairo, in the tenth and eleventh centuries. Medical schools and the first schools of pharmacy were also established in Arab societies during this period.
- *Philosophy and theology.* Philosophy prospered, as Islamic scholars mined classical sources; in fact, Arabic translations of ancient Greek texts preserved much of classical civilization that would otherwise have been lost, and the later transmission of these works to the West helped to spark the Renaissance. Legal scholars took up theories of jurisprudence, mainly of Roman origin, and developed four related but distinct codes of law that are all considered legitimate in Sunni Islam – a development that provided flexibility within consensus.
- *Mathematics.* Islamic civilization adopted the decimal system, and the use of zero, from India, and transmitted it to the West. Algebra (from Arabic *al-jabr*), trigonometry, and analytical geometry were all first developed by Arab scholars.

- *Science.* Arab scholars made particular contributions in chemistry, where they introduced the concept of the objective experiment. In astronomy, Arab observatories made observations accurate enough to determine, very closely, the size of the earth and of degrees of latitude and longitude. Optics was another area in which Arab science made remarkable strides, laying the foundation for later progress in Europe.
- *Medicine.* Arabic medical texts such as that of Ibn-Sina (Avicenna), 980–1037, were used in Europe until the seventeenth century. From the early ninth century hospitals and medical schools were established, as well as the first pharmacies and the first pharmacopoeia. The theory of infection was first propounded by an Arab physician; the first textbook in ophthalmology came from the Islamic world (Hitti 1970a: 363–9).
- *Arts.* Though Islam in its monotheistic strictures forbade use of the human image, architecture and decorative arts flourished and produced masterpieces from the Taj Mahal in India to the Alhambra in Spain. European medieval architecture was heavily inspired by Arab models (for example, the Gothic style). Musical influences included not only many instruments (lute, guitar, cymbals, tambourine, timbal, horn, rebec), but also advances in music theory and notation.
- *Geography.* Islamic civilization at its peak carried on commerce with the farthest reaches of the known world, from China and the East Indies to Central Asia and Scandinavia to East Africa. Baghdad, in its days of grandeur, boasted "miles of wharves" with "hundreds of vessels," carrying to the Abbasid capital the finest goods from around the world (Hitti 1970b: 305). Muslim traders and sailors thus became acquainted with regions only dimly known in Europe. The traveler sometimes known as "the Arab Marco Polo" (Muhammad ibn Abdullah ibn Battutah, 1304–c. 1368) not only traveled much further than Marco Polo; he also was able during most of his journeys to remain within the comfortable but extensive World of Islam.!

The scope of Arab civilization and the nature of its contributions to Europe are reflected in the many English words that come from Arabic. Some of these are: admiral, alchemy, alcohol, alcove, algebra, algorism, alkali, almanac, amber, arsenal, azimuth, candy, carafe, check, cipher, coffee, cotton, lute, magazine, nadir, orange, rice, saffron, sherbet, sugar, syrup, tariff, zenith, zero. We might also add Arabic numerals, arabesque design, cordovan leather, Damascus steel and damask fabrics, Mocha coffee, Moorish architecture, morocco leather, muslin cloth (from Mosul), and Toledo steel.

The ascendancy of Arab civilization is dramatically expressed by Philip Hitti, who notes that tenth-century Cordova, in Muslim Spain, took its place as the most cultured city in Europe and, with Constantinople and Baghdad, as one of the three cultural centers of the world. With its one hundred and thirteen thousand homes, twenty-one suburbs, seventy libraries and numerous bookshops, mosques and palaces, it acquired international fame and inspired awe and admiration in the hearts of travelers. It enjoyed miles of paved streets illuminated by lights from the bordering houses whereas, seven hundred years after this time there was not so much as one public lamp in London, and in Paris, centuries subsequently, whoever stepped over his threshold on a rainy day stepped up to his ankles in mud (Hitti 1970a: 526).

The Rise of the West

Islamic Arab civilization, by any account, was for several centuries an astounding success. What, then, explains the long period of decline that followed? As the title of Bernard Lewis's book asks, *What Went Wrong?* (Lewis 2002).

Many explanations are offered. What seems clear is that from about the tenth or eleventh centuries the pace of progress began to slow, and the first signs of stagnation appeared. In the twelfth and thirteenth centuries there was a "Closing of the Gates" regarding new interpretations of religion or religious law, creating a resistance to innovation that was reinforced by the religious control of education. Economic decline is attributed to a number of factors: the inefficiency of military feudalism and tax farming that removed incentives, the shifting of trade with the opening of new sea routes to Asia and to the New World, the appearance of potent European sea power protecting these routes and closing off the core Middle East. Another factor was political instability and internal strife within the Islamic world, weakening Islamic society and leaving it vulnerable to outside exploitation. Finally, there is the intrusion of the outside world, especially the devastating invasions of the Crusaders, beginnning at the end of the eleventh century, and of the Mongols in the middle of the thirteenth.

Some Arab scholars have also blamed the Turks. In chapter 1 we noted the rise of the Turks, originally as slave soldiers from Central Asia, beginning in the eleventh century. Blaming the Turks may be unfair; known as redoubtable warriors, they conquered and Islamized Anatolia (present-day Turkey), something that Arab armies had been unable to accomplish. It was the Turkish Mamluk regime in Cairo that stemmed the Mongol invasion, in a battle in present-day Palestine, and evicted the last of the Crusaders. And the Ottoman Turks conquered Constantinople and much of southeastern Europe for Islam, twice threatening the city of Vienna and effectively shielding the core Middle East from Europe during a period when European power was on the rise. Nevertheless, it was also the Ottoman Empire, during the latter half of its existence, that presided over the final period of decline and penetration of Western power into the Islamic heartland. By the mid-nineteenth century, the Ottoman Empire was known as the "Sick Man" of Europe, and European diplomacy wrestled with the "Eastern Question": who would get to pick up the pieces when it finally collapsed?

Whatever the reasons why the Arab world once led the West, but no longer does, the historical fact is that there was a dramatic and (from the Arab perspective) demeaning reversal of roles. At the dawn of the twentieth century, Arabs, like Jews, looked back on a past grandeur that stood in stark contrast to the humiliations and sufferings of the present. Recognition of this reality is essential to an understanding of the Arab–Israel conflict.

Arabs and other Muslims had, with justification, long regarded Europeans as culturally backward. The Toledan judge Said, in the tenth century, wrote of Europeans that "because the sun does not shed its rays directly over their heads, their climate is cold and atmosphere clouded. Consequently their temperaments have become cold and their humors rude, while their bodies have grown large, their complexion light and their hair long. They lack withal sharpness of wit and penetration of intellect, while stupidity and folly prevail among them" (Hitti 1970b: 526–7). Needless to say, the Crusades did not improve Arab perceptions of the Nordic barbarians, whose only notable skills seemed to lie in weaponry and warfare. Arabs were unlikely to forget the story of Ma'arra, in present-day Lebanon, where, according to the Crusaders' own account, "our troops boiled pagan adults in cooking-pots; they impaled children on spits and devoured them grilled" (Maalouf 1984: 39). An Arab historian born in a neighboring city later wrote: "All those who were well-informed about the Franj [Franks; European Christians] saw them as beasts superior in courage and fighting ardor but in nothing else, just as animals are superior in strength and aggression" (Maalouf 1984: 39).

Arab armies ultimately defeated and expelled the Crusaders over the course of two centuries. But deep hostility remained, especially on the Islamic side, where the Crusades remained a much more potent memory. In the following period there was little contact, so Arabs were unaware of the startling changes taking place in Europe. The Ottomans used the Christian populations they controlled in the Balkans as a source of slaves. With this attitude, they were hardly prepared to deal with a new post-Renaissance Europe mounting a new and much more formidable threat. The loss of Spain and Sicily to Christian reconquest, in the fifteenth and sixteenth centuries, was a signal that the power balance was shifting. Another was the fact that, after unsuccessfully besieging Vienna in 1683, the Ottoman Empire suffered a series of military reversals in the succeeding century, mostly against Russia, that left it much reduced and embattled. "In the late fifteenth [century]," writes a leading historian, "the disciplined professional army of the sultan, using firearms, had been a match for any in Europe . . . In the last quarter of the [eighteenth] century, however, the situation began to change rapidly and dramatically, as the gap between the technical skills of some western and northern European countries and those of the rest of the world grew wider" (Hourani 1991: 259).

The biggest shock came with Napoleon's invasion of Egypt in 1798, generally regarded as the date that Western colonialism arrived in the Middle East. The easy French victories over Ottoman forces demonstrated not only technological advantage, but also superiority in organization, training, and strategy. Muslims – Arabs and Turks alike – were suddenly faced with a Europe that had surpassed them in many areas. There were frantic efforts at quick reform, as regimes tried to close the gap by copying Western institutions and methods. In Egypt itself, the founder of a new dynasty, Muhammad Ali (who ruled from 1805 to 1848), changed the face of his country and at one point even threatened to overthrow his nominal sovereign, the Ottoman Sultan. The Ottoman regime carried out its own reform program, the *Tanzimat*, in midcentury. But the attempt to acquire modern technology, without first building the social and cultural infrastructure and values underlying this technology, was a mixed success. Much of the technology could be transferred, but attempts to liberalize institutions and cultures made little or no headway. The fact that these liberal values were associated with foreign, Western, Christian intruders was no help.

The intruders themselves seemed less interested in promoting their ideas than in expanding their control. The British took over the strategic port of Aden, on the southwestern tip of the Arabian peninsula, in 1839. They took control of Egypt, informally, in 1882, and during the 1890s they brought most of the petty rulers of the Persian Gulf into their orbit as protectorates, as a result of which these anachronistic sheikhdoms and emirates – Kuwait, Bahrain, Qatar, United Arab Emirates, Oman – are independent states today.

The French conquered Algiers in 1830, gained a foothold in Lebanon in 1861, established a protectorate over Tunisia in 1881, and finally moved into Morocco in 1911. The Russians, in the course of the century, were expanding their control of Muslim areas in both the Caucasus and Central Asia, and were bringing increasing pressure on the Ottoman Empire for leverage in the Bosphorus and the Dardanelles, the straits controlling passage between the Mediterranean and the Black Sea. And, as already noted, the European provinces of the Ottoman Empire had all won their independence by 1914.

The first stirrings of Arab nationalism had been heard by 1880 (see chapter 1), and by the turn of the century a small but visible movement had emerged. If the Turks could not protect the Islamic heartland from European depredations and cultural penetration, other solutions had to be found. Some early reformers turned to pan-Islam, urging a reunification and renewal of the Islamic world that would enable it to stand up to the new challenge. Others turned to more localized identities to rally resistance to Western colonialism; in Egypt, for example, a distinctive sense of community as Egyptians could be invoked. But others borrowed from the West itself, applying newly coined concepts of "nation" and "nation-state" to their own reality. Were they not "Arabs," sharing a common language, common culture, and common history as heirs to a great world civilization, from Morocco to Iraq? Were they less entitled than Europeans (Serbs, Montenegrins, Romanians, Bulgarians, or Albanians) to national self-determination as a nation-state based upon this ethnic identity? The term "Arab," which had been used to refer to *beduin* or to inhabitants of the Arabian peninsula, was now being embraced as a unifying identity by all Arabic speakers, apart from some smaller minorities such as Jews or Armenians who had their own distinct identities.

Arab Christians were especially prominent among early promoters of Arab nationalism. Educated Arab Christians were, first of all, more attuned to Western political ideas and ideologies such as nationalism. But, more importantly, forging a common identity as "Arabs" made them part of a political force that submerged religious differences, while as

Christians they would remain an exposed island in an Islamic ocean.

The idea of a unified Arab state, or pan-Arabism, was of course a challenge to the legitimacy of Turkish rule over Arabs, which was justified by the Sultan's status as Caliph of all Muslims. The Arab nationalists saw Turkish rule, therefore, as unjust, and advocated the overthrow of the Ottoman regime. Because of Turkish domination, this could not be done openly, and in the last two decades of the nineteenth century Arab nationalism was largely confined to small secret societies of Arab intellectuals, primarily in Beirut and Damascus.

The small size of the nationalist movement, and the fact that Arabic speakers did not all see themselves as "Arabs," does not mean that there was no sense of collective identity or political consciousness among the populations under Ottoman rule. There were in fact several levels of common identity: as Muslims, as Ottoman subjects, as members of particular clans or kinship groups, as residents of particular areas. In addition, there was identity as an indigenous population resisting outside (usually Western) intrusions. Opposition to foreigners may be the most basic level of community feeling; there was no absence of it in Ottoman territory in the late nineteenth century. This was particularly true in the "Palestinian" provinces, to which we now turn.

Palestine and Palestinism

As noted before, Ottoman administrative divisions did not correspond to historical and geographic definitions of "Palestine." After 1888, the southern area of historic Palestine was governed as the independent *sanjak* of Jerusalem, ruled directly by Constantinople, while central and northern areas were organized as the *sanjaks* of Nablus and Acre, subdivisions of the *vilayet* of Beirut, and the area east of the Jordan River was part of the *vilayet* of Damascus. The population of the Jerusalem, Nablus, and Acre districts at the beginning of the 1880s was slightly under half a million, with Arabs (Muslims and Christians) accounting for over 95 percent of this total. The population was still predominantly (two-thirds) rural.

There is a tendency to read Palestinian history backwards, looking in the nineteenth century for the roots of later failures and disasters. The result is a skewed analysis that can be highly misleading. Palestinian Arab society underwent important changes during this period, many of which contributed to a process of building a national consciousness. Donna Robinson Divine notes that "with their attention directed to explaining the loss of a Palestinian state in 1948, [scholars] have failed to appreciate Palestine's nineteenth-century history as a period of significant development" (Divine 1994: 2).

On the international level the Ottoman Empire was in decline as its relative military and economic standing sank, along with its ability to resist penetration by a rising Europe. But this does not mean that there was no progress, or at least change, domestically. European penetration itself produced important innovations and stimulated reform. Ottoman attempts to reform and modernize – the *Tanzimat* – were not entirely fruitless. Through a combination of internal pressures and external interventions, the Palestinian landscape at the end of the century was radically different from that of a century or only half a century earlier. Vast improvements in health standards, security, communication, transportation, government services, public administration, and judicial institutions transformed Palestinian life. Ottoman authority actually became more direct and effective than in the past, when the government had worked primarily through local sheikhs representing the clans and kinship groups that dominated traditional society. The Ottoman Sultan Abdul Hamid II, who ruled from 1876 to 1909, focused particularly on keeping the loyalty of Arabs, the second largest ethnic group (after the Turks themselves) in his remaining Empire, and nowhere more than in Palestine – precisely because of outside interest in the Holy Land. In this the Turks were fairly successful; despite the inroads of Arab nationalism, most Arab subjects of the Sultan remained loyal during World War I.

Of course not all reforms had the intended result. An 1858 Land Law, with subsequent refinements, tried to regularize land ownership through a system of registration and taxation. The impact, however, was to transfer much communal land, which peasants had farmed for generations, to private ownership. A new class of wealthy, and often absentee, landowners emerged, along with a large number of landless tenants (including some who lost their land because they could not pay the new taxes). These landowners, along with notable urban families and merchants prospering in the growing cash economy, pushed aside the traditional clan-based leadership. At the same time the tenant farmers, with no legal claim to the land, became vulnerable to displacement if the land was sold to new owners. These new owners might even be non-Ottoman citizens, as the government was under strong pressure from European powers to honor its obligation to allow land ownership by foreigners. This situation was a key factor in many large land purchases by the Zionist movement.

Aversion to non-Muslim foreigners – not just Jews, but all non-Muslim foreigners – was deeply rooted in Palestinian society. The legacy of the Crusades, only a dim memory in the Christian West, was very much alive in the Holy Land itself. European nations were not allowed to have a diplomatic presence in Jerusalem, and non-Muslim foreigners could not live there. Both of these bans were ended during Muhammad Ali's control of Palestine in the 1830s, but the hostility remained; the first Western consuls in Jerusalem had to be protected by armed escorts. There were riots, in some cases, when European flags were raised or church bells were rung. Perhaps the most galling aspect of the growing European presence was the constant intervention by foreign consuls under the Capitulations (extraterritorial judicial powers) to protect not only their own citizens but also Ottoman citizens who shared their faith. Ottoman authorities tried to eliminate the Capitulations, but Western powers were not about to give up a lever that had proven so useful in promoting their own presence and balancing that of their rivals.

The Ottoman Empire's international orientation was changing during this period. Earlier, Great Britain had propped up the Turks when they were threatened, organizing Great Power coalitions to force Muhammad Ali and his French backers out of Palestine and Syria in 1840, and to oppose Russia in the Crimean War of 1853–6. Russia was always the first concern in Constantinople, given the long history of conflict, but by the 1880s Britain and France had also emerged as major threats. The British occupation of Egypt (1882) was particularly important, and so was the growing strategic cooperation among Britain, France, and Russia. Consequently the Sultan, on the basis of the classic Middle Eastern adage that "the enemy of my enemy is my friend," was turning to Germany, the new European power that opposed the other three.

While these developments were felt throughout the Ottoman Empire, in the Palestinian provinces the struggle was particularly acute. This was because it was in Palestine that the efforts of infiltration and penetration were most intense. The British might take military control of Egypt, but they were not trying to alter Egyptian society or demography – and anyway, the Ottomans had not really controlled Cairo for some time. In Palestine there was a growing sense among the population that they faced a particular threat because of Palestine's unique significance. This is the beginning of a particular identity as Palestinians, in tandem with the other emerging national identity as Arabs. In the decades to come, the interplay between "Arab" and "Palestinian" identities played a key role in Palestinian discourse.

One pole of this discourse was "Palestinism": "the belief that the Arab population originating in the area of the Palestine mandate is distinct from other Arab groups, with a right to its own nation-state in that territory" (Kimmerling and Migdal 1993: p. xviii).

It is sometimes claimed that Palestinian identity developed only in reaction to Zionism. This is inaccurate; while the rise of the Zionist movement reinforced Palestinism, it did not create it. Even the resistance to foreign penetration was not new, as there were other "others" before Zionism (Europeans, Turks) who stimulated local patriotism (R. Khalidi 1997: 154).

First Encounters

How did the Arab population react to the early Zionist settlers? As we have seen, the first Zionists came at a time when the entire Ottoman Empire was engaged in a rearguard defense against European threats from a number of quarters, internal and external. European Jews were naturally regarded as part and parcel of these colonialist and imperialist threats. It was enough that the Zionists were European; they were seen as another front in the overall struggle. On the other hand, both Turks and Arabs regarded the British, the French, the Russians, and general Western cultural and economic penetration, as the major fronts; compared to these threats, the challenge posed by a handful of Jewish farmers seemed relatively inconsequential.

The existing Palestinian Jewish community was assimilated into Arab culture, for the most part. The newcomers from Europe were too few for their presence to be felt, at first, by most Arabs. Where they settled, Zionists did encounter hostility and opposition locally. But this could be dismissed as a natural xenophobic response to strangers rather than a reaction to Zionism itself. The incidents were isolated and sporadic, and did not signal (Zionists reassured themselves) any general pattern of opposition to the idea of a Jewish home in Palestine. Of course Zionist settlers were trying to recruit more settlers, and were not likely to emphasize difficulties that, they thought, would in any event go away.

But, over time, resistance to Zionism grew as Zionism itself grew. Every new Jewish settlement had property disputes with neighbors, even when efforts were made to get agreed demarcation of property lines in advance. Another major source of conflict was the displacement from purchased land of tenant farmers who, in the wake of the 1858 Land Law, had lost rights to land cultivated by their families for generations. Offers of generous compensation, beyond that required by law, did not always work; some disputes dragged on for years. In the Arab view, this should hardly be surprising. There was a pattern here: that of an indigenous population reacting to alien intruders. This did not require that this population possess a common identity as "Arabs" or "Palestinians"; it required only that they felt threatened by an influx of outsiders. This common reaction does not require a modern sense of nationalism.

Arabs from neighboring villages attacked Petach Tikvah in 1886, Gedera in 1888, Yesud Ha'ma'alah in 1890, Rehovot in 1892, 1893, and 1899, Kastina in 1896, Jewish Jaffa in 1908, and Sajera in 1909. There were in every case specific triggers to the attacks, but the general pattern speaks for itself.

In June 1891 some 500 notable Arab figures in Jerusalem sent a petition to Constantinople demanding a halt to all Jewish immigration and all land sales to Jews. The immediate trigger was the threat of a new wave of Russian Jewish settlers. The Ottoman government responded sympathetically, forbidding the entry of Russian Jews in August of that year, and of all Jews in October (Mandel 1976: 39–40). Such decrees violated the Ottoman pledge of non-discrimination on the basis of religion or race and evoked sharp counter-pressure from European powers. Between this and the usual problems of enforcement, many new settlers made it into Palestine despite Ottoman policy (see chapter 2).

This was still several years before Theodore Herzl and the founding of the World Zionist Organization (WZO) made political Zionism a recognized and visible movement. On March 1, 1899, soon after the WZO's establishment, a distinguished member of one of Jerusalem's leading families, Yusuf Diya Pasha al-Khalidi, sent a letter to the Chief Rabbi of France, who was close to Herzl, challenging the Zionist program. Al-Khalidi began by acknowledging the historic Jewish link: "Who can challenge the rights of the Jews on Palestine? Good Lord, historically it is really your country." But he then warned that neither the Muslim nor the Christian worlds would allow this to happen, and begged the Zionist movement to find a less problematic locale for its visions:

It is necessary, therefore, for the peace of the Jews in Turkey that the Zionist movement, in the geographic sense of the word, stops ... Good Lord, the world is vast enough, there

are still uninhabited countries where one could settle millions
of poor Jews who may perhaps become happy there and one
day constitute a nation. That would perhaps be the best, the
most rational solution to the Jewish question. But in the name
of God, let Palestine be left in peace. (Mandel 1976: 47–8)

Herzl responded to al-Khalidi with the familiar argument
that Jewish settlement of Palestine would bring benefits to the
existing non-Jewish population: "It is their well-being, their
individual wealth which we will increase by bringing in our
own" (W. Khalidi 1987: 92).

By this time expressions of Arab opposition to Zionist
settlement were coming with increasing frequency. In the
same year, 1899, Muhammad Tahir al-Husayni, Mufti of
Jerusalem (and father of Hajj Amin al-Husayni, Mufti of
Jerusalem and dominant Palestinian Arab leader during the
British Mandate period) proposed that all Jews who had
entered the Jerusalem *sanjak* since 1891 should be expelled,
and that terror should be employed to achieve that end.
Furthermore, the debate had spread to Arab intellectual
circles outside Palestine. Muhammad Rashid Rida, a Syrian
living and writing in Egypt who is considered one of the
leading pre-nationalists in the Arab world, wrote in an
Egyptian newspaper in 1898:

You complacent ones, raise your heads and open your eyes.
Look at what peoples and nations do. Are you happy to see
the newspapers of every country reporting that the poor of
the weakest peoples [the Jews], whom the governments of all
nations are expelling, master so much knowledge and understanding of civilization methods that they are able to possess
and colonize your country, and turn its masters into laborers
and its wealthy into poor? (Muslih 1988: 75)

The evidence is overwhelming that the Arab inhabitants of
Ottoman Palestine, far from feeling indifferent or permissive
toward the immigration of European Jews to their homeland,
consistently opposed such immigration. Had they been able
to settle the question democratically, there is little doubt that

they would have voted to exclude Zionist settlers – and for that matter any "Western" interlopers. The Ottoman government, responding both to Arab demands and to its own interests, tried to carry out such a policy. The fact that it failed was due, at least in part, to political realities beyond its control.

The Debut of Arab Nationalism

In the last decade before World War I the ferment in the Ottoman Empire increased, Western pressures intensified, and the Arab–Zionist conflict went public. Tied to all of this was the appearance of Arab nationalism as a significant force in the region.

In 1905 Najib Azuri, a Lebanese Christian who had served in the Ottoman bureaucracy in Jerusalem, published in Paris *Le Reveil de la Nation Arabe* (The Awakening of the Arab Nation), the first "textbook" of secular Arab nationalism. Azuri called for an Arab state, independent of the Turks, from Iraq to the Suez (the Egyptians were not yet considered "Arab"). Palestine received considerable attention; in the passage quoted at the beginning of this chapter, Azuri predicted that "the fate of the entire world" would depend on the outcome of the Arab–Jewish struggle, which would continue until one side had won a total victory (a "zero-sum" view of the conflict). This was a rather remarkable projection, given that both national movements were still in an embryonic stage. The book includes many anti-Zionist and even anti-Semitic passages, indicating that from the outset some Arab nationalists saw the Zionist issue as a central part of their program.

In 1908 Azuri published an article proposing that the independent *sanjak* of Jerusalem be raised to the status of a *vilayet*, thus making Palestine a political unit on the highest level in the Ottoman Empire. This was necessary, he said, because "the progress of the land of Palestine depends on it" (R. Khalidi 1997: 28, 151–2). This may have been the first political, and not just geographic, use of the term.

In July 1908 Ottoman army officers forced Sultan Abdul

Hamid II to restore the constitution of 1876, which he had suspended in 1878; in the following year the Sultan was deposed. This "Young Turk" Revolution brought out into the open both the growing Arab nationalist movement and the growing conflict over Zionist settlement in Palestine. Arab leaders expected that a restored Parliament and other liberal reforms would give them a greater voice in affairs of state; the Young Turks, however, were interested primarily in preserving the Empire, and in pursuit of their own nationalist visions embarked on a campaign of "Turkification" among minorities. This only spurred Arab nationalists to redouble their efforts, this time as an organized and visible political movement offering a clear and compelling alternative to the Ottoman framework: a unified Arab state. While most Arabs remained loyal Ottoman subjects in World War I, the strength of Arab nationalism was sufficient for the British to instigate an "Arab Revolt" against the Ottoman enemy.

The Palestinian provinces were at the center of this turmoil, with both Arab nationalism and "Palestinism" achieving greater visibility and greater support. The first major Palestinian newspapers, *al-Karmil* in Haifa and *al-Quds* in Jerusalem, appeared in 1908; in 1911 *Filastin* was founded in Jaffa. The terms "Palestine" and "Palestinian" were coming into general use, and the Zionist threat received increasing attention not just in Palestine but also in neighboring Arab countries. Rashid Khalidi's survey of ten Arab newspapers (two Palestinian papers, five in Beirut, two in Cairo, and one in Damascus), in the 1908–14 period, found over 600 articles dealing with the Zionist issue. By this time, clearly, Zionism was on the Arab agenda. Furthermore, the Arab view of Zionism was uniformly negative in all but one of the newspapers (the exception was one of the Cairo papers) (R. Khalidi 1997: 122–4).

In the restored Ottoman Parliament, the deputy from Jaffa, Hafiz al-Said, raised the issue of Zionism in June 1909. The two deputies from Jerusalem both spoke against Jewish settlement in Palestine. One of them, Ruhi al-Khalidi, later told a Hebrew newspaper that individual Jews should be allowed to enter freely.

But to establish Jewish colonies is another question. The Jews have the financial capacity. They will be able to buy many tracts of land, and displace the Arab farmers from their land and their fathers' heritage. However, we did not conquer this land from you. We conquered it from the Byzantines who ruled it then. We do not owe anything to the Jews. The Jews were not here when we conquered the country. (Mandel 1976: 77).

In a similar parliamentary debate in 1911, the second deputy from Jerusalem, Said al-Husayni, contended that "the Zionists' aim was to create a Jewish state extending from Palestine and Syria to Iraq" (Mandel 1976: 113).

Arab opposition to Zionism also tied the Zionists to the Capitulations and the special protection that settlers were receiving from foreign powers. *Al-Asma'i*, a Jaffa newspaper, declared that "they harm the local population and wrong them, by relying on the special rights accorded to foreign powers in the Ottoman Empire and on the corruption and treachery of the local administration" (Mandel 1976: 81). Shukri al-Asali, the governor of Nazareth, wrote a long and bitter open letter in 1910 about the disloyalty of the Zionists:

They have deceived the Government with lying and false-hood when they enroll themselves as Ottoman subjects in the registers, for they continue to carry foreign passports which protect them; and whenever they go to Ottoman courts, they produce their passports and summon foreign protection . . . If the Government does not set a limit to this torrential stream, no time will pass before you see that Palestine has become a property of the Zionist Organization and its associates. (Mandel 1976: 89)

What is apparently the first poem directed against the Zionist intrusion appeared in *Filastin* in November 1913. It was written by Sheikh Sulayman al-Taji, an Arab political figure from Jaffa, and it demonstrates that, even at this early stage, the objective conflict over land was beginning to evoke subjective prejudices and hatreds:

Jews, sons of clinking gold, stop your deceit;
We shall not be cheated into bartering away our country!
Shall we hand it over, meekly,
while we still have some spirit left?
Shall we cripple ourselves?
The Jews, the weakest of all peoples and the least of them,
are haggling with us for our land;
How can we slumber on?
We know what they want
– and they have the money, all of it . . .
And you, O Caliph, guardian of the faithful,
have mercy on us, your shield . . .
Bearer of the Crown, does it please you
that we should witness our country
being bought from us, wrenched from us?

(Mandel 1976: 175–6)

Palestinians and other Arabs, by this time, had reached a fairly solid and consistent consensus about the project of a Jewish "return" to their ancestral homeland. Put simply: Palestine is at the heart of the Arab world, and has had an Islamic and Arab majority population since the ninth century – for a millennium. It still has a 90 percent Arab majority. If the right of self-determination has any meaning at all, Palestinian Arabs must be permitted to defend their homes, their livelihoods, their culture, and their way of life against the uninvited intrusion of an alien nation that openly declares its goal of taking over their country by transforming its demography. Jews have enjoyed the status of *dhimmi* (protected people) in Islamic lands, so long as they accepted the existing framework and assimilated culturally. The Zionists are a different matter. Zionists come from Europe, infected with the colonialist mentality that justifies the conquest and subjugation of non-Western peoples and lands. They have no intention of adjusting to the Palestinian culture and way of life; instead they intend to impose their designs upon the local people. We will never accept a non-Muslim state in the heart of the Arab and Islamic worlds, and so long as this is their goal, there is an irreconcilable conflict between us.

By the time World War I erupted, therefore, the seeds had been sown, and the basic outlines of future conflict were evident to a careful observer. The issues had been defined, and most of the arguments had been laid out already. What remained was for these doleful projections to play out with the stately inevitability of a Greek tragedy.

4 | The Emergence of Israel

The State of Israel! My eyes filled with tears, and my hands shook. We had done it. We had brought the Jewish state into existence ... From this day on we would no longer live on sufferance in the land of our forefathers. Now we were a nation like other nations, master – for the first time in twenty centuries – of our own destiny. The dream had come true – too late to save those who had *perished* in the Holocaust, but not too late for the generations to come.

Golda Meir (Meir 1975: 226)

The British Mandate

By 1914 the Jewish population in *Eretz Yisrael/Filastin* was an estimated 94,000, about 13.6 percent of the 689,300 total (Bachi 1974: 5). The new yishuv (Jewish community in Palestine), those committed to Zionism, now overshadowed the old *yishuv* of more traditional non-Zionist and anti-Zionist Jews. Considering the obstacles, this was quite an achievement, but it seemed very unlikely that it would produce a Jewish state. What the Zionists had built was a framework with an ideological vanguard of highly committed pioneers; what they lacked was the multitude who would fill in this framework. The prospects for mass immigration, moreover, were rather bleak. Most Jews fleeing Russia continued to pick other destinations. More importantly, Ottoman policy remained hostile; during the Great War that followed, Turkish authorities made a huge dent in the existing *yishuv* by deporting many foreign passport-holders.

For lack of a better option, Zionist leaders were still trying to break through the brick wall in Constantinople. Two promising young pioneers, David Ben-Gurion and Yitzhak Ben-Zvi, traveled to the Ottoman capital to master Turkish and study Ottoman law. As events turned out, of course, this was a rather short-sighted decision.

Fortunately for the Zionists, the Ottoman government also made a bad decision: choosing to side with the Central Powers in World War I. Once again external events rescued the Zionist movement when it had run out of steam. Perhaps the Turks had no real choice: if the Allied Powers won the war, Britain and France would almost certainly concede to Russia its long-sought foothold in the straits, at Turkish expense. Be that as it may, when the Ottomans aligned themselves with Germany, the path was open for the Allies to do exactly that. The three powers proceeded to parcel out Ottoman territory among themselves in secret agreements (primarily the 1916 Sykes–Picot agreement) that indeed gave Russia control of the straits, while also handing Syria and Lebanon to France, promising most of present-day Iraq and Jordan to Britain, and projecting an international dominion in Palestine.

Great Britain also instigated an "Arab Revolt" within the Ottoman Empire in order to hasten its demise. Their agent in this cause was the Ottoman-appointed governor of the holy cities, the Sharif of Mecca, Husayn ibn Ali, head of the Hashemite dynasty and thirty-seventh in direct descent from the Prophet. The British promised to Husayn, also in secret negotiations, their support in the establishment of an Arab state or states under Hashemite rule in the Arabian peninsula, Syria, Iraq, and – in the Hashemite interpretation – Palestine (great controversy followed on this last point, which depended upon which Ottoman administrative unit was intended by the English word "district"). Clearly the British were going to have some trouble reconciling this commitment and their previous transaction with the French.

But this was not the last British promise in the Middle East. Engaged in an apocalyptic world war, Britain was also courting the Zionist movement as a means of winning Jewish support in Russia and the United States, and possibly gaining an ally on the ground, near the vital Suez Canal, in the future Middle East. The British government also feared that the German enemy might soon make a pro-Zionist move of its own. Finally, some British leaders, including Prime Minister David Lloyd George, were "Gentile Zionists" drawn to the idea of Jewish revival in the Holy Land on religious and biblical grounds.

Consequently, on November 2, 1917, British Foreign Secretary Lord Arthur Balfour released the following policy statement in the form of a letter to Lord Lionel Rothschild, head of the British Zionist Federation:

> His Majesty's Government view with favor the establishment in Palestine of a national home for the Jewish people and will use their best endeavors to facilitate the achievement of this object, it being clearly understood that nothing shall be done which may prejudice the civil and religious rights of existing non-Jewish communities in Palestine or the rights and political status enjoyed by Jews in any other country.

This is the famous Balfour Declaration. It was only a statement of British policy, but it became legally relevant when it was written into the British Mandate for Palestine by the League of Nations. The British government had debated the statement at length and circumscribed it carefully: it spoke of a "national home," not a state; it was to be "in Palestine," not "of Palestine"; and the rights of the non-Jewish population were to be respected (in the Jewish and British readings, this meant the individual rights of Arabs and not Arab national rights). Despite the qualifications, Zionists welcomed the statement as a major victory, and the establishment of a Palestine Mandate, with the building of a Jewish national home as one of its guidelines, conferred international legitimacy on the Zionist enterprise. For Arabs, the declaration and Mandate were simple colonialism, with the British presuming to dispose of territory they did not rightfully possess.

With the fall of the Russian, Austro-Hungarian, and Ottoman Empires, and the defeat of Germany, the remaining Great Powers could finally come to terms on partition of the Middle East. Britain and France dominated the drawing of a new post-war map of the region, which is still the basic map today. The Ottoman Empire was replaced by an ethnic Turkish state reduced to Anatolia. Iraq became a League of Nations Mandate under British rule, while the French took on mandates for Syria and Lebanon – all of this more or less in accord with the earlier agreements. Palestine became a British rather than an international Mandate, and at first included present-day Jordan as well as Palestine. But the British were still scrambling to reconcile their various commitments, especially after the French expelled Faysal, son of Sharif Husayn and would-be Hashemite ruler, from Syria. Britain decided, therefore, to organize the territory east of the Jordan River (77 percent of the total area) as a semi-autonomous emirate named "Transjordan," under the rule of Abdullah ibn Husayn, another son of Sharif Husayn. Faysal ibn Husayn was given a newly created throne in Iraq.

This left the 23 percent of the original territory lying west of the Jordan River, between internationally recognized borders with Egypt to the south and Lebanon and Syria to the north, as the final Palestine Mandate. There were vocal elements in the Zionist camp who objected that the biblical Land of Israel had included the East Bank of the Jordan, and there were also Palestinian Arabs who criticized the severing of Transjordan from Palestine. But the British division of the Mandate, confirmed by the League of Nations in 1922, led to the separate development of the two areas, and the borders set at that time became the generally accepted definition of "Palestine."

Within the new Palestine, the British had a built-in conflict to resolve. They were mandated both (1) to help build a Jewish national home and (2) to prepare the population for self-government. Since Arabs in Palestine overwhelmingly opposed the idea of a Jewish national home there, the task facing the British was daunting. It seemed more likely that they would earn the condemnation of both sides than the approval of either. But they did embark on an honest effort to find common ground. In the first stage, apart from separating Transjordan, the British government under Colonial Secretary Winston Churchill issued a White Paper stating very plainly that a "national home" did not mean making all of Palestine into a Jewish nation. Furthermore, Jewish immigration would be limited by the "absorptive capacity" of the country.

The critical problem was that on this issue, immigration, there was not and could not be any middle ground. Immigration was the core issue, the Holy Grail, in the dreams and fears of both sides. For Jews, only by achieving majority status could they fulfill the 2,000-year-old dream; any limit on Jewish immigration was too much. For Arabs, the ultimate nightmare was losing majority status in their own land; any Jewish immigration was too much. This was truly a zero-sum confrontation; no compromise would satisfy either side. Thus each new *aliyah* (wave of Jewish immigration) triggered Arab demonstrations and riots, and each wave of protest and violence produced the instinctive British response: an investigating commission. Five such royal commissions were established during the Mandate period; typically, each of them pointed out that the guidelines of the Mandate were contradictory and recommended backing down a little on the commitment to a Jewish national home. Typically, both sides rejected such a compromise as either too much or too little, and the situation returned to its original, unstable state. As a result of the deadlock, the British were unable to develop national institutions that would bring Arabs and Jews together; each community developed its own institutions, and the separation between them intensified over time.

There were, however, two realities that favored the Zionist cause. The first was that the gate, which had formally been closed under Ottoman rule, was now at least partly open; the British might be limiting immigration, but they did feel committed to permitting a carefully regulated, steady influx of Jewish immigrants. The second reality was that persecution of Jews in Europe not only continued but reached a crescendo in the 1930s and 1940s, while other traditional havens had closed their gates. This created enormous pressure on the British to admit more desperate Jewish refugees to Palestine.

Because of deportations and hardships, the Jewish population had fallen during the war years by as much as one-third, but by the time of the 1922 British census, it was back up to 83,790, or 11.1 percent of the total. This increased to 174,606 (16.9 percent) in the 1931 census and to an estimated 630,000 (32 percent) at the end of 1947 (not including an estimated 100,000 illegal immigrants) (Bachi 1974: 5).

For Jews, therefore, this was a period of achievement and hope. The eternal Jewish link to Eretz Yisrael had been internationally recognized; this was the "charter" that Herzl had sought in vain. At first there was even hope that Arabs might agree to a Jewish homeland, and the WZO negotiated briefly with the Hashemites. After all, there was a large Arab world of which Palestine was but a tiny corner, but for Jews it was their only homeland. But at least Jews now had, potentially, a secure haven from persecution. Palestine served this function as, once again, the waves of immigration reflected anti-Semitic pressures in countries of origin: the third aliyah, 1920–3, from Russia; the fourth aliyah, mid-1920s, from Poland; the fifth aliyah, mid-1930s, from Germany and other countries threatened by Nazism.

But were Jews any more secure in Palestine? Given Arab attacks in 1920, 1921, 1929, and 1936–39, wasn't history simply repeating itself? Not at all, in the Jewish view. There was a critical difference in Palestine: in their homeland, Jews were free and able to organize in their own defense. Following the first attacks in 1920, a Jewish defense organization – Haganah (Defense) – was founded to protect Jews and Jewish settlements from threatened violence. In the course of time, this became the foundation of the military force with which the *yishuv* was able to secure its existence against seemingly impossible odds.

And now it was more important than ever for Jews to have at least one secure haven. During the 1920s, countries of free immigration, beginning with the United States, had closed their gates. By the late 1930s, as the position of Jews in Central and Eastern Europe became increasingly precarious, there were no havens apart from Palestine. Those who managed to make it to Palestine, under British numerical quotas, were no longer a small, unrepresentative ideological vanguard. Now whole Jewish communities, or large segments of them, were turning to Palestine as the only port in a world of storms. The classic case was that of German and Austrian Jews, relatively few of whom had been active Zionists, who fled en masse to the only refuge available – Palestine – in response to Nazi barbarity. They, in turn, were lucky in comparison with the Jews of Poland and Eastern Europe, who were trapped in the Holocaust after the British had all but shut this one last gate of rescue.

Politically, the *yishuv* was divided among Labor Zionists, who combined Zionism with socialism, religious Zionists, General Zionists who rejected socialism, Revisionist Zionists who advocated more militant policies, and the ultra-Orthodox (the "old *yishuv*") who rejected Zionism.

By the early 1930s Labor Zionists dominated the politics and institutions of the *yishuv*, usually in coalitions with religious Zionists and General Zionists. David Ben-Gurion, as Secretary-General of the Histadrut (Labor Federation) and later Chairman of the Jewish Agency Executive, became the preeminent Jewish leader. Ben-Gurion combined a commitment to restructuring Jewish life with a very realistic view of power realities. During this period he made several attempts to reach an overall accommodation with key Arab leaders; in 1933 and 1934 he met, for example, with Musa Alami, Government Advocate in the Mandate administration, proposing that Arabs concede Palestine and Transjordan to the Zionists in return for Jewish support in the creation of a federation of independent Arab states. No Arab leader, however, was interested in such a deal (Furlonge 1969: 102–5).

Though also divided along political, social, and kinship lines, Palestinian Arabs were focused on the injustice embodied in the Mandate itself. For Arabs throughout the region, the idea of "mandates" was a betrayal by European powers who had promised self-determination and independence to those who had suffered under the Turkish yoke. Instead,

Arabs found themselves defined in Article 22 of the League of Nations Covenant among "peoples not yet able to stand by themselves under the strenuous conditions of the modern world," who were therefore to be subjected to the tutelage of the Mandatory powers "until such time as they are able to stand alone." Arab civilization had stood alone, of course, when Europe was still in the Dark Ages. The entire concept of a "mandate" was an insult and a travesty demonstrating the extent of Western arrogance; it was simply a mask for imperialism and colonialism. There were in fact armed revolts against European rule throughout the interwar period, in Egypt, Syria, Iraq, Libya, and Morocco as well as Palestine, all part of a history of 170 years of indigenous resistance to foreign occupation (R. Khalidi 2004: 25–30).

In Palestine the situation was even worse, since the Mandate was also seen as a cover for designs to alter the basic demography of the nation over the protests of the vast majority of its people. Palestine had been Muslim and Arab for over a millennium; its people were entitled to the same basic right of self-determination claimed by all peoples, unconditionally and without delay. Jews, it was pointed out, had dwelt peacefully in Muslim and Arab lands and could continue to do so on an individual basis. But Jews had no national rights in Palestine, since Palestine was an inalienable part of the Islamic heartland, and in any event Jews did not constitute a nation. Judaism was a religion, whose free practice had always been tolerated in Islamic societies. The problem was not Jews but Zionists, who sought to introduce a foreign, European culture, refused to assimilate to the framework of an Islamic society, and sought to displace this society with their own.

In other words, as they saw it the Arabs of Palestine faced the threat of being subjugated in their own land. All of the major elements of Mandate rule – liberal immigration, new laws on land sales, economic initiatives favoring new enterprises, measures of "divide and rule" toward the Arab community – favored the development of Jewish newcomers over the indigenous population. Even the official commissions of inquiry established by the British themselves, Arab observers pointed out, recognized the legitimacy of these concerns, though it seldom resulted in a meaningful change of course. As for Jewish refugees, Arabs pointed out that they could not be held responsible for the persecution of Jews elsewhere. Since this persecution was taking place in the Christian world, the Christian world should find a solution that did not impose the burden on innocent third parties. Palestinians were being asked to pay for the sins of others; this was clearly an unjust demand that could be pressed only because of the temporary weakness of the Islamic and Arab worlds at this point in history. Furthermore, all the usual channels for peaceful political protest and change were blocked, leaving Palestinians no option except to go outside the law in order to defend their basic existence as a people.

The dominant Palestinian Arab leader to emerge in this period was al-Hajj Amin al-Husayni, from a prominent Jerusalem family that had long held key religious offices in the Muslim community. Al-Husayni's career was a microcosm of the changes in orientation and identity among Palestinians of his generation. Initially a loyal subject of the Sultan, al-Husayni served in the Ottoman army during World War I until the Hashemite call for an Arab Revolt won his loyalty. Hoping that union of Palestine with Syria would defeat Zionism, he continued to support Faysal's claim to a throne in Damascus until the French put an end to it. Al-Husayni then became one of the leaders of the new Palestinian nationalist movement, without abandoning his pan-Arab or pan-Islamic inclinations (Mattar 1988: 12–18).

In 1921 al-Husayni was appointed by the British as Mufti of Jerusalem, the top Muslim post in Palestine. The following year he was also elected Head of a new Supreme Muslim Council. From this position of power the new Mufti was able to dominate Palestinian politics, undercutting political movements and parties based, by and large, on other notable families. The Mufti was known for his unbending opposition to any compromise with Zionism or any accommodation that would include official recognition of a Jewish community in Palestine. In 1936–9 Arab unrest finally erupted into what they termed "the Great Revolt," feeling that they had been left with no option except revolt. The Mufti fled to avoid arrest by the British for his role in the uprising, and later discredited himself in Nazi-controlled Europe, where, in the words of his biographer, he "cooperated with the most barbaric regime in modern times" (Mattar 1988: 99).

A Mischievous Pretence?

By the mid-1930s Zionist Jews and Palestinian Arabs both recognized the seriousness of the conflict between them. In the beginning, Zionists had been able to deny the existence of a problem by persuading themselves that Arabs would welcome the transformation of Palestine into a Jewish state because of the individual benefits that they would gain. Palestinian Arabs, for their part, had not realized at first that the small community of European Jewish newcomers represented an entirely new kind of challenge, in contrast to the Jews who had been content to live as individuals in Arab societies. Now both sides began to take seriously the collective ethnic and national identities and claims of the other.

This does not mean, however, that either side had yet abandoned its exclusive claim to Palestine. Most Zionists still looked forward to achievement of a Jewish majority in an undivided Palestine; they would then give Arabs, as a minority, the kind of decent treatment and respect that they, as Jews, had always sought but seldom enjoyed. On the other side, Palestinian Arabs now saw the Zionist threat as real, but were determined to maintain the character of an undivided Palestine as an Arab and Muslim state. Both sides still saw it, in other words, as a zero-sum game: a winner-take-all contest for total stakes. David Ben-Gurion put it very simply: "We and they want the same thing. We both want Palestine" (Teveth 1985: 166).

Given consensus on the borders of *Filastin/Eretz Yisrael*, there were, and are, only a limited number of logical possibilities for resolution of the conflict.

As outlined in figure 4.1, the first choice is between leaving the territory, as defined by the British, undivided, or dividing

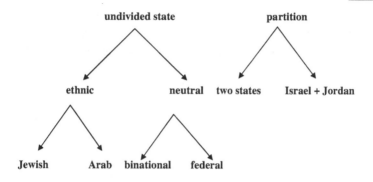

Figure 4.1 Possible solutions of the Israeli–Palestinian conflict.

it into separate political units. If it is left undivided, it could become either a state identified with a dominant ethnic group, like most nation-states today, or it could aspire to ethnic neutrality like some states with power-sharing arrangements ("consociationalism") among ethnic groups, such as Switzerland, Belgium, and Canada. If it is to be an undivided ethnic state, then of course there remains the not insignificant question of whether it is to be a Jewish state or an Arab state – and in either case, what happens to residents of the non-dominant nationality. If it is to be an ethnically neutral state, there is a choice between a binational state, carefully constructed so that central governmental powers are divided between Jews and Arabs, or a federal system of some sort based on the decentralization of powers to constituent Jewish and Arab territorial units.

The second major option – dividing Palestine – was first proposed in 1937 by the British Peel Commission, which was appointed to investigate the causes of the 1936–9 uprising. Partition has been at the center of most international initiatives and resolutions since then. Within the general framework of partition there have always been two major possibilities: partition of Palestine between a Jewish state and a Palestinian Arab state (the "two-state" solution), or partition between a Jewish state and one or more of the existing contiguous Arab states – usually Jordan, since that state was itself initially a part of the Palestine Mandate. This latter possibility, often overlooked, was in fact the solution preferred by the Peel Commission and was the de facto situation during the 1948–67 period.

In its final report, the Peel Commission concluded that "an irrepressible conflict has arisen between two national communities within the narrow bounds of one small country ... There is no common ground between them." Trying to find some kind of common Palestinian framework was, therefore, "a mischievous pretence. Neither Arab nor Jew has any sense of service to a single State." The Commission highlighted the contradiction that had always been at the heart of the Mandate: "To put it into one sentence, we cannot – in Palestine as it now is – both concede the Arab claim to self-government and secure the establishment of the Jewish National Home." The only workable solution was to establish two sovereign states: an Arab state of about 80 percent of Palestine united with Transjordan, and a Jewish state in the other 20 percent of Palestine (basically the coastal plain from Tel Aviv north and the Galilee) (Palestine Royal Commission 1937: 370–1, 374, 381).

In response to the Peel recommendation, Palestinian Arabs, who still constituted a decisive majority, resisted partition or even autonomy for the Jewish minority. Palestine had been Arab and Muslim for centuries; was one to reward trespassers by surrendering even a part of what they illegitimately laid claim to? If your home is invaded and the invaders agree to occupy only the ground floor, is this truly a fair and just "compromise"?

On the Jewish side, the vision of an undivided Eretz Yisrael gave way to a pragmatic acceptance by a majority of a Jewish state in part of Palestine. The Jewish leadership, over the protests of Revisionist Zionists who continued to oppose any division of Palestine (even the East Bank, for that matter), accepted the principle of partition proposed by the Peel Commission, though not the specific borders in the proposal.

The 1936–9 uprising took place against a backdrop of gathering war clouds in Europe. The rise of Nazi Germany and the onslaught of anti-Semitism in Europe brought a new surge in Jewish immigration to Palestine; in light of the lack of havens elsewhere, the British were compelled to open the gates a little more widely. But as Germany gained strength and momentum with the repudiation of World War I treaties, union with Austria, dismemberment of Czechoslovakia, and alliance with Italy, Britain came under strong pressure to shore up its position in the Arab and broader Islamic worlds. Defense of the Suez Canal, and of Britain's extensive interests in the Middle East and the Indian subcontinent, weighed more heavily than the waning commitment to a Jewish national home in Palestine.

After having first introduced the idea of partition as a solution, the British quickly retreated. In 1939 they released another White Paper, stating with finality that there would be no Jewish state and projecting independence for undivided Palestine in ten years, provided that sufficient progress in building a government of shared powers had been made. The crux of the matter, however, was that Jewish immigration would end after five years, and the Jewish share of the population would consequently be stabilized at about one-third. Further sale of land to Jews in Arab areas would also end. The White Paper did envision power sharing with the Jewish minority, but the bottom line was that Palestine would stay undivided and predominantly Arab. The White Paper did not meet the Arab demand for immediate independence; but for Zionists it was a total calamity. For how could Jews openly oppose Britain when it was facing a showdown with Nazi Germany? Ben-Gurion's response tried to walk a fine line: the Zionists would fight the White Paper as if there were no war, and fight the war as if there were no White Paper (Ben-Gurion 1939).

And World War II did become, in the Jewish view, a question of survival. At one point the German army was poised at El Alamein, in Western Egypt, ready to overrun Cairo and Palestine, putting an end to the Jewish national home. On the other hand, Jewish volunteers fighting in the British army acquired military training and experience that was to prove decisive short years later in fighting Arab armies.

Holocaust and Partition

Without World War II, would the Jewish state have emerged? Once again, it seemed that the drive had faltered short of its goal. Yet once again, it was revived by an unfailing resurgence of massive anti-Semitism.

From the Jewish perspective, the Holocaust – the killing of one-third of the Jewish people, the largest mass murder in history – created an unanswerable humanitarian case for a Jewish state. Who could forget that as satanic savagery descended on Europe's Jews, the nations of the world had closed those few routes of escape left open? As the Zionist leader Chaim Weizmann told the Peel Commission in 1936, for tyrannized Jewish refugees the world "is divided into places where they cannot live and places into which they cannot enter" (Palestine Royal Commission 1937). The British admitted to Palestine even fewer refugees than the White Paper had projected. As for other possible refuges: a poll of US opinion showed that 67.4 percent favored keeping refugees out of the United States, 18.2 percent supported admitting them within the very limited existing quotas, and only 4.9 percent favored raising the quotas (Morse 1968: 212). An international conference convened in Evian, France, in 1938 to find places of refuge for Jews under Nazi tyranny, but only the Dominican Republic offered to take more refugees. This enabled Hitler to taunt the West for its hypocrisy: "We, on our part, are ready to put all these criminals at the disposal of these countries, for all I care even on luxury ships" (Morse 1968: 212).

The Nazi Final Solution – the systematic annihilation of millions of human beings – was implemented only after it became clear that mass deportation, the first Nazi "solution," would not work because there was nowhere to go. If a Jewish state had existed, Zionists lamented, some or most of the six million could have been saved. The impact of the

Holocaust on Jews everywhere can hardly be overstated. The sheer horror of it foreclosed debate.

After the Holocaust, almost all Jews accepted the basic tenet of Zionism: Jews needed a state of their own, if only to insure their physical survival. For too long Jews had been passive objects in history rather than actors; this sense of ever-present disaster was later captured by the Israeli poet Yehuda Amichai:

> The city in which I was born was destroyed by cannon.
> The ship by which I emigrated was later sunk, during
> the war.
> The barn in Hamadiya where I loved was burnt down.
> The kiosk in Ein Gedi was blown up by enemies.
> The bridge by Ismailiyeh, which I crossed
> and recrossed on the evening of my love
> was ripped to pieces.
> My life is being wiped out behind me according to a
> precise map.
> How long will the memories hold out?
> The little girl of my childhood was killed, my father died.
> Therefore do not choose me as a lover or a son,
> as a bridge-crosser, tenant or citizen.
>
> (Carmi 1981: 572)

The Holocaust also had a tremendous impact on the entire Western world. As the dimensions of the horror became known, shock and guilt shaped attitudes toward "the Palestine issue." Sympathy for the creation of a Jewish state grew. Harry Truman, the US President who in many ways seemed to represent the common man, typified this response:

> The fate of the Jewish victims of Hitlerism was a matter of deep personal concern to me. I have always been disturbed by the tragedy of people who have been made victims of intolerance and fanaticism because of their race, color, or religion . . . But the organized brutality of the Nazis against the Jews in Germany was one of the most shocking crimes of all times. The plight of the victims who had survived the mad genocide of Hitler's Germany was a challenge to Western civilization, and as President I undertook to do something about it. (Truman 1965: 158)

Truman had an opportunity to act because Great Britain faced a deteriorating situation on the ground in Palestine at a time when its resources were being stretched thin worldwide. This was the period in which Britain withdrew from India and passed on to the USA the primary responsibility for opposing Communist threats in Turkey, Greece, and elsewhere. While Europe lay exhausted, the United States at war's end accounted for about half the world's GDP and had become, de facto, the hegemonic power in the Middle East and most other regions of the world. Earlier on, the British had drawn the US government into the Palestine issue by proposing a joint Anglo-American Committee of Inquiry to look into the problems of displaced Jews in Europe and immigration into Palestine. In its report (May 1, 1946), the Anglo-American Committee recommended the immediate admission of 100,000 Jewish refugees into Palestine – a recommendation that the British government declined to implement.

As part of its general retrenchment, in early 1947 the British dumped the Palestine problem in the lap of the new United Nations (UN), successor to the now-defunct League of Nations. The UN formed a United Nations Special Committee on Palestine (UNSCOP), of 11 nations, to investigate. A seven-member majority of UNSCOP returned to the principle of partition, recommending the creation of both Arab and Jewish states, with economic union and the internationalization of Jerusalem. Three UNSCOP members presented a minority plan, supported by Arab and Muslim states, that called for an undivided Palestine with limited local self-government for Jews (one nation, Australia, abstained).

On November 29, 1947, the UN General Assembly adopted the partition plan by a vote of 33 to 13, with ten abstentions (GA Resolution 181). Strikingly, both the Western bloc and the Soviet bloc supported partition; at the time, the Soviet Union viewed creation of a Jewish state as a useful lever against British imperialism. Soviet spokesmen in the United Nations spoke eloquently, if only this once, in support of Zionism and for ending British rule. The borders proposed (see map 4.2) were more favorable to the Jewish state than

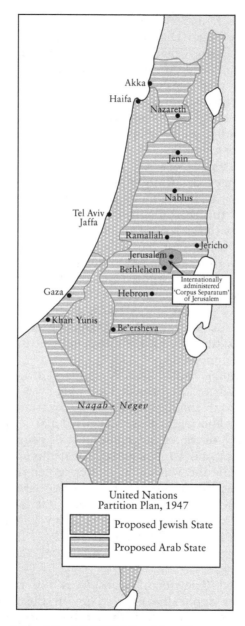

Akka

Haifa
Nazareth

Jenin

Nablus

Tel Aviv
Jaffa

Ramallah
Jericho

Jerusalem
Bethlehem

Internationally
administered
'Corpus Separatum'
of Jerusalem

Gaza
Hebron

Khan Yunis
Be'ersheva

Naqab - Negev

United Nations
Partition Plan, 1947

Proposed Jewish State

Proposed Arab State

Map 4.2 1947 UN Partition Plan.

the Peel plan had been, giving it 56 percent of Palestine (including the Negev Desert as room for expansion). But the UN Security Council made no move to enforce the General Assembly plan, while the British refused to implement any plan not accepted by both sides. Instead, the British proceeded simply to withdraw from Palestine; fighting between the two sides broke out immediately after passage of the partition plan, and grew apace as the British presence dwindled in the following months.

The Palestinian Jewish leadership (except for the Revisionists) regarded Resolution 181 as a major victory conferring international legitimacy and recognition on the Jewish state, and for this reason agreed to accept the proposal as it stood, even without Jerusalem. The Jewish leaders lobbied intensely for passage of the plan in the General Assembly. Palestinian Arab leaders pointed out that the proposal gave the Arabs, who still constituted two-thirds of the population, only 44 percent of the land, while leaving a large Arab minority of about 42 percent in the Jewish state. But this argument was secondary, since Palestinian Arabs opposed the principle of a Jewish state; more favorable borders would not have changed this opposition.

For Palestinian Arabs, the UN vote was a defeat that followed one disaster and preceded another, even worse, catastrophe. The Arab community had been devastated as a result of the 1936–9 fighting, which had caused massive destruction and casualties, uprooted large numbers of people, dispersed the leadership, and left an extremely demoralized population. And while the Palestinian drive for self-determination had been brutally suppressed, neighboring Arab states had one by one achieved their independence (at least formally) during these same years: Iraq in 1932, Egypt in 1936, Syria and Lebanon in 1943, Transjordan in 1946. In 1945 these five states, together with Saudi Arabia and Yemen, formed the Arab League.

Why, asked Palestinian Arabs, was the right of self-determination applicable everywhere in the Middle East except in Palestine? Why was the Arab majority in Palestine held hostage to the attempt to impose an alien immigration?

In the Arab case submitted to a US–British committee of inquiry in 1946, Palestinians argued that they were descendants of the indigenous inhabitants "since the beginning of time," and that the Jewish claim "is based upon a historical connection which ceased effectively many centuries ago." Palestinians could not submit to being turned into a minority in their own state; they "claim the democratic right of a majority to make its own decisions." Furthermore, the Zionist presence had not brought material benefits to Arabs; on the contrary, it had isolated them from their Arab brethren, disrupted normal economic development, and threatened to leave them landless. By geography and history, in short, Palestine was "inescapably part of the Arab world." Partition, or the imposition of a binational state, were both inadmissible as a denial of majority rule: "If it is unjust to the Arabs to impose a Jewish state on the whole of Palestine, it is equally unjust to impose it in any part of the country" (Laqueur and Schueftan 2016: 57–62).

With a number of newly independent Arab states by their side, Palestinian Arabs also felt in a stronger position than they had been in 1936–9. In the earlier confrontation, they had faced the forces of a Great Power with little assistance from other Arabs, who were engaged in their own struggles. Now they had strong and growing vocal support from seven independent Arab states, while the British were leaving and they faced a Jewish community of only about three-quarters of a million with little military tradition or experience. Arabs everywhere saw the Palestinian battle as a part of the common struggle against Western imperialism and colonialism, and the Arab governments were under great pressure to intervene in the emerging military conflict. In addition, some of these regimes had their own interests in intervening: the Hashemite states (Transjordan and Iraq) appeared to be thinking again of the greater Hashemite state envisioned after World War I, and this evoked opposition from Egypt and elsewhere. When full-scale war erupted in Palestine, therefore, it was unlikely to be limited to parties within the Mandate borders.

The War of Independence/An-Nakba: The Second Stage of the Conflict

Fighting between Jews and Arabs in Palestine began after adoption of the partition plan at the end of November 1947. This first phase of fighting, taking place while British troops were still in nominal control, was largely guerrilla warfare between irregular Palestinian Arab forces and the military organizations of the Jewish *yishuv*: the mainstream *Haganah* and the more radical *Etsel* (*Irgun*) and *Lehi* movements of the Revisionists. In early April *Haganah* launched an offensive aimed at creating contiguous territorial control over the area of the Jewish state plus a corridor to Jerusalem.

By the time of the final British withdrawal, May 15, 1948, Jewish forces had managed to hold on to most of the territory allotted to the Jewish state, and even to overrun some Arab areas, such as the city of Jaffa. In addition, a large number of Arab refugees had already fled the areas of fighting, creating the beginning of the refugee issue. But there was a general expectation that the intervention of Arab states, after the British departure, would reverse this outcome.

On May 14, a Provisional State Council of Jewish leaders declared the independence of the Jewish state, to be named Israel. Basing its legal case on Resolution 181 as well as the League of Nations Mandate, the declaration also cited the Holocaust as evidence of "the need to solve the problem of the homelessness and lack of independence of the Jewish people" by means of a Jewish state that would "endow the Jewish people with equality of status among the family of nations." The new state promised "full social and political equality of all its citizens, without distinction of religion, race, or sex," and called on neighboring states to make peace. The ecstasy of the moment was electrifying, as conveyed in the recollection of Golda Meir at the beginning of this chapter.

On the following day, as expected, five Arab states (the four neighbors and Iraq) sent military forces into Palestine. The war that followed was fought episodically. In the first month, Israeli forces stopped the Egyptian army on the coast

20 miles short of Tel Aviv, kept a corridor to Jerusalem open despite occupation of the West Bank by the Arab Legion of Transjordan, and held the Syrians to minimal gains in the north. This was followed by a month-long truce imposed by the UN, followed in turn by "The Ten Days" of fighting (July 8–18) during which Israeli forces took the offensive and captured strategic areas beyond the partition lines. A second, unlimited truce was imposed on July 18; it was punctuated by isolated outbreaks of hostilities on the Egyptian front in mid-October and late December, and with Palestinian forces in Galilee in late October. These campaigns left all of Galilee, and most of the Negev region, in Israeli hands.

During the early months of 1949 four separate bilateral armistice agreements were negotiated between Israel and Egypt, Transjordan, Syria, and Lebanon (but not with Iraq, which had no border with Israel). The armistice agreements brought the fighting to a close, but did not address any of the political issues. Opposing armies remained where the fighting had left them (see map 4.3). Egypt clung onto a narrow strip of the southern coast, today's Gaza Strip.

Transjordan's Arab Legion, the most effective Arab fighting force, occupied the central regions that became known as the West Bank. Syria withdrew from its remaining toehold in Palestine in return for demilitarization of that area.

This left Israel in possession of about 78 percent of the former Palestinian Mandate, as opposed to the 56 percent allocated to the Jewish State in the 1947 partition resolution. Much of this expansion came from the determination to hold Jewish West Jerusalem, and to broaden as much as possible the corridor linking it to the rest of Israel. In addition, Western Galilee, which was to have been part of the Arab state, was absorbed into Israel.

The defeat of five regular Arab armies by the new state of Israel is explained by (1) the fact that, despite a 50 to one advantage in total population, the Arab states actually put fewer forces in the field than did Israel (Morris 2001: 217, 241); (2) Israel's strong leadership and unity contrasted with Arab disunity; (3) Israel's advantage with internal lines enabled it to focus on one enemy at a time; (4) Arab armies

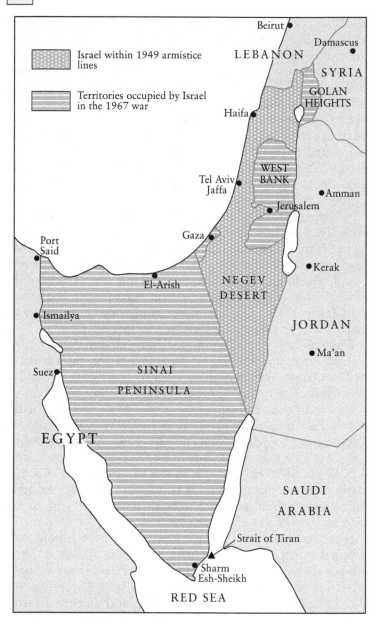

Map 4.3 1949 armistice lines and 1967 cease-fire lines.

had a poor level of training, equipment, and leadership, tied to government corruption on a broader level; and (5) the motivation of Jewish soldiers, many of them Holocaust survivors, who felt they were fighting for physical survival.

The Arab–Israeli war of 1948 established the context of the Arab–Israeli conflict, marking its passage from a conflict between two communities within Palestine to a new second stage as a conflict between states. It is hard to imagine a more complete contrast than its impact on the two sides. For Jews, coming so quickly after the greatest tragedy in their history, the re-emergence of a Jewish state after 2,000 years was one of the greatest historical moments, if not the very greatest, in their long history. But for Palestinians it was simply *an-nakba*, the disaster, as it has been referred to ever since. Few nations have ever been defined so completely by tragedy: perhaps, ironically, only the Jews.

The 1948 war transformed the confrontation in a number of ways:

- *The communal clash became an interstate conflict.* Previously Arab and Jewish communities in Mandatory Palestine had been the main contenders, but now the focus shifted to the new state of Israel and the Arab states, who before this had been partisan bystanders. The Palestinians disappeared as an independent actor in the drama; there was, for the time being, no recognized organization or spokesman representing all Palestinians. Arab governments, having little incentive to make peace with a nation they considered illegitimate, adopted a policy of total ostracism: borders with Israel were sealed, all communication and transportation links severed, and anything Israeli was boycotted.

- *The 1949 armistice lines became* de facto *borders.* Though armistice lines are not legally political borders, the 1949 lines acquired great legitimacy over the years as the point of reference between "Israeli territory" and "Arab territory." This left Israel with roughly one-third more territory than allotted in the partition plan. Jerusalem was divided, with East Jerusalem (including the Old City) held by the Transjordanian Arab Legion and West Jerusalem by Israeli forces. By occupying East Jerusalem and the rest of the West Bank, Transjordan was the only Arab winner; it soon annexed this area and renamed itself "Jordan." King Abdullah negotiated secretly with Israel for a time, but was assassinated in July 1951 by opponents of peace with Israel. His grandson and successor, King Husayn, did not pursue the option further.

- *Israel achieved general international recognition.* Based on the legitimization of a Jewish state in Resolution 181, Israel was admitted to UN membership and established diplomatic relations with most other independent states, apart from Arab and Muslim regimes. At this time the UN was dominated by Western and Latin American countries; when Asian and African nations later tripled UN membership, their identification with the Palestinians made the world body much less sympathetic to Israel.

- *The Arab state projected in the partition plan was never created.* Since Arab states and the Palestinians rejected the principle of partitioning Palestine, they did not establish an Arab state in the framework of partition. The more heavily populated Arab areas were in the hands of Egypt and Transjordan; Transjordan annexed the West Bank and Egypt administered the Gaza Strip without allowing Palesinian self-rule there. In essence, the war created a *de facto* partition remarkably reminiscent of the Peel plan, with Jordan and Egypt ruling the Arab areas of Palestine.

- *The new Jewish state acquired a substantial Arab minority.* While most of the Arabs in areas that became part of Israel fled or were expelled, at war's end about 150,000 remained in place, constituting about 19 percent of the new state's population (a figure that scarcely changed over the years). In the absence of a clear policy, security considerations dominated in policies toward the new minority (Dowty 1998, 2001a). Formal citizenship rights were extended, but Arabs were marginalized in the power-sharing of Israeli politics and faced *de facto* discrimination. Most Arab-inhabited localities were put under a "Military

Government" from 1948–1966, with strict controls on movement and political activities.

- *The war created a massive Palestinian refugee issue.* Since this issue remains to this day one of the most contentious unresolved questions, we will examine it more closely below. Even the numbers are disputed, but a British estimate of 600,000–750,000 for the original refugee population of 1947–9 covers the likely range and the initial UN estimate was 726,000 (Morris 2004: 602–3). Since Palestinian refugees rejected resettlement as a solution, the UN did not deal with them through its normal refugee machinery. Instead the UN created a separate body, the United Nations Relief and Works Agency for Palestine Refugees in the Near East (UNRWA), to address their humanitarian, social, and educational needs only, and not long-term solutions. The refugees have always maintained that the solution to the problem lay, very simply, in the implementation of UN General Assembly Resolution 194 of December 11, 1948, which provides that "refugees wishing to return to their homes and live in peace with their neighbors should be permitted to do so at the earliest practicable date, and that compensation should be paid for the property of those choosing not to return."

Who was responsible for creating the refugee problem? Did the refugees flee on their own, or did Israeli forces expel them? The most complete answer to this question has been provided by Benny Morris, an Israeli scholar who was the first to make extensive use of Israeli sources made available in the 1980s. While partisans on both sides have taken issue with Morris, his careful village-by-village analysis is clearly the place to begin. What emerges, not surprisingly, is a more complex picture than the simplistic portraits favored by partisans. In some cases refugees fled before enemy forces arrived, as often occurs in war; in some cases they were expelled by Israeli forces; and there are murky cases with elements of both situations. Since many factors were involved in most cases, Morris argues, accurate quantification is impossible (Morris 2004: 598).

The situation also varied greatly in different phases of the war. In the first four months, November 1947–March 1948, there were almost no cases of expulsion, but a significant number of relatively well-to-do Arabs fled in order to escape the widespread fighting. During the *Haganah* offensives of April–June 1948 a psychosis of flight was created, with most residents of cities and villages captured by Jewish forces fleeing either before or during battles. Morris concludes that there was no explicit decision or systematic plan for expulsion, but that it was generally understood that certain vital areas should be cleared, and many who did not flee were expelled after the battle. The Jewish claim that Arab leaders ordered their own people to leave is generally unfounded, Morris finds, but he does document some cases in which local Arab commanders and officials made such appeals.

In the third stage, June–August 1948, a third exodus took place during the "Ten Days" fighting in July, with a greater readiness to expel inhabitants but also a growing opposition to flight among Arab Palestinian leaders and states. In the final stage of fighting, November–December 1948, outcomes differed on different fronts but some areas, especially on borders, were deliberately cleared of residents. The general trend over time was from internal causes of flight (such as demoralization and fear on the Arab side) to external forces (primarily pressures or expulsions). At the same time, the more extreme claims of both sides are discredited (Morris 1988: 286–96; Morris 2004: 588–601; for critiques of Morris from a pro-Palestinian perspective, see Masalha 1991 and W. Khalidi 2005; for a pro-Israeli critique, see Karsh 2003 and Karsh 2005).

The Palestinians, in any case, were a shattered community. About half of the Palestinian Arab community became refugees, scattered in the West Bank, the Gaza Strip, Jordan, Syria, and Lebanon. Another 150,000 remained in territory under Israeli control, where they were cut off from contact with the rest of the Arab world, and the rest were inhabitants of the West Bank and Gaza who fell under Jordanian or Egyptian rule. Palestinian institutions, organizations, and leadership were decimated; all other parties, Jewish or Arab, seemed intent on erasing Palestinian identity. The bitterness and despair that Palestinians experienced was expressed in a "literature of exile." Fawaz Turki, writing a "journal of Palestinian exile," exclaimed:

> The nation of Palestine ceased to be. Its original inhabitants, the Palestinian people, were dubbed Arab refugees, sent regular food rations by the UN, and forgotten by the world ... Beneath the glamor [of Israel] lies the tragedy of another people who suffered for no reason, who were uprooted from their homeland, and who had never in their history practiced persecution in their rencontre with Jews, but who were made to pay the price of a crime [the Holocaust] that others had committed. (Turki 1972: 29)

Given the strength of the poetic tradition in Arabic culture, many of the most eloquent statements of the Palestinian perspective came from poets.

Rashid Hussein, "Tent #50 (Song of a Refugee)," recorded both the despair and the defiance of the refugee experience:

> Tent #50, on the left, is my new world,
> Shared with me by my memories ...
> Two doors has my tent, two doors like two wounds,
> One leads to the other tents, wrinkle-browed
> Like clouds no longer able to weep;
> And the second – a rent in the ceiling – leading
> To the skies, revealing the stars
> Like refugees scattered, and like them, naked.
> Also the moon is trudging there
> Downcast and weary as the UNRWA,
> Yellow as though it was the UNRWA
> Under a load of yellow cheese for the refugees.
> Tent #50, on the left, that is my present,
> But it is too cramped to contain a future.
> And "Forget!": they say, but how can I?
> > Teach the night to forget to bring
> > Dreams showing me my village
> > And teach the wind to forget to carry to me
> The aroma of apricots in my fields!
> > And teach the sky, too, to forget to rain.
> Only then may I forget my country.
> > (Parmenter 1994: 64)

One of the central messages in Palestinian writings during these years is that the Palestinians are defeated and dispersed, for the moment, but that they will not disappear. There is a general feeling that the Arab world is on the rise; the 1950s were the years of Gamal Abdul Nasser and Arab nationalism. The new, revolutionary Arab regimes will stand behind the Palestinians and will correct the injustice done to them, and possibly for that reason Palestinian particularism is less evident. Palestinians readily identified with the cause of Arab unity, which promised to be their deliverance.

Israel was seen as an inherently theocratic, racist, and discriminatory state that would not be able to survive against the rising tide of popular liberation and anti-colonialism in the world. Furthermore, refugees would insist on the absolute "right of return," to their original homes, as expressed literally in Resolution 194. It was clear that few if any refugees would accept compensation and resettlement; repatriation was the only acceptable solution.

The Jewish response to this was that the Palestinians and the Arab states had defied the UN and initiated the war, publicly threatening – three years after the Holocaust – to kill all Jews. The Secretary-General of the Arab League, Abd ar-Rahman Azzam Pasha, said just before the war broke out that "it does not matter how many [Jews] there are. We will sweep them into the sea!" (Kirkbride 1976: 23–4). Having failed to achieve this success, it was sheer effrontery to ask for a fresh start and another chance – for example, by going back to the borders of the 1947 partition plan. The Arab states continued with a policy of total rejection of Israel's existence, total boycott of Israel, and repeated threats of a "second round" to destroy Israel. Arab propaganda had become increasingly racist and extreme. In such circumstances, for Israel to make unilateral concessions on strategic issues would be the height of folly.

As for the refugee question, Israelis argued that there would be no such problem if the Arabs had not defied the United Nations. The claim that Israel deliberately and systematically expelled Palestinians was disproved by the presence of the 150,000 who did not flee, and were given citizenship in the state of Israel. Furthermore, one should ask how many Jews were allowed to remain in areas conquered by Arab armies, such as the Jewish Quarter of the Old City or the Etzion bloc of settlements south of Jerusalem. The answer was: none.

As for UN Resolution 194, it must be read as a whole; the refugee clause is only one paragraph in a much longer resolution setting up a framework for reconciliation. In such a framework the refugee issue will be addressed, but it cannot be dealt with in isolation, while Arab states still consider themselves at war with Israel. Furthermore, the exodus of Palestinians must be seen against the exodus of Jews forced out from Arab countries during the decade after the 1948 war. With great difficulty, these refugees were absorbed into Israeli society, tripling the population within the first ten years. Israel was thus fulfilling its historic mission by offering a haven to distressed and threatened Jewish communities; Arab states should do no less in integrating their Palestinian brethren into their own societies. Abba Eban, Israeli representative to the United Nations, put it in these words:

> Should not the representatives of Arab states, as the authors of this tragedy, come here in a mood of humility and repentance rather than in shrill and negative indignation? Since their governments have, by acts of policy, created this tragic problem, does it not follow that the world community has an unimpeachable right to claim their full assistance in its solution? (Laqueur and Rubin 1995: 154)

Nasser and Nationalism

The two decades between the 1948 war and the 1967 war mark the peak of the interstate "Arab–Israeli" phase of the conflict. With the Palestinians temporarily eclipsed as a player, the stage – the entire Middle East stage – was dominated by Egypt's charismatic Gamal Abdul Nasser. Nasser was the prime mover in a 1952 military coup that overthrew the Egyptian monarchy, and he remained the key figure in Arab nationalism until his death in 1970. There were moments when it appeared that Nasserism might sweep all before it, including the new and vulnerable Jewish state on its eastern border.

Important changes were taking place in international politics during these years. First, the rise of the Third World, as Asian and African states threw off colonial rule and formed a bloc of "non-aligned" states tied to neither side in the Cold War. Decolonization became a part of the dominant world view in the United Nations and elsewhere, and Nasser became a major figure in the new bloc.

Secondly, the Arab world passed through a process of radicalization, with coups not only in Egypt but also in Syria (1949), Iraq (1958), Sudan (1958, 1969), Yemen (1962), and Libya (1969), and with threats of coups in Lebanon, Jordan, and elsewhere. Algeria was the scene of a long and bloody war for liberation that popularized the doctrine of guerrilla warfare as a means of fighting established governments. By the end of the decade the Arab world was split down the middle, with clashes not only between radical and traditional regimes but also among radical regimes as they competed to lead the movement to Arab unity. In this competition the Palestinian issue took center stage, as it represented a cause that united all Arabs. In the meantime, rivalries among radical regimes showing their support for the Palestinians could trigger violent outbreaks or war – as happened in 1967.

A third change had particular bearing on the Middle East. After the death of Josef Stalin in 1953, the Soviet Union discovered the Third World, where the fight against imperialism and colonialism gave the Soviets tremendous leverage in the "battle for hearts and minds." By supporting "struggles for national liberation," they could leapfrog over encircling Western alliances – NATO, CENTO, SEATO – and strike directly at Western influence in such key areas as Southeast Asia, North Africa, and even Latin America. The Middle East, with its strategic location as a crossroads and its oil reserves, was a priority target. In September 1955 the Soviet Union entered the Middle East arena dramatically with the announcement of a major arms deal between Nasser's Egypt and Czechoslovakia (the Czechs being a front for the

Soviets). This broke the Western monopoly over arms supplies to the region, threatening to upset the military balance and put Israel in jeopardy.

The Middle East was an arena in the Cold War from its inception. The United States was drawn deeply into the region, primarily in order to keep the Soviet Union out and to guard Western access to Middle Eastern oil and strategic passages. This created an interest in maintaining regional stability – since instability created opportunities the enemy could exploit. This meant, among other things, containing regional wars so that they did not become dangerous confrontations between superpowers.

But the Arab–Israel conflict presented dilemmas for which there was no easy answer.

How could the United States prevent Arab–Israeli wars, which would only drive the Arabs further into the Soviet camp, without openly guaranteeing Israeli survival or providing weapons to match those going to Egypt? An open alliance with Israel would hardly help win hearts and minds in the Arab world.

Moreover, the prospect of Arab–Israeli wars was always high during these years. Prime Minister Ben-Gurion favored punitive military responses in order to compel Arab acceptance of Israel, while Moshe Sharett (Foreign Minister 1948–56, Prime Minister 1954–5) led those who advocated a more diplomatic and less military policy. Sharett's approach was dominant only in the short period after he succeeded Ben-Gurion as Prime Minister in 1954; when he was forced aside with Ben-Gurion's return to the Prime Ministership in 1955, the more "activist" line prevailed, setting the stage for the Suez campaign a year later.

All of these new dimensions and dilemmas can indeed be seen in the 1956 Suez Crisis. Apart from the threat posed by the new Soviet-supplied weaponry in Egypt, Israel was beset by increased cross-border raids by *fedayin* (self-sacrificers) from the Gaza Strip and by Egypt's complete closure of the Strait of Tiran, at the southern tip of the Sinai peninsula, to Israeli sea and air traffic. This last move, also in September 1955, closed Israel's only outlet to East Africa and Asia

(Egypt having already barred Israeli ships from the Suez Canal). Feeling that it had legitimate cause, the Israeli government decided in principle on preemptive war with Egypt, pending a suitable opportunity.

The opportunity came with a crisis in relations between Egypt and the West. When the United States abruptly withdrew its promised funding for the Aswan Dam, centerpiece of Egypt's development plans, in July 1956, Nasser retaliated by nationalizing the Suez Canal from its British and French owners. Britain and France were ready to reverse this audacious move militarily, but were held back by President Dwight Eisenhower and Secretary of State John Foster Dulles, who felt that such neo-colonialism might push the entire Third World into Soviet hands. Finally despairing of the US diplomatic moves on Suez, the two European powers secretly negotiated with Israel to create a conflict in which they could intervene and, incidentally, reoccupy the Canal Zone. Israel did its part at the end of October, invading Sinai and advancing to within a few miles of the Canal Zone; the British and French began their "intervention," but were forced by immense international and domestic pressure to back down before their goal was achieved.

The collusion with Israel was one of history's most transparent plots; it fooled no one, and anger over the attempted deception fueled the vociferous response. Most notably, Eisenhower and Dulles were enraged, and invoked bilateral sanctions against their own allies. Israel held on to the Sinai and the Gaza Strip for a few weeks, finally withdrawing in return for the stationing of a UN peacekeeping force, the first ever created, to stabilize the Egypt–Israel border and ensure free passage through the Strait of Tiran. The United States also gave Israel a written guarantee that it would act with other nations to keep Tiran open to Israeli ships.

The Suez Crisis left a mixed legacy. It clearly marked the eclipse of the colonial powers, at least in the Middle East. It was a personal triumph for Nasser, despite Egypt's military defeat in Sinai; for the first time since Western colonialists had entered the region, an indigenous leader had defied the leading imperialist powers and, by cleverly exploiting new forces in world politics, had compelled them to back down. In the following years, Nasser's prestige and power in the Arab world reached new peaks. But at the same time, Israel did gain a stable border with Egypt and the opening of its access to the East – at least for the next ten years.

For Palestinians, the appeal of Arab nationalism lay in its goal of unifying the Arab world. This implied an Arab state stretching from Morocco to Iraq. A unified Arab state of such dimensions, or even one considerably smaller, would be the key to liberation of Palestine. Such a state would be a mortal danger to Israel; it would dwarf the Jewish state in resources, manpower, and international influence. The intent was clear; in one speech Nasser declared that "Egypt has decided to dispatch her heroes, the disciples of Pharaoh and the sons of Islam, and they will cleanse the land of Palestine . . . There will be no peace on Israel's border because we demand vengeance, and vengeance is Israel's death" (Middle Eastern Affairs 1956: 461).

When Syria merged with Egypt in 1958 to form the United Arab Republic, under Nasser's rule, Israel found itself facing this rising major enemy on two fronts. If Arab unity gained more momentum, as seemed likely, the implications for Israel were dismal. Nasser himself, speaking in Damascus in 1960, put it very clearly:

> I would like to tell you, Brethren, that all that we are now doing is just a part of the battle for Palestine. Once we are fully emancipated from the shackles of colonialism and the intrigues of colonialist agents, we shall take a further step forward towards the liberation of Palestine. When we have brought our armed forces to full strength and made our own armaments we will take another step forward towards the liberation of Palestine, and when we have manufactured jet aircraft and tanks we will embark upon the final stage of this liberation. (Laqueur and Schueftan 2016: 90)

Arab observers during this period continued to characterize the conflict in zero-sum terms; there was no possibility of compromise, given the total incompatibility of the goals and aspirations of the two sides. The Arab world had the potential resources to erase Israel from the map, once past weaknesses were remedied and this potential was realized. But by the early 1960s, there were some signs that "Palestinism," a greater emphasis on Palestinian identity, might be re-emerging. Palestinians still identified strongly with Arab nationalism and counted on the Arab states to supply the military muscle necessary to defeat Israel. But the peak of the drive for Arab unity passed; Syria broke away from Egypt in 1961, and Nasser became bogged down in a civil war in Yemen. There were doubts that the broader support of the Arab world was so reliable or would be so effective, and there was some feeling that Palestinians should take the lead in their own liberation. As Fawaz Turki wrote:

> My generation of Palestinians, growing up alienated, excluded, and forgotten, rejected this legacy [of waiting for others to act]; yet when we looked around us we could see either the desert to shed our tears in or the whole world to hit back at. Having nothing and with nothing to lose, we proceeded to do the latter. (Turki 1972: 16)

During these years doctrines of guerrilla warfare and popular resistance were resonating throughout the Third World. The success of Algerian Arab rebels against the French inspired Palestinian Arabs. A number of Palestinian fighting groups were established, most importantly the Palestine Liberation Movement (Fatah, from its Arabic initials in reverse order). Fatah was founded sometime in 1957–62 (sources differ), was supported initially by Syria, and was headed by Yasir Arafat, a scion of the Husayni family who had headed the Palestinian Students' Union in Cairo. From 1965, Fatah and other groups carried out cross-border raids into Israel that helped bring on the 1967 war (which was the intention). The Egyptians, trying to stay in front, sponsored the 1964 creation of the Palestine Liberation Organization (PLO), designed to serve as an umbrella organization for all Palestinian factions.

For Israelis, these were years of danger and growing threat. The 1948 war had not led to normalization; Arab governments seemed more committed than ever to the destruction of Israel. Moreover, Arabs had gained the assistance of the Soviet Union as a source of modern weaponry – something that Israel found hard to offset (only France was willing to sell Israel equivalent arms). The fear of Arab states acquiring superiority over Israel in conventional weapons led to Prime Minister Ben-Gurion's decision to develop a capacity in nonconventional arms. Following the 1956 Suez crisis, military cooperation between Israel and France (engaged in war in Algeria) remained at a high level, and in October 1957 France agreed to help Israel build a nuclear reactor capable of producing fissionable material with military potential (Cohen 1998: 59). The existence of the reactor, under construction at Dimona in southern Israel, was revealed by US sources in December 1960. Since Israel did not join the Nuclear NonProliferation Treaty (in force since 1970), the reactor did not fall under international inspection or safeguards.

The new Palestinian fighting groups that emerged in the 1960s were, from the Israeli perspective, even more extreme than the radical Arab regimes. Such groups defined the conflict as a war to the finish with Israel in which all "revolutionary" means were legitimate and all "Zionists" were legitimate targets. The romance of violence that such groups embraced seemed to put them outside any civilized framework.

The level of violence against Israelis, soldiers and civilians alike, seemed to be rising inexorably. In the six years before the Suez Crisis, reported Abba Eban to the UN Security Council, according to the Israeli record

> in violation of the Armistice Agreement there have occurred 1843 cases of armed robbery and theft, 1339 cases of armed clashes with Egyptian armed forces, 435 cases of incursion from Egyptian controlled territory, 172 cases of sabotage perpetrated by Egyptian military units and *fedayin* in Israel. As a result of these actions of Egyptian hostility within Israel, 364 Israelis were wounded and 101 killed. In 1956 alone, as a result of this aspect of Egyptian aggression, 28 Israelis were killed and 127 wounded. (United Nations Security Council 1956: 14)

This was only on the Egyptian front. In such a situation, Israelis asked, what else could any state do but strike back at the sources of the attacks, either as prevention or as deterrence? "Retaliation" was not a nice word, but what else could be done?

The Suez Crisis, in the Israeli reading, again indicated that in the final analysis Israelis could count on no one but themselves. The British and the French had abandoned them, while the United States applied extreme pressure for Israeli withdrawal – in return for which Israel received a vague commitment on free passage through the Strait of Tiran.

At the same time, Israel asked the Arab states only for peace and normalization on the basis of existing borders (that is, the 1949 Armistice lines). Golda Meir, now Israeli Foreign Minister, expressed the Israeli view concisely in a 1962 speech to the UN:

> Year after year Israel has come on this rostrum with one demand
> – peace between it and its Arab neighbors ... Negotiations
> and conciliation are proclaimed from this rostrum as the
> method to solve all other problems in the world except this
> one, which must, according to these spokesmen, be resolved
> by force. For every other nation, they claim co-existence,
> practiced in peace. For Israel, non-existence, to be achieved
> by war. (Meir 1962: 166)

There were also some voices in Israel that still advocated a Jewish state in all of Eretz Yisrael, defined as either the British Mandate after 1922 (that is, with the West Bank and Gaza), or in some cases as the British Mandate before 1922 (that is, including also the East Bank, meaning Jordan). But the issue was largely dormant in Israeli politics during the next two decades; even the one major party still dedicated to an undivided *Eretz-Yisrael* (*Herut*, representing the Revisionists) seldom raised the issue. After all, in the 1948–9 war for survival, the Jewish state had emerged with control over 78 percent of Palestine rather than the 56 percent allotted in the UN partition plan. This, for most Israelis during this period, was a tremendous achievement and a quite acceptable basis for a settlement.

Furthermore, the *de facto* partition that had taken place in 1948 seemed to be gaining legitimacy with the passage of time. The period from 1956 to 1967 was relatively quiet and stable, with UN peacekeepers stationed on the borders between Israel and Egypt, its most dangerous adversary. Despite the vocal rejectionism of Arab nationalists, it did not appear that any of the Arab governments, or Israel, was likely to challenge the *status quo* within the foreseeable future. Nor did it appear that the small Palestinian movements would be able to drag the Arab states into an unwanted war.

When Israeli military intelligence prepared its annual "national strategic assessment" in May 1967, therefore, it stated that there was "no chance" of a war during the coming year (Black and Morris 1991: 211).

This turned out to be one of the most grievous misjudgments among the many that mark the history of this conflict.

5 The Re-Emergence of the Palestinians

From out of the long years of trial in ever-mounting struggle, the Palestinian political identity emerged further consolidated and confirmed ... Palestinian resistance was clarified and raised into the forefront of Arab and world awareness, as the struggle of the Palestinian Arab people achieved unique prominence among the world's liberation movements in the modern era. The massive national uprising, the Intifada, now intensifying in cumulative scope and power on occupied Palestinian territories, as well as the unflinching resistance of the refugee camps outside the homeland, have elevated awareness of the Palestinian truth and right into still higher realms of comprehension and actuality.

Palestine National Council, Declaration of Independence, 1988

The War that No One Wanted?

The 1967 war was a major turning point in the Arab–Israel conflict. Assigning responsibility for its outbreak is therefore a key issue in ongoing debates over Israeli occupation of Arab territories or the rights of Arab states. But it can be argued, quite plausibly, that neither Israel nor the Arab governments actually wanted war, before the chain of events that began in mid-May 1967. If so, this unintentional war tells us much about unpredictable risks and limited rationality in the conflict.

With United Nations Emergency Force (UNEF) peacekeepers deployed between Egypt and Israel, that key border had been stable for ten years. Israeli shipping moved unhindered to and from the southern port of Eilat, through the Strait of Tiran. Egypt's Gamal Abdul Nasser was preoccupied with the Arab world, promoting projects of Arab unity; most recently, Egypt had become bogged down in a civil war in Yemen, tying up many of its best troops. Other borders were less stable, as new Palestinian "guerrilla" groups, usually operating from Jordanian territory, hit Israeli targets across the border. This triggered the usual cycle of reprisals, but neither Jordan nor Syria appeared eager for war without Egyptian participation.

How, then, did all parties find themselves, within short order, at war? The bare outline of what happened in May and June 1967 is not complicated. There was a high level of tension between Israel and Syria, which in itself was not unusual. The Soviet Union warned Egypt that Israel was about to launch a major strike on Syria; in response, Egypt moved troops into the Sinai peninsula toward its border with Israel and requested the withdrawal of UNEF forces separating the two sides. After reoccupying the position at Sharm Esh-Sheikh that controls the maritime passage to the Gulf of Aqaba, on May 22 Egypt announced its renewed closure to Israeli ships. As the crisis intensified, Egypt, Syria, and Jordan concluded mutual defense agreements. After a period of futile diplomacy, Israel launched an air and land attack on June 5, and in six days of fighting conquered the Gaza Strip and Sinai from Egypt, the West Bank from Jordan, and the Golan Heights from Syria.

But beyond this outline, perceptions are diametrically opposed. From the Arab perspective, every Arab move was defensive. Clearly Egypt was not contemplating war at a time when many of its best forces were bogged down in Yemen. Mahmoud Riad, then Egyptian Foreign Minister, argued later that Israel was in "dire crisis" and needed war "not only in fulfillment of its central dream of expansion but, more so, to maintain the integrity and cohesiveness of the young State and the continued loyalty and support of the diaspora Jews." Statements by Israeli leaders, in Riad's view, seemed to threaten Damascus itself; Soviet intelligence backed this up (Riad 1981: 17).

On May 12, for example, United Press International reported that a "high Israeli source said Israel would take limited military action designed to topple the Damascus army regime if Syrian terrorists continued sabotage raids inside Israel." This source was later identified as General Aharon Yariv, the head of Israeli military intelligence (Morris 2001: 304).

Egypt moved forces to its eastern borders to offset Israel's escalation, as a measure of prudent self-defense and to deter an Israeli attack on Syria. In Riad's account, Egypt asked United Nations Secretary-General U Thant for only a partial UNEF withdrawal: "I did not ask for the withdrawal of UN troops from Gaza and Sharm Esh-Sheikh; my request was restricted to a withdrawal from our international borders" – in other words, the Egypt–Israel land frontier from the Gaza Strip south to Eilat. U Thant's position was that there could be no partial withdrawal; it was all or nothing. Consequently, in Riad's words, "Egypt could not back down on its demand and had to accept a complete withdrawal" (Riad 1981: 18).

This raised the issue of Israeli passage through the Strait of Tiran; when Egyptian forces reoccupied positions at Sharm Esh-Sheikh controlling this waterway, would Egypt also reimpose its closure to Israel? Despite an Egyptian law banning Israeli ships there, Riad felt that "navigation in the Gulf of Aqaba was a matter to which a solution could be secured, either through the ICJ [International Court of Justice] . . . or through the redeployment of UN forces at Sharm Esh-Sheikh, once Israeli threats were eliminated." In any event, Egypt pledged not to attack Israel, and kept this pledge. It was Israel that attacked, in a massive surprise move on three Arab neighbors in the early hours of June 5 (Riad 1981: 18–24).

But from the Israeli perspective, every Israeli move was also defensive. Clearly Israel was not contemplating war, to judge from the sense of surprise, if not fear and dread, that gripped both leaders and public during the countdown to war. Abba Eban, then Israeli Foreign Minister, remembered that "the early part of 1967 had been turbulent, but no more than during other years." Syrian-supported terrorism was a problem, but Israel had no intention of occupying Damascus and trying to overthrow the regime. When the Soviet Union accused Israel of mobilizing 11–13 brigades on its Syrian border, Israel invited Soviet Ambassador Dmitri Chuvakhin to inspect the area himself. "Chuvakhin's response was that his function was to communicate Soviet truths, not to put them to a test" (Eban 1977: 316–19). (Given the short distances involved, even if Israel had been planning an attack, it would have been unnecessary and self-defeating to broadcast its intent by mobilizing large forces in the tiny finger of territory opposite Syria.)

Egypt's expulsion of UNEF was based, therefore, on Soviet disinformation. But the "decisive question" in Eban's account was "whether Nasser would actually blockade the Straits of Tiran ... If the blockade was imposed, Israel would be challenged to defend or abandon a vital national interest." Israel had the legal right to defend its free passage through an international waterway. The decision taken, and conveyed to Cairo, was that "if Egypt will not attack us, we will not take action against Egyptian forces at Sharm Esh-Sheikh – until or unless they close the Straits of Tiran to free navigation by Israel" (Eban 1977: 326–8).

When news of Nasser's closure of the Strait reached him in the early hours of May 23, Eban recollects that "I knew that nothing in our life or our history would ever be the same." Nasser's reckless move reflected "the ecstatic mood sweeping over the Arab world" (Eban 1977: 330–3). By May 26, Nasser was openly declaring that he had initiated the crisis in order to destroy Israel: "Recently we felt we are strong enough, that if we were to enter a battle with Israel, with God's help, we could triumph. On this basis, we decided to take actual steps ... The battle will be a general one and our basic objective will be to destroy Israel" (Laqueur and Schueftan 2016: 99). Muhammad Hassanein Haykal, Nasser's confidant, claimed that Egypt had pushed

Israel into striking first, but that Egypt's response would be overwhelming: "Israel cannot accept or remain indifferent to what has taken place . . . Israel has to reply now. It has to deal a blow . . . Let Israel begin. Let our second blow be ready. Let it be a knock-out" (Laqueur and Schueftan 2006: 102).

Swept up in this mood, King Husayn of Jordan flew to Cairo on May 30 and signed a mutual defense pact with Egypt similar to an earlier Egyptian–Syrian treaty; Israel thus faced a three-front war. However, after two weeks of futile diplomatic efforts to mobilize effective international action against Egypt's closing of the Strait, Eban was now ready to join the rest of the Israeli cabinet in a resort to arms. Israelis from left to right now agreed that there was no alternative. The decision was made on June 4 in a unanimous vote of 18 to 0 (Eban 1977: 400).

Only three weeks before, we should recall, none of the major parties (apart from some small Palestinian fighting groups) had wanted or intended an armed conflict in the near future. The 1967 war demonstrates the potential for unintended collisions, and the limits of rationality, in such confrontations. The miscalculation by the Soviet Union showed that outside powers have greater capability to set events in motion than they have to control the consequences. The failure of UN peacekeeping underlined the limits of cooperative international frameworks when local parties believe that vital interests, and perhaps their very survival, are at stake. The 1967 war was, in short, a cautionary tale that is still studied for its lessons by both analysts and practitioners.

Perceptions of responsibility for the 1967 war thus remain, not surprisingly, deeply divided. To Arabs it was a war of Israeli aggression fought under the flimsy pretext of "freedom of navigation." Israel, after all, launched the war with a surprise attack, capturing territory on which it had long held designs. To Israelis it was a war for survival, fought against a steady drumbeat of threats to Israel's very existence. Israelis never forget the fear of annihilation that prevailed on the eve of the war, or the digging of mass graves in anticipation of vast civilian casualties. Against this backdrop, the course of the war itself was shorter and more easily described than the crisis that preceded it.

Israel's attack began early on June 5 with a massive aerial bombing of Egypt's airfields, successfully crippling the Egyptian Air Force. When the Jordanian army opened fire on Jewish Jerusalem, honoring its commitment to Egypt, similar attacks were carried out on Jordanian and Syrian air bases. Since dominance in the skies is particularly critical in desert warfare, Israel's victory on the ground was practically assured. Within days the Israeli army had captured all of the West Bank from Jordan, as well as the Gaza Strip and the Sinai peninsula, up to the Suez Canal, from Egypt. At the end of the week, a short and sharp campaign wrested the Golan Heights, dominating the upper Jordan Valley, from Syria (see map 4.3).

To Israelis this conflict, labeled triumphantly the "Six Day War," represented deliverance from the dread of destruction to a new reality in which Arab states would surely have to sue for peace. Israel's strategic position was enormously improved; instead of Egyptian forces sitting less than 50 miles from Tel Aviv, Israeli troops now deployed on the Suez Canal. Eastern Jerusalem, including the Old City and holy sites so important in Jewish tradition, was now in Israeli hands (and was quickly annexed to Israel). After 1967 fear of conquest by an Arab army receded from Israeli consciousness, not only because of Israel's demonstrated edge in conventional military power, but also because of the development by the late 1960s of an undeclared Israeli nuclear deterrent that factored into both regional and global relations (Cohen, 1998: 259–76). In short, Israel now held the important bargaining cards.

To Arabs, however, this was simply the June War, and it represented the unfortunate culmination of the long Jewish campaign to control all of Palestine. Israel now occupied all of former Mandatory Palestine, as well as Egyptian and Syrian territory that had never been part of Palestine. How far did Israeli territorial ambitions extend? The issue was no longer survival and self-determination for the Jewish people, but survival and self-determination for Arabs caught in the path of Jewish self-determination.

In a word, the 1967 war turned the Arab–Israel conflict upside down. It marked the final stage in the reversal of power relationships. Zionists who had at first sought a foothold in historic Palestine now controlled all of it; Palestinians who saw all of Palestine as their heritage now clung to a remaining foothold under Israeli occupation.

The Peculiar Legacy of 1967

Militarily, the 1967 war was an exhilarating triumph for Israel and a humiliating defeat for Palestinians and other Arabs. But in terms of its impact on the shape of the Arab–Israeli conflict, the picture is much more complicated. What the 1967 war did, above all, was to derail the process of *de facto* partition and to reopen competing options. Israel had not challenged the 1949 armistice lines, which had gained (and still hold today) great legitimacy as *de facto* international borders. Before 1967, Israeli governments regarded the 1949 lines as the maximum territorial deal obtainable; the question was whether Israel would have to move back from these lines in any future settlement. Only a small minority on Israel's nationalist right kept alive the vision of expansion beyond those lines. Arab states for their part had no incentive to accept and recognize Israel within any given borders, but the passage of time would have dulled any inclination to challenge the 1949 armistice lines. Indeed, both Jordan and Egypt had gained from the *de facto* partition created in 1949.

The Palestinians, who were eclipsed as actors in the conflict after 1948 by Arab governments, would have had much less space in which to re-emerge as active challengers. While this re-emergence would certainly have occurred sooner or later, it would more likely have been led by Palestinian elites in the West Bank and Gaza, operating through the Jordanian and Egyptian governments, rather than by radical liberation movements based primarily in the Palestinian refugee camps of Lebanon and Syria.

What the 1967 war did, in Avner Yaniv's words, was "to salvage from oblivion the twin ghosts of Jewish maximalism and Palestinian particularism" (Yaniv 1990: 105). It effectively voided any thought of resolving the Arab–Israeli conflict through negotiation between Israel and the Arab states alone, without a Palestinian actor. Further, it led to a renewal of intense demographic conflict, since visions of a unitary state in all of Palestine make demography much more contentious than it would be between two states separated by a border.

In Israel, a unitary state again seemed realistic to some, as the "ghost of Jewish maximalism" returned to haunt the scene. The war brought to life contentious issues that had been locked in cold storage for 20 years, involving not just the future of the territories occupied but also the very nature of Israel itself. Was Israel to be a compact and relatively homogeneous Jewish state, or a state of two peoples? Contrary to much conventional wisdom, opposition to withdrawal from the West Bank, Gaza, and the Golan Heights among Israeli Jews did not grow slowly over time, but actually peaked shortly after the war; the general long-term trend after that – until recent years – was toward greater willingness to withdraw (Stone 1982: 36–45; Shamir and Shamir 1993: 5–8). This reflects the sensitivity of Israeli opinion to Arab policies and attitudes; in 1967, Arab governments still rejected any dealings with Israel, while subsequent moderation of these policies evoked moderation in Israeli thinking.

Supporters of *Eretz Yisrael Ha'shlema* (The Whole Land of Israel) very quickly challenged partition on the ground, beginning with the establishment of an "illegal" settlement in Hebron in 1968. (The Israeli government, still under Labor Party domination, authorized "legal" settlements in particular areas of strategic importance – Jordan Valley, Golan Heights – or prior Jewish residence – Old City of Jerusalem, Etzion bloc – while the unauthorized "illegal" settlements sought to prevent future Israeli withdrawal by settling in the heart of Arab population centers or in places of historic religious significance such as Hebron.) Settlement growth (over 406,000 settlers by 2016 in the West Bank, not including East Jerusalem) is testimony to the ability of a committed minority to establish facts. The settlers enjoyed government support when the sympathetic *Likud* party was in power (1977–92, 1996–9, 2001–5, 2009–), but even during periods of Labor rule there was a prevailing permissive attitude, rooted in the traditional pioneering ethos, that led Prime Ministers to allow the continuing expansion of settlements. To Palestinians this was seen as evidence of intent to incorporate the West Bank and Gaza into Israel, and thus as rejection of the basic principle of partition.

The "ghost of Palestinian particularism" that re-emerged was embodied in the rise of the Palestine Liberation Organization (PLO) and in its take-over by Yasir Arafat's Fatah (Palestine Liberation Movement) in 1968. As support for the PLO in the West Bank and Gaza grew over the years, the door to a negotiated settlement based on partition seemed to close; Jordan might have eventually formalized its division of Palestine with Israel in an agreement, but it was unrealistic to expect the same from an organization whose founders and historic base of support came not from indigenous West Bank and Gaza residents but from refugees seeking to return to homes across the 1949 armistice lines, in Israel itself.

Paradoxically, while the 1967 war made negotiation more difficult, it also made it more unavoidable. The previous *de facto* partition could gain acceptance without negotiation, which was fortuitous since the Arab states had no incentive to recognize formally the reality of a Jewish state whose existence they continued to oppose in principle. Or, put another way, Israel had little or nothing to offer the Arab states in return for accepting Israel's unwelcome presence.

But after 1967 the likely solutions required redivisions and redeployments, which could be done only through negotiated *quid pro quo* deals. However, such negotiated deals might actually end the conflict; for the first time, there appeared to be a basis for a final settlement that would be acceptable to both sides. Neither Israel nor the United States wanted to repeat the experience of 1957, when Israeli withdrawal was traded for arrangements that fell apart at the first serious challenge; President Lyndon Johnson later wrote that "twenty years of fragile truce, of hatred and anxiety, had yielded three dangerous armed conflicts. This time, I was convinced, we could not afford to repeat the temporary and hasty arrangements of 1957" (Johnson 1971: 303).

Israel had taken territory from three Arab states, giving it a powerful bargaining chip. The Arab states, for their part, could reject or accept peace with Israel, giving them an important card in negotiations as well. Why not, then, trade Israeli withdrawal for Arab acceptance? Israel would return territories occupied in 1967 in return for Arab recognition and a final peace treaty. This "land for peace" formula was adopted in UN Security Council Resolution 242 of November 22, 1967, which has been the point of departure for all subsequent Arab–Israeli diplomacy. Since Resolution 242 has been so central, it is important to take a close look at it:

The Security Council,

Expressing its continuing concern with the grave situation in the Middle East,

Emphasizing the inadmissibility of the acquisition of territory by war and the need to work for a just and lasting peace in which every state in the area can live in security,

Emphasizing further that all member states in their acceptance of the Charter of the United Nations have undertaken a commitment to act in accordance with Article 2 of the Charter,

1. Affirms that the fulfillment of Charter principles requires the establishment of a just and lasting peace in the Middle East which should include the application of both the following principles:
    (i)   Withdrawal of Israeli armed forces from territories occupied in the recent conflict;
    (ii) Termination of all claims or states of belligerency and respect for and acknowledgement of the sovereignty, territorial integrity and political independence of every state in the area and their right to live in peace within secure and recognized boundaries free from threats and acts of force;
2. Affirms further the necessity
    (a)   For guaranteeing freedom of navigation through international waterways in the area;

(b) For achieving a just settlement of the refugee problem;

(c) For guaranteeing the territorial inviolability and political independence of every state in the area, through measures including the establishment of demilitarized zones;

3. Requests the Secretary General to designate a special representative to proceed to the Middle East to establish and maintain contacts with the states concerned in order to promote agreement and assist efforts to achieve a peaceful and accepted settlement in accordance with the provisions and principles in this resolution;

4. Requests the Secretary General to report to the Security Council on the progress of the efforts of the special representative as soon as possible.

Resolution 242 was the product of hard bargaining among the permanent members of the Security Council: the Soviet Union demanded immediate Israeli withdrawal, the United States sought to secure Arab acceptance of Israel and a final settlement, and Great Britain played a mediating role in tying these two elements together. It is, therefore, a carefully balanced resolution: "inadmissibility of the acquisition of territory by war" is linked to "need to work for a just and lasting peace," and the withdrawal of Israeli forces is paired with the end of all claims of belligerency, mutual recognition, and secure and recognized boundaries. It is, furthermore, only a framework for negotiation, setting forth five principles that should guide the process of reaching a just and lasting peace; the only operational clauses in the resolution involve the appointment of a special representative to further this negotiation.

In certain key respects Resolution 242 is tantalizingly – and intentionally – ambiguous, leaving vast space for conflicting interpretations. Israel has always emphasized that it is only a framework for negotiations; it does not call for unilateral Israeli withdrawal except as part of an overall settlement, and even then does not specify "all" territories or "the" territories, leaving the exact border to be negotiated. Arab representatives argue that "territories occupied in the recent conflict" logically implies all such territories, not just some of them, and point out that nothing in the resolution requires a formal, written, and signed treaty covering all issues. Arab states can meet their obligations under Resolution 242 simply by refraining from acts of war against Israel ("termination of all claims or states of belligerency"), while positive steps such as territorial withdrawal could and should be implemented without need of further negotiations.

Of the Arab states involved, only Egypt and Jordan accepted Resolution 242 at the time. Syria accepted it indirectly a few years later, after the 1973 war. The PLO and other Palestinian groups rejected it totally at the time, since Resolution 242, reflecting the definition of the conflict that had prevailed in the 1948–67 period, envisioned negotiations only between Israel and the neighboring Arab states. The word "Palestinian" does not appear in the resolution, and the only indirect mention is the brief reference to "the refugee problem." At a time when Palestinians were reasserting their particular identity and national rights, and striving to take the leading role in the struggle with Israel, this was simply unacceptable.

To summarize: Israel now had the leverage to pursue a peace based on partition, since it held all of the land that might form any future Palestinian state. But precisely because of this position of strength, internal opposition to territorial compromise was very strong at the outset. Another problem, with the rise of the PLO and the eclipse of Jordan, was the absence of a credible partner willing and able to negotiate within this framework. The PLO moved slowly over the years toward acceptance of the partition framework, but it was not until 1988 that it formally accepted Resolutions 181 (of 1947) and 242.

The 1967 war also marked a higher level of international involvement in the Arab–Israel conflict. To begin with, Soviet ties with its client states, Egypt and Syria, had played a key role in the path to war, and the conflict was waged with the global powers trying to prevent an outcome that would benefit the other side. After the war the defeated Arab states were even more dependent on Soviet support, especially in the rebuilding of their military forces, and the higher intensity level led to even greater polarization of the conflict along Cold War lines.

The Israeli victory helped to cement US–Israeli ties, and in the following years the "special relationship" between the two states flourished. Before 1967 US aid to Israel had been almost entirely non-military and only once exceeded $100 million in a given year. After the war the total jumped to $160 million in 1969 and to $643 million in 1971, most of it in military loans (it would jump again, even more dramatically, after the 1973 war) (Congressional Research Service 2010). While the defeat of Soviet clients relieved some pressures on US diplomacy, the aftermath of the war also left serious unresolved issues: the closure of the Suez Canal (blocked by Egypt during the war), the future of Israel-held territories, the threat of further radicalization in the Arab world.

One of the key issues in US–Israel relations, in the late 1960s, was the status of Israel's nuclear weapons program. This issue was handled behind closed doors, as preferred by both nations, following reports that Israel had managed to hastily assemble crude nuclear devices during the 1967 war. This was the period in which the United States, in tandem with the Soviet Union, was leading the drive to conclude the Nuclear Non-Proliferation Treaty (NPT) and secure universal adherence to it among non-nuclear-weapon states. From available evidence, it appears that the outcome was a 1969 US–Israel agreement, between President Richard Nixon and Prime Minister Golda Meir, that Israel would not "go public" with its nuclear weapons capability and that the United States would not insist on Israel joining the NPT. This understanding has apparently remained the basis of both nations' policies (Cohen 1998: 336–7; Cohen 2010: 23–33).

The Decade of Sadat: Entering the Third Stage of the Conflict

Although it was not apparent at first, the post-1967 period marked the beginning of disengagement by Arab states from the "Arab–Israeli" conflict, parallel to the re-emergence of the Palestinians. The conflict over the next two decades became less of an interstate confrontation and gradually entered a third stage as, once again, a clash between Jews and Arabs within historic Palestine, culminating in the creation of a direct relationship between Israel and the PLO in 1991 (see chapter 6).

This process was tied to the remarkable personality of Anwar Sadat, President of Egypt from the time of Nasser's death in 1970 until his own assassination in 1981. Sadat's program for disengaging Egypt was not clear at first, perhaps, because his pursuit of a negotiated settlement led initially to a renewal of armed conflict.

In the post-1967 euphoria that prevailed in Israel during these years, there was little sense of urgency about negotiations with Arab states. Israel held the strong cards, and could afford to wait until Arab governments came to the table. The mood was captured in Defense Minister Moshe Dayan's oft-quoted comment that "I'm waiting for the phone to ring" (Oren 2002: 315). Furthermore, if and when "land for peace" agreements were negotiated, Israel intended to demand changes in the pre-war armistice lines. East Jerusalem, including the Old City and its Jewish Quarter, had already been annexed to Israel. Other likely claims were indicated by government sponsorship of Jewish settlements. Some were on sites where Jewish settlements had existed before 1948, such as the Etzion bloc south of Jerusalem. Most were set up in strategically important spots: the Jordan Valley, the Golan Heights, the Egypt–Gaza border. As formulated in the "Allon Plan" of Labor Party leader Yigal Allon, the intention was to hold onto these areas but return the heavily populated areas of the West Bank to Jordan, linked by a corridor through the Jordan Valley. One consequence of favoring a Jordan-based solution was that the Labor governments of this period consistently suppressed the development of an independent leadership on the West Bank – leaving the arena open to the PLO.

In accord with their design, the Labor governments of the late 1960s and early 1970s, under Prime Ministers Levi Eshkol (1963–9), Golda Meir (1969–74), and Yitzhak Rabin (1974–7), opposed Jewish settlement outside of the designated areas. In this they were challenged by the emergence, from 1968, of a settler movement dedicated to establishing a renewed Jewish presence throughout the homeland, and making the return of territory to Arab rule a political and practical impossibility. This movement, identified informally as *Gush Emunim* (Bloc of the Faithful), was inspired by a strong religious and historical nationalism, and enjoyed close ties with religious and right-wing parties, in particular the National Religious Party.

On the Arab side, the very extent of the 1967 defeat was a huge psychological barrier to negotiation. Egypt, Jordan, and Syria had all lost territory and had, for the first time, clear incentives to talk to Israel, but they were also determined not to appear to be supplicants begging for Israel's favor. When pressed by Soviet President Nikolai Podgorny to pursue diplomacy, Nasser replied that "any discussion on political concessions is only a reward for aggression and that is illogical both politically and mentally" (Farid 1991: 11). Arab leaders convened in Khartoum, the Sudanese capital, at the end of August 1967, to consider their next move, and in the final communiqué called for "no recognition of Israel, no peace and no negotiations with her." The "three no's of Khartoum" were seen in Israel as total rejection of a diplomatic solution; if the other side refuses even to negotiate, what is left? Arab observers, however, have argued that Khartoum did not close the door to political compromise, so long as it did not involve direct contact with Israel or a formal peace agreement. Agreements providing for Israeli withdrawal from occupied territory, in return for Arab non-belligerence, could have been reached through third-party mediation, and would have been in perfect accord with the Egyptian and Jordanian interpretation of Resolution 242, passed three months later.

In one respect, at least, the Khartoum summit did give a clear indication of what was to come. Although lip service was paid to Palestinian rights, Palestinian leaders were not invited to the meeting, nor were their concerns high on the agenda. Clearly the priority of Arab governments had shifted to recovery of territories occupied by Israel in 1967; in fact, they were beginning a process of disengagement from the front lines of the conflict that would play out over the coming decades. There was now a "1967 file" as well as a "1948 file" on the Arab side, and increasingly the 1948 file was shunted aside as attention focused on ending Israeli occupation of Sinai, Gaza, the West Bank, and the Golan Heights. This was true even among Palestinians, since the 1967 war brought about one million of them under direct Israeli military occupation.

Egypt's first recourse was to wage a "war of attrition" along the Suez Canal line, where Cairo enjoyed an advantage in numbers and firepower. Israel used its air force to offset Egyptian artillery, eventually conducting deep strikes into Egypt and impelling the Soviet Union to deploy new air defense systems in Egypt. A cease-fire negotiated by the United States ended open hostilities in late 1970, but the impasse remained: Egypt demanded total Israeli withdrawal in return for something less than a full peace, while Israel insisted on full peace in return for something less than total withdrawal.

After succeeding Nasser in October 1970, Anwar Sadat became convinced that Israel would not make the necessary concessions unless Egypt demonstrated that it still had military options. Sadat's aim was to change the psychological relationship by showing that Egypt could still inflict heavy costs on Israel and at the same time remove the burden of humiliation that limited Egyptian flexibility. As Sadat recounted, "I used to tell Nasser that if we could recapture even 4 inches of Sinai territory ... and establish ourselves there so firmly that no power on earth could dislodge us, then the whole situation would change – east, west, all over. First to go would be the humiliation we had endured since the 1967 defeat" (Sadat 1979: 244).

Sadat coordinated his planned attack with Syria, and on October 6 – the holy day of Yom Kippur in the Jewish calendar – both nations struck across the respective cease-fire lines on the Suez Canal and the Golan Heights. Achieving both strategic and tactical surprise, the two nations achieved considerable initial success: Egypt established a firm foothold east of the Canal, and Syria reoccupied most of the Golan

Heights before being thrown back a few days later by hastily mobilized Israeli forces. By October 19 Egyptian forces were threatened by an Israeli counterattack across the Canal, and fighting ended on October 24 to the background accompaniment of a threatened confrontation between the United States and the Soviet Union.

The 1973 war brought US–Soviet rivalry in the Middle East to a new pitch of intensity. US President Nixon and Secretary of State Henry Kissinger suspected that the Soviet Union had encouraged the Egyptian–Syrian attack, in violation of mutual understandings, and matched Soviet arms shipments to the region with a highly visible resupply airlift to Israel. In the final days of fighting, it seemed that the Soviet Union might be about to intervene in force to prevent impending Egyptian collapse; the United States countered with an increased level of military alert (DefCon 3, labeled by the media as a "nuclear alert"). For a moment it appeared that the Arab–Israel conflict could become the catalyst for global conflagration (Dowty 1984: 273–7).

The aftermath of the war, however, brought a great boost to the US position in the region when Egypt reversed its entire orientation and forged close ties to the United States, becoming the second largest recipient (after Israel) of American assistance. Sadat seemed to be working on the assumption that only the United States could induce Israel to offer farreaching concessions, making US ties with Israel an asset rather than a liability in regional politics. In the years that followed, in fact, the Soviet Union was almost totally excluded from a meaningful role in Middle East diplomacy as Kissinger, and his successors, shuttled between Israel and Arab capitals.

Though the military results in 1973 were mixed – Egypt remained on the eastern bank of the Canal, while Syria actually lost territory – Sadat achieved his political goals. He had shaken up Israeli thinking, which since 1967 had regarded further Arab military attacks as foolhardy and thus highly unlikely. The "myth of Israeli invincibility" had been shattered. He also aroused the United States into taking a more active role, as US Secretary of State and National Security

Advisor Henry Kissinger carried out rounds of "shuttle diplomacy" among the various parties. The barrier of humiliation on the Arab side was overcome; memories of 1967 were replaced by images of the heroic crossing of the Canal. The path was now cleared for negotiation.

The first official face-to-face diplomatic meeting since 1949 took place shortly after the war, in December 1973, when Egypt and Jordan (but not Syria or the Palestinians) sat at the table with Israel at a two-day conference in Geneva. But Kissinger's shuttles soon became the central diplomatic pivot, and produced disengagement agreements between Israel and Egypt (January 1974) and Israel and Syria (May 1974). A second-stage "Interim Agreement," returning an additional slice of Sinai to Egyptian control, was reached in September 1975.

After 1967, the issue of the occupied Palestinian territories became the central axis of Israeli politics. Two seemingly contradictory trends characterized Israeli opinion over this period. In the first place, there was slow growth of support for "territorial compromise," meaning greater willingness to withdraw from occupied territories. But at the same time, in terms of party politics, there was a shift to the right in Israeli politics, with the rise of the *Likud* and the end of Labor domination. To explain this apparent contradiction, we need to look more closely at the divisions in Israeli politics (Aronoff 1989).

Doves, who generally referred to occupied Palestinian territories as "the West Bank and the Gaza Strip," saw them as bargaining cards to be traded for recognition and peace – initially through negotiation with Jordan, since the PLO was not considered a viable negotiating partner. Hawks used the historic Jewish designation – "Judea and Samaria" – for the West Bank and advocated its integration into Israel on historical, nationalist, and security grounds.

The appearance of a religious nationalist ideology was largely a post-1967 phenomenon. The key figure was Rabbi Zvi Yehuda Kook, who declared that redemption was to be achieved in the present age by restoring Jewish rule to the remaining areas of the Land of Israel that had been, by divine providence, captured in the 1967 war. A religious vision thus became a radical political program to carry out the sacred task of reclaiming Judea and Samaria by intensive Jewish settlement in all areas of the historic homeland.

Jewish settlement in these areas challenged the model of a two-state solution; clearly the settlers envisioned a unitary Jewish Land of Israel. It also reopened a demographic struggle that had not existed when Israel was separated from the West Bank and Gaza by a clear border.

The growth of religious nationalism is part of the backdrop to the dramatic 1977 "upheaval" in Israeli politics, when half a century of Labor domination of Zionism ended with an electoral victory for the right-wing *Likud* party led by Menachem Begin. Begin was the successor of Vladimir (Ze'ev) Jabotinsky, the founder of Revisionist Zionism and advocate of militant Jewish nationalism. The success of the *Likud* was only in part based on security issues; a more fundamental factor was the rise of the *Sephardim* – Jews of Asian or African background – who constituted roughly half of the Israeli population and had been alienated from the Labor-dominated *Ashkenazi* (European) establishment, which had conveyed attitudes of cultural superiority and condescension toward *Sephardim*. But whatever the causes, one of the results of the upheaval was an Israeli government unswervingly committed to the expansion of Jewish settlements in the territories. In 1977 there were still only about 4,000 Jewish settlers beyond the Green Line (the 1949 armistice lines); due in part to the efforts of the new Minister of Agriculture, Ariel Sharon, this number grew quickly.

As for the Palestinians: excluded from Resolution 242, excluded even from the Khartoum summit, they ceased to rely on the Arab states for their deliverance and began to take over their own cause. The trend toward reassertion of a distinctive Palestinian identity, evident before the 1967 war, swept all before it in response to the Arab defeat. Arab states could not defeat Israel in an all-out war; furthermore, they were obviously focused on their own occupied territories rather than on the injustices of 1948. Palestinians would have to fight their own fight; for this purpose, the then popular theory of revolutionary guerrilla warfare provided a ready model. By 1969 the Palestinian fighting groups, led by Yasir Arafat's *Fatah*, took over the PLO, established in 1964 as an umbrella organization representing all Palestinians. They then rewrote the PLO Charter; the changes they made illustrated the new direction of Palestinian politics.

The new 1968 Charter paid less attention to Palestine as a pan-Arab issue and more attention to Palestinian identity and particularity. Palestine, within the Mandate borders, was declared "an indivisible territorial unit." Any partition of this territory, including the creation of Israel, was illegal, and anything other than the "total liberation of Palestine" was rejected. Jews as a people had no valid claims in Palestine, since Jews were, in fact, *not* a people: "Judaism, being a religion, is not an independent nationality." Only Jews who resided in Palestine "before the beginning of the Zionist invasion" would be accepted as Palestinians. The Charter also associated the Palestinian cause with "movements of national liberation" throughout the world, labeling Israel as "a geographic base for world imperialism," and using the language of "armed struggle" ("the only way to liberate Palestine").

Efforts to apply the guerrilla model to the West Bank and Gaza did not prove successful, however; this was not Algeria or Vietnam. Efforts to use Jordan as a sanctuary and base of operations ended when the Jordanian government, feeling that its own survival was at stake, expelled the Palestinian guerrilla movements from its territory in 1970–1. Neither Egypt nor Syria permitted the PLO to launch attacks from its territory, leaving Lebanon as the last possible base of operations on Israel's border. The Lebanese government was too weak to keep the PLO from establishing itself in southern Lebanon, making that border, previously peaceful, into a zone of conflict and eventually igniting civil war among the always contentious factions within Lebanon.

As direct military confrontation was impossible, PLO groups turned to surprise attacks on unprotected – usually civilian – targets. By most definitions this was terrorism; PLO spokesmen argued that in wars of national liberation all of the oppressor's institutions and population are legitimate targets. Apart from the arguable psychological impact, the attacks did little or nothing to weaken Israel. The gain for the Palestinians came from the publicity it gave to their cause and the boost to their own morale and self-respect.

At the same time, the Palestinian political and diplomatic offensive was achieving significant gains. In October 1974, with the coerced acquiescence of Jordan, the Rabat Arab summit meeting declared the PLO to be the sole legitimate representative of the Palestinian people. The following month Yasir Arafat was invited to address the UN General Assembly, and in November 1975 the General Assembly, in a vote of 93 to 18 with 27 abstentions, approved a resolution that listed Zionism as "a form of racism or racial discrimination." The dominance of Third World post-colonial nations in the United Nations had created a much more sympathetic forum for the Palestinian cause; by this time the PLO had diplomatic relations with more states than recognized Israel.

Two forces were now pushing the PLO into more serious consideration of political solutions rather than pursuit of military victory. The first was the simple fact that Palestinians were having much more success politically than militarily. Secondly, there was now a West Bank and Gaza constituency focused, understandably, on getting the Israeli army out of their lives, rather than on the "1948 file" that concerned the refugee communities of Jordan, Syria, and Lebanon – the historic base of the PLO. An immediate issue was the proposal for a Palestinian state in the West Bank and Gaza: should the PLO support or oppose the idea? In accord with the 1968 Charter that rejected partition, hard-liners opposed the idea on the grounds that it would be regarded by the world at large as a permanent solution to the conflict, thus "liquidating" the Palestinian struggle for total liberation. The fixed aim should remain, in this view, a "secular democratic Palestinian state" in all of Palestine.

In a compromise reached by the Palestine National Council in June 1974, the PLO reaffirmed its rejection of UN Resolution 242, its commitment to armed struggle, and its goal of liberating the whole of Palestine. But at the same time, "the PLO will consider any step toward liberation which is accomplished as a stage in the pursuit of its strategy for the establishment of a democratic Palestinian state." In other words, the PLO would accept Palestinian rule in part of Palestine, so long as this was seen as a stage toward the accomplishment of the total liberation of Palestine.

The "Palestinism" that was transforming the identity of Palestinian Arabs in exile was also felt among the Arab minority in Israel. Isolated from other Arabs for two decades, they now had contact with Palestinians in the West Bank and Gaza strip. Living standards and educational levels had also improved considerably, so that the demoralized population of 1948, having been relatively quiescent in the interval, were now ready to become more active and more assertive on behalf of themselves and other Palestinians. Numerous new movements, many with a radical tinge, began to appear. On March 30, 1976, a general strike called to protest land confiscations turned into massive demonstrations in which six Israeli Arabs were killed; the date has since been marked by the community as the time it came of age politically.

Against this backdrop, Anwar Sadat made his second unexpected move, one even more unexpected than the first. The 1973 war had cleared the way for separate agreements between Egypt and Israel, but in 1977 there was still no final agreement, and Israel still occupied most of the Sinai peninsula. In Sadat's words, "I realized that we were about to be caught up in a terrible vicious circle precisely like the one we'd lived through over the last thirty years." The basic problem, he concluded, was still the "psychological barrier" between the two sides: "we had been accustomed . . . to regard Israel as taboo" (Sadat 1979: 302–3). To overcome that barrier, Sadat announced in the Egyptian People's Assembly that he was willing to go anywhere, including Israel, to prevent further bloodshed. He was immediately invited by Israeli Prime Minister Menachem Begin to visit Israel and address the Israeli Knesset.

In one of the stranger ironies in the history of the conflict, it was Begin, the superhawk, who made Israel's first major breakthrough in the peace process. From Begin's point of view, Sadat's initiative did not present a problem. Israeli territorial hawks did not have the same kind of attachment to the Sinai that they had to the West Bank, and the chance to detach Israel's most powerful enemy from the opposing coalition was a strategic opening that no Israeli government could pass up.

There was, however, a real issue: linkage to the Palestinian question. Sadat was giving priority to Egypt's interest in recovering Sinai, and in general he was pursuing a course of disengagement from the front lines of the conflict – but he did not want to abandon the Palestinians completely, or be seen as having done so. A peace treaty between Egypt and Israel, he insisted, had to be accompanied by resolution or at least significant progress on Palestinian issues. But for Begin, much of the appeal of a deal with Egypt was precisely that it left him in a stronger position to resist withdrawal from the West Bank.

At the Camp David summit meeting in September 1978, US President Jimmy Carter mediated a compromise: there would be two agreements, one for Egypt–Israel peace and the second a framework for a West Bank/Gaza resolution, but they would not be formally linked. Consequently an Egypt–Israel peace treaty was signed in March 1979, and within three years Israel had withdrawn from Sinai, which was demilitarized, and normal diplomatic relations were established between the two nations. The Egypt–Israel peace treaty proved to be durable, surviving the assassination of Anwar Sadat by Islamic militants in 1981 as well as Israeli intervention into Lebanon and the first Palestinian uprising (*intifada*) in the 1980s.

But the West Bank/Gaza agreement was never implemented. This agreement called for a five-year transition period during which Israeli troops would withdraw and the Palestinian population there would elect a self-governing authority. During this transition period, the final status of the territories would be negotiated. Talks began as scheduled on procedures and powers for this autonomous authority, but it became clear that Begin's conception of autonomy was very circumscribed: it would apply to persons rather than to territory, and would be limited to control of local affairs. The talks were hampered also by the fact that neither the Palestinians nor Jordan were willing to participate or cooperate in any way. In fact, Egypt was ostracized by Arab and Muslim states for signing a peace treaty with Israel, and it took more than a decade for the restoration of diplomatic ties and the readmittance of Egypt to the Arab League.

The Lebanese Tangle

The Egypt–Israel peace treaty was, beyond all doubt, a singular breakthrough in the Arab–Israel conflict. It was no longer inconceivable that an Arab state would make peace with Israel; one state, and the most important one at that, had just done so. With the strongest Arab state now out of the equation, the military calculus was radically altered. Even with whatever assistance it might muster from Jordan, Lebanon, and Iraq, Syria could not seriously contemplate a full-scale one-front war with Israel. Not surprisingly, there has been no full-scale war between Israel and any Arab state since the peace treaty with Egypt.

On the everyday level, peace between the two nations made less of an impact. The Israeli public was excited by the first open border with an Arab state, and in the first few years flocked to see the Pyramids and other previously forbidden sights. Egyptians were less excited, and there was little flow in the opposite direction. Egypt observed the minimal requirements of normalization to the letter, but no more; social, cultural, and even economic relationships remained stunted. To Israelis it was a "cold peace," not the friendly amity that many had anticipated.

Furthermore, even this cold peace did not extend to other borders. Jordan was too weak and exposed to follow Egypt's lead. Syria had accepted the framework of Resolution 242 in 1973, but refused to separate the Golan Heights issue from a resolution of Palestinian claims. For that matter, Israeli public opinion was more strongly opposed to withdrawal from the Golan Heights than from any other front (except Eastern

Jerusalem), because of the Syrian hard-line stance and the strategic importance of the Golan.

Another critical factor was the prominence of the *Likud* in Israeli politics. *Likud* was either the dominant governing party, or an equal governing partner for over 30 of the 39 years between 1977 and 2016. It was *Likud* that returned Sinai to Egypt, but regarding the West Bank – the heartland of biblical Israel – the party was at that time strongly opposed to anything beyond granting limited autonomy to Arab residents. *Likud* declared that there was no Palestinian negotiating partner; the PLO was simply a terrorist organization. Peace could be negotiated with the Arab states, but Israel would not withdraw from the West Bank or Gaza or, for strategic reasons, from the Golan. Furthermore, Jews had the right to live anywhere in *Eretz Yisrael*; why should any part of the historic homeland, of all places in the world, be closed to Jews? This did not mean that *Likud* leaders wanted at that time to annex the West Bank or Gaza, with their large Arab populations, to the state of Israel. Such a move would endanger the Jewish majority in Israel. But if Israel would neither withdraw from the territories nor annex them, what was the policy? As expressed in the 1977 *Likud* platform, it was that "Judea and Samaria will not be handed to any foreign administration; between the [Mediterranean] Sea and the Jordan [River] there will only be Israeli sovereignty" (Laqueur and Schueftan 2016: 206). In the *Likud* interpretation, this was compatible with autonomy for Arab residents, including the autonomy outlined in the Camp David agreements.

In the meantime, the buildup of a PLO base in southern Lebanon represented a new threat that the Israeli government felt it could not ignore; also, as this was the last land frontier from which the PLO could strike Israel, sealing it would put an end to the PLO as a military threat. In 1978 Israel had intervened and established a buffer zone on the Lebanese side of the border, controlled by anti-Palestinian Lebanese forces. When Ariel Sharon became Defense Minister after Begin's re-election in 1981, he sought a more radical and far-reaching solution: Israel would ally itself with the Maronites and other anti-Palestinian Lebanese factions; together they would expel PLO and Syrian forces from the country; and a new Maronite-dominated Lebanon would make peace with Israel.

Sharon failed to get cabinet approval for this ambitious plan, but won consent for a scaled-down version in which Israel would clear the PLO from a zone extending 40 kilometers (about 25 miles) into Lebanon. The campaign, known as "Peace in Galilee," was launched in June 1982, and won strong public backing at first. It was even welcomed by Lebanese glad to be rid of the PLO forces in their towns and villages. But Israeli troops did not halt at the 40-kilometer line, moving instead – on Sharon's orders – to besiege PLO forces in the heart of Beirut. Sharon explained each further advance of the Israeli army as a matter of military necessity; in the end, most cabinet members concluded that he was in fact implementing his original, more ambitious design by stealth and deceit (Schiff and Ya'ari 1986).

Whatever Sharon's plans, they were dealt a lethal double blow in September. First, Bashir Gemayel, Israel's favored Maronite ally and newly elected President of Lebanon, was assassinated. Immediately afterward, Maronite forces entered the Palestinian refugee camps of Sabra and Shatilla, in Israeli-controlled Beirut, and massacred an estimated 700–800 Palestinian civilians before being stopped – after some 38 hours – by Israeli forces (Kahan Commission 1983). This triggered a vociferous international reaction, against a backdrop of growing condemnation of Israel's campaign in Lebanon. In Israel itself, opposition to the war had also been growing, and the Sabra/Shatilla massacre catalyzed this opposition into a massive protest movement that eventually forced the government, and Sharon, to back down. Some 400,000 demonstrators – about ten percent of the country's population – gathered in one Tel Aviv rally to demand the appointment of a governmental investigating commission.

An investigating body – the Kahan Commission – was established, and in its report concluded that Israeli commanders, up to Sharon himself, bore indirect responsibility for the atrocities committed (Kahan Commission 1983). A number of commanders were forced from office, and Sharon was forced to resign as Defense Minister, though he remained in the cabinet as a minister without portfolio. Israel subsequently withdrew from southern Lebanon in two stages, in 1983 and 1985, leaving behind as before a buffer zone patrolled by an Israeli-supported Lebanese force, the Southern Lebanese Army. A peace treaty negotiated with a pliant Lebanese government in May 1983 was never ratified by Beirut, and was eventually denounced as Lebanon came increasingly under Syrian influence.

The only major tangible gain for Israel, in the end, was the coerced departure of PLO forces from southern Lebanon and Beirut, carried out shortly before the bloody events of September. The PLO's new headquarters were in Tunis, 1,500 miles from its avowed theater of operations. But radical Islamist groups that had arisen in response to the Israeli presence soon took the place of the PLO. These groups, *Hizballah* principally, also introduced the macabre new phenomenon of suicide bombers into the Arab–Israel arena.

The rise of Islamic extremism introduced a new dimension not only to relations between Israelis and Arabs, but also in the regional and international context.

The leadership of the PLO, meanwhile, continued to move in the direction of a two-state solution. Arab leaders proposed two plans during this period – the Fahd Plan of August 1981 and the Fez Plan of September 1982 – clearly based on the two-state model, though not including explicit mention of Israel's right to exist. These plans were accepted by Arafat and the *Fatah* leadership of the PLO, but not by the more radical organizations inside or outside the PLO (or by Israel, for that matter). The PLO was less enthusiastic about the Reagan Plan, put forward in September 1982, that called for Palestinian participation without mentioning the PLO, and suggested self-government on the West Bank and Gaza "in association with Jordan."

Shaking Things Up: The First *Intifada*

Throughout the early and middle 1980s there were new initiatives to bridge the gap between Israelis and Palestinians on the basis of a two-state solution, but all fell short. Two major obstacles dominated the discussion. One was the question of Palestinian representation: so long as the PLO rejected UN Resolution 242, refused to accept the existence of Israel, and continued to condone terrorism as generally defined, it would not be accepted as a legitimate negotiating partner by Israel or the United States. The other obstacle was political stalemate in Israel, where National Unity Governments including both Labor and *Likud* ruled from 1984 to 1990; since *Likud* still opposed anything more than autonomy for West Bank and Gaza residents, it blocked diplomatic initiatives that went beyond that.

Thus when Israeli Prime Minister (1984–6) and Foreign Minister (1986–8) Shimon Peres of Labor worked with King Husayn to convene an international conference on Israeli–Palestinian issues, he was blocked by his *Likud* governing partner under Foreign Minister (1984–6) and Prime Minister (1986–8) Yitzhak Shamir (Peres and Shamir "rotated" as Prime Minister and Foreign Minister during these four years).

For Palestinians, frustration boiled over finally in the sustained period of unrest known as the *intifada* (an Arabic word meaning literally "shaking off," but also used to denote a political uprising). There had been protests and violent confrontations throughout the 20 years of occupation, but nothing of this scope or duration. For Palestinians, this was a natural outpouring, from the grass-roots level, of the accumulated grievances of a people long denied the basic right of self-determination and subjected to the harassments of an occupation army. A number of Israeli practices in particular aroused resentment and anger. One concerned the methods of interrogation used to extract information; reports of various monitoring bodies made it clear that standard procedures included sleep and food deprivation, verbal abuse and threats, intense noise, hooding, forced standing, binding in painful positions, solitary confinement, enclosure in tight spaces, exposure to extreme temperatures, denial of access to toilets, genital abuse, shakings, and beatings (El-Serraj 1995). Other controversial measures whose legality was seriously challenged included the demolition of homes of security offenders (a collective punishment), deportation (illegal without the consent of the country of destination), and administrative detention – which can be legal if done with proper safeguards, but such safeguards break down when detention is employed on a massive scale rather than individually.

From the Palestinian perspective, such practices were ample justification for efforts to overturn the occupation, including the use of force. But from their perspective, the major thrust of the *intifada* was nonviolent, consisting of strikes, boycotts, and demonstrations. Since Palestinians had no firearms, the most they could do was to throw stones, and "the sacred stone" became a symbol of the uprising. Above all, the *intifada* restored to Palestinians a sense of pride and the perception of being, finally, in charge of their own destiny; it was a glorious chapter in Palestinian history.

Inevitably, the grassroots uprising in the occupied territories served to strengthen the shift among Palestinians to a focus on the occupation rather than the 1948 issues. West Bank and Gaza residents stressed their loyalty to the PLO, but at the same time their activism was pushing the PLO to give greater attention to the immediate concern of getting the Israeli army out of the territories occupied in 1967. In addition, the *intifada* convinced King Husayn that it was time to withdraw any remaining Jordanian claim to the West Bank, which he did in July 1988 – pulling the rug out from under the Israeli Labor Party, which was still officially advocating "the Jordanian option."

The *intifada* also catalyzed the emergence of radical Islamist groups. Fundamentalist Islamic movements had made headway among Palestinians, as elsewhere in the Muslim world, during the previous decade. *Islamic Jihad*, a group inspired by the Iranian model, had already appeared on the scene. In mid-1988 a new group named *Hamas* (the initials of Islamic Resistance Movement) was formally organized; in its Charter, *Hamas* sought "to raise the banner of God over every inch of Palestine," since Palestine was an Islamic trust (*waqf*). "So-called peaceful solutions" were strongly rejected, and Jews were described in the language of classic anti-Semitism (Laqueur and Schueftan 2016: 340-47). The new militant Islamist groups thus came to play the rejectionist role among Palestinians that had been played in the past by radical leftist parties.

From the Israeli perspective, the *intifada* came as a surprise. Despite the signs of gathering unrest in the territories, Israelis tended to believe that Palestinians would respond to the demise of conventional military options by agreeing to negotiate. After all, there was considerable evidence of a trend among Palestinians toward acceptance of a two-state solution. Furthermore, Israelis saw the occupation of the West Bank and Gaza as relatively humane, at least compared to many other military occupations in the world. The Israeli army maintained a posture of low visibility in the territories, and was ill-equipped and ill-trained to deal with civil unrest. As a result the response was confused, ineffective, and often heavy-handed. Officially Israel observed the recognized legal norms for occupying forces, but in a situation of massive unrest and low-level violence, normal procedures broke down. The laws of military occupation were simply not adequate for situations of prolonged occupation or of general insurrection.

Moreover, Israelis pointed out, legal issues were not the core of the conflict. Even if deportation, demolition, and other questionable measures were halted, and administrative detention were employed strictly within acceptable legal standards, and all Israeli soldiers were to scrupulously observe the "rules of engagement" and other accepted norms, basic demands on both sides would remain unmet. Palestinians would continue to oppose the very fact of Israeli occupation, however civilized and refined it might become. For Israelis as well, the basic issue was not the legality of particular measures, but the political issue of what was to come after the occupation.

In the meantime, Israelis argued, the material condition of the Palestinian population had actually improved dramatically in the twenty years of occupation. Income and consumption levels had improved enormously in the West Bank and Gaza since 1967; a 1987 government report claimed that the

Gross Domestic Product (GDP) of Judea and Samaria had risen 400 percent, and the GDP of Gaza 430 percent, in this time (Israel Ministry of Defense 1987: 14–17). Palestinians pointed out, however, that growth in private consumption is not the only relevant economic measure. Improvement in living standards was due more to income from work in Israel than from economic development in the territories themselves. The Israeli government had little incentive to invest in West Bank or Gaza industries that would compete with Israeli producers in the new captive market they had acquired.

Given this confusion, what impact did the *intifada* have on Israeli opinion? Within a year or so after the onset of the *intifada*, surveys recorded a definite dovish shift on the basic question of territorial compromise. Some of these results are shown in table 5.1, in answer to the question: "What concessions would you make on the West Bank (Judea and Samaria) in order to reach a peace settlement with the Arab states?".

The dovish trend on basic issues can also be seen in regard to the controversial question of Israeli negotiations with the PLO. Support for negotiation with the PLO, provided it recognized Israel and renounced terrorism, grew from 43 percent in September 1986 to 58 percent by March 1989 (Smith Research Center 1986–9). Conditional support for talking with the PLO thus moved from a minority to a majority opinion after the *intifada*.

Both Labor and *Likud* moved very gradually in a dovish direction in apparent response to shifting public opinion and, on a deeper level, to changes in the Arab world (Inbar and

Table 5.1 Impact of the *intifada*: territorial concessions (in percentage)

	March 1987	Jan. 1989	May 1991
Some, most, or all of the territories	54	65	69
None of the territories	45	35	31

Sources: Katz 1988, 1989; Katz and Levinsohn 1991. All data from Continuing Survey of the Israel Institute of Applied Social Research

Goldberg 1992: 45–66). In Labor, the Allon Plan (for the return of most of the West Bank to Jordan), once championed by those on the left in the party, became the position of those on the right. The focus for resolving the conflict shifted from Jordan to the Palestinians. By 1989 *Likud* had accepted Labor's conditional formula for talking with the PLO; both parties also agreed that Arafat had not yet met these conditions. The electorate was still divided between those who favored partition solutions in their various versions (a Palestinian entity of some kind, redivision with Jordan, or a Palestinian–Jordanian confederation) and those who favored unitary solutions (autonomy or other forms of functional compromise based on continuing Israeli control of the territories), but the tide was running in favor of the former.

On the Palestinian side, the *intifada* gave PLO leaders more confidence to face negotiations, while it also shifted power among the Palestinians from the 1948–9 refugees to West Bank and Gaza residents more willing to consider a compromise solution. But while the *intifada* could put the Palestinian issue back on the agenda, and impose higher costs on Israel, it could not force unilateral Israeli withdrawal. The *intifada* might make Israelis more willing to leave the territories, but in order to reap this benefit, the Palestinians would have to negotiate.

In December 1988, PLO leader Yasir Arafat renounced terrorism and called for a negotiated peace based on coexistence of Israel and a Palestinian state. This statement clearly changed the rules of the diplomatic game, leading to the opening of direct contact between the USA and the PLO. It did not go far enough to qualify the PLO as a bargaining partner in the eyes of most Israelis, but clearly the stage was set for a new chapter in the Arab–Israel conflict.

6 | The First Pass at Peace

When I think of what happened on the lawn of the White House I am reminded of an entertaining story by Yehuda Amihai, "Inverted Love," in which a man and a woman, drunk on the eve of Independence Day and finding themselves in the apartment belonging to one of them, go to bed and make love; the morning after they behave with scrupulous politeness, introducing themselves to each other and parting with a handshake but with no exchange of addresses.

Israeli Deputy Foreign Minister Yossi Beilin (Beilin 1999:135)

The Oslo Breakthrough

The first *intifada*, beginning in December 1987, created for the first time an apparent majority among both Palestinians and Israelis in support of a two-state solution to the conflict. By the end of the 1980s, converging forces had pushed mainstream opinion on both sides toward the previously unthinkable: direct negotiation with the established leadership of the other side.

The *intifada* restored Palestinian pride and self-reliance, but in itself brought little concrete advance toward self-determination or territorial sovereignty. In order to convert its psychological gain into political change, Palestinian leaders would have to enter the diplomatic arena and deal directly with Israel. The shift of power to the "inside" – residents of the West Bank and Gaza – from the traditional "outside" leadership in Tunis and elsewhere made this less unthinkable; Palestinians living under occupation had little choice but to deal directly with Israeli officials. In addition, the collapse of the Soviet bloc at the end of the decade meant that the PLO and other radical parties in the area could no longer rely on the automatic Soviet counterweight to Western pressures and influences. The United States was, increasingly, the only super-power in town; the PLO and other former Soviet clients would have to deal directly with the West. And US pressure, as well as that of its moderate Arab clients such as Egypt, Jordan, and Saudi Arabia, consistently pushed Palestinians to choose the course of moderation and political compromise. Finally, the specter of Islamic fundamentalism (*Hamas* and other groups) gave both the PLO and Israel reason to move while the window of opportunity was open, and before religious extremism could slam it shut. For Palestinians, *Hamas* posed the prospect of unending martyrdom in pursuit of unachievable goals; for Israelis, it made Yasir Arafat look much less radical than before, or, at least, the lesser of two evils.

Within a year the PLO officially accepted UN General Assembly Resolution 181 – the Partition Plan of 1947 – and UN Security Council Resolution 242 of 1967. By these steps the Palestinian mainstream formally endorsed the "two-state solution" to the conflict, envisioning a Palestinian state alongside the Jewish state, rather than in place of it.

Among Israelis the *intifada* brought growing recognition that there was no purely military solution to Palestinian unrest. Occupation could not be continued indefinitely, and political compromise would therefore be necessary. As noted in chapter 5, Israeli opinion shifted by 10–15 percent toward greater support for withdrawal from some or all of the West Bank and Gaza as part of a peace agreement, and greater support for negotiating with the PLO if it recognized Israel and renounced terrorism. At the same time, Jordan's withdrawal of its claim to the West Bank in July 1988 forced Israeli advocates of territorial compromise to move from the previously favored "Jordanian option" to the previously unthinkable notion of a two-state solution with Yasir Arafat's PLO as partner. Support for an independent Palestinian state in the West Bank and Gaza, which had never exceeded ten percent in the past, grew to 25–30 percent – with 61 percent in a 1990 poll predicting that a Palestinian state would emerge whether they wanted it or not (Smith Research Center 1986–9; Arian 1992, 1995; Katz, Levinsohn, and Al-Haj 1991).

Given these trends, the 1991 Gulf War proved to be only a temporary diversion in the passage toward negotiation. Iraq's Saddam Hussein tried to tie his invasion of Kuwait to the Israeli–Palestinian conflict, conditioning his retreat on Israeli withdrawal from the occupied territories. This sparked an enthusiastic response on the Palestinian street, forcing the PLO (and King Husayn of Jordan as well) to cozy up to Iraq. During the war itself, Iraq's launching of several dozen SCUD missiles against Israeli cities evoked public celebration among some Palestinians, to which both Israeli hawks and doves responded angrily. For a moment, it seemed that Israeli support for direct negotiations was another casualty of the war.

This mood was soon overtaken, however, by other after-effects of the war. First of all, Palestinian adulation of Saddam Hussein led to loss of support from the oil-producing states and a severe financial crisis for the organization. In its weakened state, the PLO was pushed even more strongly than before to consider political and diplomatic options rather than an armed struggle for which the wherewithal was evaporating. It was also impelled to deal with a strengthened United States, which, in accord with commitments made to gain the support of moderate Arab states against Iraq, was about to launch a serious diplomatic offensive to resolve or at least moderate Arab–Israeli tensions. US Secretary of State James Baker embarked on a series of consultations aimed at bringing all the parties to the conflict together at the same negotiating table – something that had never been achieved before.

By this time it was assumed that Palestinians would be represented at any general peace conference; the remaining issue was how they would be represented. The Israeli government, now a narrow right-wing coalition after the breakup of the National Unity Government in 1990, continued to reject out-right any dealing with the PLO. After intense negotiation, it was agreed that Palestinians would form a joint delegation with Jordan, and that they would be represented by West Bank and Gaza residents approved by both the PLO and Israel, but not officially tied to the PLO. This proved to be a polite fiction, as the delegates chosen made it clear that they looked to PLO headquarters in Tunis for their instructions.

With much fanfare, the first all-inclusive peace conference on the Arab–Israel conflict – the first gathering in which credible representatives of all parties met face to face – convened in Madrid on October 30, 1991. Israeli Prime Minister Yitzhak Shamir conveyed little enthusiasm for a forum in which Israel faced four Arab delegations (five, counting the Palestinians separately) and the two super-powers; Eytan Bentsur, Deputy Director-General of the Israel Foreign Ministry, later noted that "meetings of Israel's delegation, led by Shamir, were riddled with doubt, suspicion, and even dread concerning what the future might bring. It was patently evident that the prevailing desire was nothing more than to get the Madrid conference over and done with" (Bentsur 2001: 121). On the Palestinian side, Hayder Abd al-Shafi, head of the Palestinian delegation at Madrid, lamented the official exclusion of the PLO: "An invitation to discuss peace, the peace we all desire and need, comes to only a portion of our people. It ignores our national, historical, and organic unity ... We have been denied the right to publicly acknowledge our loyalty to our leadership and system of government" (Laqueur and Rubin 2008: 394).

Following the script that had been painstakingly hammered out, the ceremonial sessions in Madrid were adjourned after three days of often vituperative speeches, and the actual negotiations began in a number of bilateral and multilateral forums. The five multilateral forums represented an innovative effort to involve the entire region and some outside states in talks on functional issues (water, refugees, economic development, arms control, and the environment) in order to build a more cooperative environment for bilateral negotiations on the key issues. But the idea of depoliticizing issues where there were strong motives for cooperation, however well conceived, did not travel far in the heavily politicized Middle East. Despite some initial progress, the multilateral tracks became inactive as the general atmosphere worsened at the end of the decade.

The four bilateral negotiations, held in Washington, went in four different directions. With a peace treaty already in place, Israel and Egypt had little to talk about. There were more substantive issues between Israel and Lebanon, but because of Syrian opposition the Lebanese could not move until there was progress between Israel and Syria. Israel–Syria talks faced a number of difficult obstacles. Syria demanded the return of every inch of the Golan Heights, including areas acquired by encroachment before 1967, in return for something less than full peace and normalization, while Israel pressed for a full-scale normalization, despite the strong Syrian distaste for such intimacy, for something less than full withdrawal from the Golan. Syria also insisted that, unlike Egypt, it would not make peace with Israel until the Palestinian issue was also resolved. Not surprisingly, the Israeli–Syrian talks quickly deadlocked.

The fiction of a joint Jordanian–Palestinian delegation soon broke down, and *de fac*to separate talks took place. With few major problems between Israel and Jordan, conclusion of a peace treaty clearly depended on a Jordanian decision that the time was right for such a move. But negotiations between the Shamir government and the Palestinian delegation made no immediate progress. The PLO in Tunis, in the words of one of its top leaders, Mahmoud Abbas (Abu Mazen), "knew that the *Likud* would not take one single step toward a settlement" and therefore put their hopes in the election of a new Israeli government in 1992 (Abbas 1995: 90). Also, the PLO leadership clearly did not want the Israeli–Palestinian channel to make substantial progress without the PLO itself directly and officially representing the Palestinian side.

In June 1992 Yitzhak Rabin led Labor to its first election victory since 1973, and formed the first Israeli government without *Likud* since 1977. The stage was set for new departures. With the Washington talks still deadlocked, and with a helping hand from the Norwegian Foreign Ministry, a secret direct channel between the Israeli government and the PLO was created. After months of secret negotiations in discreet Norwegian venues, agreement on mutual recognition and a framework for a comprehensive peace treaty were achieved and dropped like a bombshell on the international scene. For the first time, the two core actors in the Arab–Israel drama would sit at the same table, negotiating directly and openly through their recognized representatives. For the first time, the legitimate leadership of both sides had accepted a common framework for resolution of all outstanding differences.

Though the US role in this process had been slight – mainly as a midwife in the later phases – the signing ceremony was held on the White House lawn, on September 13, 1993, in recognition of the importance of the United States in implementing the agreement. The famous photograph of the handshake between Yitzhak Rabin and Yasir Arafat conveys some of the undertones of the event, with US President Bill Clinton propelling an obviously reluctant Rabin and a beaming Arafat in each other's direction. It was clearly one of the most dramatic moments in the long history of the conflict, and one of the most surreal.

An exchange of letters between Rabin and Arafat established mutual recognition between Israel and the PLO, which committed itself to a peaceful resolution of all outstanding issues, assumed responsibility for preventing acts of violence by "all PLO elements and personnel," and promised to drop from the Palestinian Covenant all provisions that denied Israel's right to exist. The Declaration of Principles committed the two parties to creating a "Palestinian Interim Self-Governing Authority" in the West Bank and the Gaza Strip for a five-year period, during which time "permanent status" negotiations would take place to reach agreement on all issues of a final peace treaty: Jerusalem, refugees, Jewish settlements, security arrangements, and borders. Prior to election of the Self-Governing Authority, the PLO would take over the Gaza Strip and the Jericho area. The entire

framework was strikingly similar to the Camp David autonomy framework negotiated by Anwar Sadat in 1978, except
for the Gaza-and-Jericho-first provision and the diminished
roles of Egypt and Jordan.

However, the Declaration of Principles, like UN Resolution
242, was ambiguous enough to allow completely different
readings of the document. For Palestinians, the key was the
long-awaited Israeli withdrawal set out in UN Resolutions,
as confirmed by the repeated references to these resolutions.
Also, the five-year interim was defined as a "transition,"
clearly indicating that it was to lead to a new dispensa-
tion; what could this possibly be, other than Palestinian self-
determination – i.e. a Palestinian state? The idea that Israeli
territorial claims in the West Bank and Gaza could be put
forward after five years of Palestinian self-government was
plainly unrealistic. Among other things, the Declaration stated
that "the two sides view the West Bank and the Gaza Strip
as a single territorial unit, whose integrity will be preserved
during the interim period." And in a larger sense, Palestinians
were already making a monumental historical concession by
conceding the existence of Israel in 78 percent of Mandatory
Palestine; where was the historic justice in further reducing
the 22 percent left to a Palestinian state when there were
more Palestinians (including refugees and others outside of
Palestine) than there were Israeli Jews?

The Israeli reading of Oslo put primary emphasis on the
commitment to end all violence and resolve all future conflicts peacefully. If the PLO was being transformed into a
governing authority, it had to accept the basic responsibility of all governments not to allow its citizens to attack
neighboring populations. If this commitment was not met,
the PLO could hardly claim the legal or moral right to com-
plain about nonfulfillment of other parts of the agreement.
In any event, the Declaration clearly put all of the final status
issues on hold until the third year of the transition period,
at which point Israel would be free to make whatever proposals on borders, refugees, or security arrangements that it
felt were appropriate. Above all, as Israelis saw it, Oslo was
based on the PLO's acceptance of Israel's permanence and

the framework of a two-state solution; Palestinian actions and statements that contradicted this framework led to the reasonable conclusion that the PLO signature on the document was dishonest. In particular, the fact that the PLO did not amend the Palestinian Covenant according to the procedures laid down in the Covenant itself raised suspicions among Israelis that the aim of destroying Israel had not been banished from the hearts and minds of PLO leaders.

Though large majorities on both sides supported the Oslo agreement, there was also significant and vocal opposition from more hawkish circles that did not. Among Palestinians, *Hamas* and other Islamic militants, together with some elements of the old radical left, condemned the agreement from the outset. For the many who openly opposed a two-state solution, this was hardly surprising; but even some willing to contemplate coexistence with Israel were dissatisfied. In their eyes, the PLO which Israel recognized was one that had submitted to Israeli demands; there was no guarantee that it would gain even the 22 percent of Palestine in the West Bank and Gaza. Above all, it had put aside all of the '1948 issues': "The PLO leaders who concluded the deal with Israel have all but buried the refugees' right of return" (al-Hasan 1993). In the end, six of the 18 members of the PLO Executive Committee resigned in protest over Arafat's "capitulation."

Israeli opponents of a two-state solution were also quick to condemn the Oslo agreements (Aronoff and Aronoff 1998). Foremost among these were the settlers in the West Bank and Gaza and their supporters, who saw the Palestinian Self-Governing Authority as the first step in a process that would lead to the evacuation of their settlements or (less likely) their incorporation into a Palestinian state. *Likud*, the National Religious Party, and other right-wing parties and groups attacked the agreement as a surrender to terrorism and a threat to Israeli security. The PLO had not, they argued, given up its basic aims, and would use its foothold in Palestine to launch the next stage of its violent struggle for the liberation of all of historic Palestine. The basic constituency of the PLO was still the 1948 refugees and their descendants, who would never accept a Palestinian state in the West Bank and Gaza as fulfillment of their historic dreams and demands. In the end, the margin of approval for the agreement in the Knesset was only 61 to 50, with nine abstentions.

Extremists among the opponents of Oslo soon instigated violent attacks intended to derail the peace process. In a pattern that recurs throughout the recent history of the conflict, a diplomatic and political breakthrough was followed by an increase in dramatic assaults designed to provoke cycles of violence. *Hamas* and *Islamic Jihad* launched a series of attacks on Israeli soldiers and settlers for which they openly claimed credit. On the other side, a Jewish settler, Baruch Goldstein, massacred 29 Muslim worshippers at the Tomb of the Patriarchs, in Hebron, on February 25, 1994. The Israeli government managed to limit such terrorist attacks against Palestinians to sporadic incidents, though attacks by some settlers on their Arab neighbors remained a constant problem. The new Palestinian Authority (PA), on the other hand, was ineffective in curbing attacks on Israelis, either because it lacked the necessary authority to take on the radical Islamists, and/or because its leaders saw a continuing low level of violence as a useful weapon against Israel. In addition, the appearance of Palestinian suicide bombers, inspired by the model of *Shi'a* "martyrs" in Lebanon, made the prevention of attacks in civilian centers much more difficult, and made such attacks even more repulsive to Israelis.

The Rocky Road to Peace

Given all the obstacles, the implementation of the Oslo framework was plagued by problems and delays from the first. The negotiation of the first step, Israeli withdrawal from about 80 percent of the Gaza Strip and from the Jericho area, was to have been completed within two months; it actually took almost seven months. Nevertheless, the return of Yasir Arafat and the PLO leadership from Tunis on July 1, 1994, and the establishment of the first-ever Palestinian administration on Palestinian soil, was a dramatic event that temporarily revived some of the initial enthusiasm, at least on the Palestinian side.

The next step, an "Interim Agreement" covering all aspects of the transition period, was to have been completed within nine months after the Oslo Declaration; it actually took two years, until September 1995. This agreement, known as Oslo II, established the PA and gave it immediate jurisdiction over the major cities of the West Bank (Area A), and civil jurisdiction with shared security control over most of the towns and villages (Area B) (see map 6.1). Areas A and B together initially comprised about 28 percent of the West Bank, but together with territory controlled in Gaza this put the vast majority of the Arab population outside Jerusalem under PA jurisdiction. The remaining 72 percent of the West Bank (Area C) consisted of sparsely inhabited areas, Israeli settlements, and military reserves, all of which remained under Israeli control.

Elections were held in January 1996 for a President and a Palestine Legislative Council; Arafat was elected President by an 87 percent majority, and his Fatah party supporters won 50 of the 88 Council seats. In April, the Palestine National Council (PNC, a PLO body) voted to invalidate the articles of the Palestinian Covenant that called for the destruction of Israel, a step promised in both Oslo I and Oslo II. But since the PNC did not specify which articles were being removed, critics in Israel continued to claim that the Covenant had not been properly amended according to its own provisions; some future Palestinian government could claim that the call for Israel's demise was still operative.

Conclusion of a final peace treaty with Jordan was less complicated. Israel and Jordan had long enjoyed a furtive relationship, given their common opposition to the PLO and their common pro-Western orientation. Jordan's King Husayn had been deterred from going public only by his weak position and the fact that a majority of his subjects (even without the West Bank) were Palestinians. But once the PLO had itself "dealt with the devil," the road was open. Within a year Israel and Jordan concluded a peace treaty that covered all outstanding issues; the fact that Jordan no longer claimed the West Bank meant that there were no significant territorial issues to resolve. There were, in addition, a number of potential areas of economic and environmental

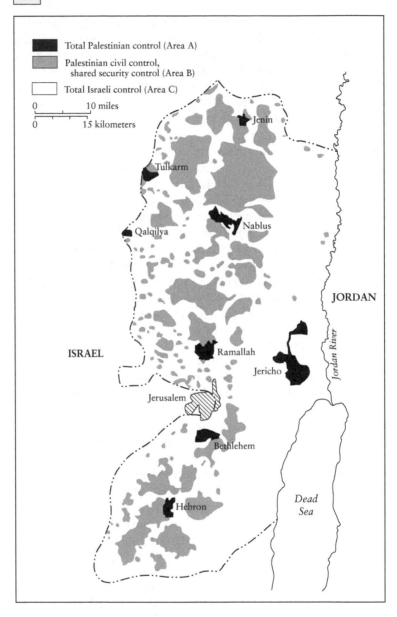

Map 6.1   1995 interim agreement (Oslo II).

cooperation that would benefit both parties. Israel also obtained a Jordanian pledge not to permit foreign armies (read: Iraq, Syria, Iran) on Jordanian territory, a matter of great strategic import to both nations. Israel now had permanent peace treaties with two of its neighbors, leaving only Syria, Lebanon, and the Palestinians as active adversaries.

Peace with Lebanon was also not problematic in principle; there were no significant territorial issues, and there would have been a treaty in the 1980s but for Syrian interference. Peace with Syria was thus the key to peace with Lebanon. By the 1990s this no longer seemed totally out of the question; Syria still represented the hard edge of Arab radicalism, but, like other nationalist regimes, it had softened its tone over the years. Syria had joined the coalition against Iraq in 1990–1, had attended the Madrid conference and had participated in bilateral talks with Israel – the first direct talks between the two states. When Labor came to power in Israel, the possibility of applying the "land for peace" formula was revived. Rabin was ready to withdraw from the Golan Heights in return for peace with Syria, with the extent of withdrawal dependent on the extent of the peace. For a full peace with full normalization of relations, he intimated, there could be a full withdrawal. The Golan would be demilitarized. Syria had finally conceded that any withdrawal could be phased, and that, while demilitarization should apply on both sides of the frontier, the areas involved need not be equal.

For a time, Syrian leaders adopted a more moderate tone, and there were signs that the government was preparing the public for peace with Israel. But a seemingly arcane difference on the definition of "total withdrawal" bedeviled the negotiations and remains unresolved today. For Israel, full withdrawal meant to the international border between the Palestinian Mandate and Syria that was established by Great Britain and France after World War I. This border incorporated all of the Sea of Galilee in Palestine, but on the northeast side of the lake it ran only ten meters from the shoreline. Since it is impossible to defend ten meters of shoreline, the Syrian army occupied this strip of land after 1948, as well as some other smaller indefensible pockets of land elsewhere (principally the Al-Hama springs where Syrian, Jordanian, and Israeli territory meet). For almost 20 years Syrians were able to swim and fish in the Sea of Galilee, a memory that remained cherished in the mind of Syrian ruler Hafez al-Assad. Syria therefore demanded a return to "the lines of June 4, 1967," which for Israel would represent an *ex post facto* legitimization of Syrian encroachment.

Since Syria refused to conduct direct negotiations with Israel, the United States served as conduit between the two sides. In July, 1994, Prime Minister Rabin authorized US Secretary of State Warren Christopher to convey to Syrian President Hafez al-Assad that Israel would withdraw to the positions of June 4, 1967, provided that its needs were met; as Christopher stressed to Asad, this concession was valid only in the context of a complete agreement, and in the meantime it remained "in our pocket, not yours" (Ross 2004: 145–8; Rabinovich 1998: 147). From that point, however, the Syrian government regarded this Rabin "deposit" as the point of departure for any further negotiations, even after Rabin was removed from the scene by an assassin's bullets a little over a year later.

On the Israeli–Palestinian front, support for the peace process fluctuated in response to events, including both the ups and downs of the process itself and violent incidents perpetrated by the extremists. Support rose to a high point after Oslo II was concluded, and by this time some of the concrete benefits of the process were also becoming more visible. From Israel's perspective, normalization of Arab relations was progressing, the Arab boycott was withering, and economic ties with some Arab states were developing. Lower-level relations were established with Morocco, Tunisia, Mauritania, and Oman; by late 1995 Israel had diplomatic relations with nearly all non-Arab Muslim states, and with 155 nations altogether (as compared with only 68 a decade earlier). The changed political climate also helped the economy, with big jumps in tourism and foreign investment following upgraded credit ratings in international markets.

The Arabs of Israel – who increasingly identified themselves as "Palestinians" – had particular cause to celebrate the breakthrough between Israel and the PLO, since they fully expected that an easing of Israeli–Palestinian conflict would lead to an easing of their own situation. But these hopes were largely dashed, as neither Israel nor the PLO put their claims on the agenda: Israel because it considered the question to be an internal matter, and the PLO because it did not want to muddy the water. Consequently the Arab minority in Israel, while still seeing itself as an integral part of the Palestinian people, began pressing its case separately. There was also a shift in focus from the achievement of equal rights to demands for changes in the structure of the state. The source of the inequality, it was now argued, lay in Israel being an ethnic Jewish state, and the solution was recognition of two peoples, Jewish and Arab, sharing power in "a state of all its citizens." An expression of the new collective identity of Israel's Palestinians, and of its ties to other Palestinians, was commemoration of the *Nakba* (disaster) on Israeli Independence Day, beginning in 1997 (Peleg and Waxman 2011).

But there were obvious benefits to Palestinians outside Israel from the peace process to this point. Nearly all of the residents of the West Bank and Gaza outside Jerusalem were now under Palestinian rule in their daily lives, though many remained subject to an Israeli security presence. What remained of the occupation was far less visible, though the fragmentation of the Oslo II map did create problems in travel that had not existed before. By 1999 donor nations had made commitments of over $4.1 billion in aid and had delivered almost $2.5 billion of this (United Nations Office of the Special Coordinator in the Occupied Territories 1999). According to Palestinian statistics, the Palestinian Gross Domestic Product grew from $3.3 billion in 1994 to $4.9 in 1999, an increase of 48 percent (Palestinian Central Bureau of Statistics 2004). However, for Palestinians the real change would come only at the end of the transition period, when they expected to become fully independent in a viable sovereign Palestinian state. Since they had made their major concession at the very outset of this transition period, by conceding the existence of Israel in most of historic Palestine, this made the period of waiting more difficult to endure. It was a recipe for frustration.

What Went Wrong?

Oslo II represented the high point of the peace process. Following conclusion of the agreement, 58 percent of Israelis stated that they supported the peace process, and another 15 percent said they were "in the middle" on the issue (Tami Steinmetz Center for Peace Research 1995). Among Palestinians, 72 percent supported the Oslo II agreement (Palestine Center for Policy and Survey Research 1995). But this positive atmosphere did not endure for long. Hard-line opponents of the agreement were galvanized into action on both sides. Most critically, an Israeli religious extremist killed Yitzhak Rabin on November 4, 1995, throwing the entire process into a period of turmoil from which, in many ways, it never recovered.

The immediate reaction to Rabin's murder was a wave of support for the peace process, but this declined in the following months as Palestinian extremists launched a series of attacks on Israeli civilian targets inside Israel. Shimon Peres, Rabin's successor as head of the Labor Party and as Prime Minister, lacked his predecessor's credentials and credibility on security issues. Perhaps more critically, a wave of four attacks in nine days, during the 1996 election campaign, helped to tip the balance against Peres, who thus for the fifth time failed to lead his party to victory. The new leader of *Likud*, Benjamin Netanyahu, defeated Peres in a direct contest for the Prime Ministership by one percent of the vote. In order to achieve this, however, Netanyahu had promised to continue the peace process, honoring commitments made by the Labor government but pledging to drive a harder bargain in the future. In doing this he gained enough votes from the center to win, but put himself in a problematic position, since most of his followers, and most of the cabinet that he put together, had opposed the Oslo process.

To continue the peace process, Netanyahu would have to overcome his own past positions: opposition to recognition of the PLO, refusal to deal with Yasir Arafat, rejection of anything beyond autonomy for the Palestinians in "Judea and

Samaria," and insistence on the right of Jews to live anywhere in the historic Land of Israel. In light of this glaring contradiction at the very heart of his government, it is remarkable that it endured for three years and even pushed the peace process forward in some respects.

In September 1996 the first widespread Palestinian unrest since Oslo erupted when the new Israeli government opened a Herodian tunnel in the Old City of Jerusalem to public access. Because it bordered the Temple Mount/Noble Sanctuary, the third holiest site of Islam, and because it ran under a Muslim section of the city, the excavation of this tunnel had been a sensitive issue to Muslims. A wave of violence swept the territories, serving as a reminder that renewed unrest, whether legal by the terms of Israel–PLO agreements or not, was the most likely result of stagnation or frustration on the Palestinian side. It was the main card left in the weak hand that the Palestinians held; it was not clear that Arafat could entirely prevent such disruptions even if he tried, and he was unlikely to try if Israel did not concede something that he could claim as a gain.

In January 1997 Israel and the PLO concluded an agreement on Israeli redeployment from most of Hebron, a loose end from Oslo II whose resolution had been delayed by the events of early 1996. In September 1998 Netanyahu's government concluded another agreement, the Wye River Memorandum, which provided for Israeli withdrawal from a further 13 percent of the West Bank. With these further redeployments, 41% of the West Bank came under Palestinian civil control (17% in Area A and 24% in Area B), with 59% (Area C) remaining under Israeli control. The areas under the jurisdiction of the Palestinian Authority now included an estimated 96% of the Palestinian population in the West Bank. At this point discussion of further Israeli withdrawals was overtaken by events: a new Israeli government, efforts to jump immediately to final status issues, and the outbreak of the second intifada. Consequently the legal framework for Israeli and Palestinian positions in the West Bank remains as defined in the Wye agreement (map 6.2).

The Wye accord also included provision for the third (and hopefully final) amendment of the Palestine Charter to remove

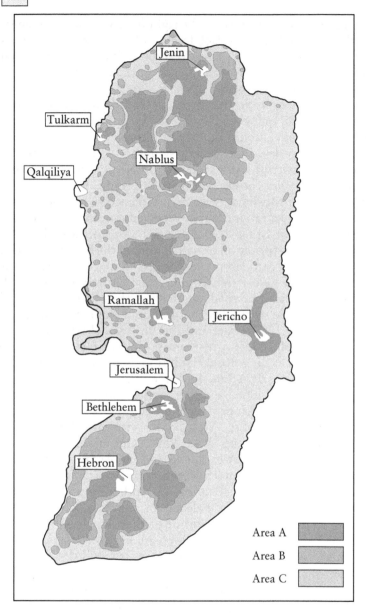

Area A

Area B

Area C

Map 6.2 Redeployment following 1998 Wye River Memorandum.

offending clauses delegitimizing Israel, which duly took place at a PNC meeting in the presence of President Bill Clinton. These two steps were important as indications that the *Likud* had come to terms with the peace process as a reality and would work within the existing framework. On the other hand, it was not clear how far Netanyahu would or could travel along this path, since he faced considerable opposition within his own party and cabinet. Observers noted that the interim solution after Oslo II was in fact very similar to what many in *Likud* had long advocated as a final settlement to the conflict, and they therefore suspected that Netanyahu's strategy was simply to stall the process at this point.

But even the Wye agreement was too much for some of Netanyahu's coalition, leading to defections that brought down his government and forced early elections in 1999. In the second Israeli election featuring a separate vote for Prime Minister, new Labor leader Ehud Barak soundly defeated Netanyahu and launched an ambitious effort to get the peace process back on track. Like the three Israeli Prime Ministers before him (as well as most after him), Barak first tried to make a deal with Syria. The logic of giving priority to Syria was compelling: Syria represented a more serious threat, a settlement seemed less complex (the proposed land-for-peace formula had worked with Egypt and Jordan), and a Syrian settlement would provide additional leverage for a final assault on thornier Palestinian issues. Furthermore, in late 1999 Syrian President Asad seemed interested in peace with Israel, possibly seeking to reclaim the Golan Heights while his health held (he died in June, 2000). Direct talks, under US sponsorship, finally took place in Shepherdstown, West Virginia, in January 2000.

At Shepherdstown Barak was pressed by Syrian Foreign Minister Farouk ash-Shara to confirm the "Rabin deposit" committing Israel to withdrawal in the Golan to the actual lines of deployment on June 4, 1967, rather than the 1923 international border between Syria and Palestine. Confronted with growing Israeli domestic opposition to any deal with Syria, Barak was unwilling to give such a pledge without substantial Syrian concessions that would help him win support at home. Consequently the negotiations failed, and at a subsequent March meeting in Geneva between Asad and US President Bill Clinton, the Syrian President reverted to a hardline position and made it clear that peace with Israel was no longer urgent (Ross 2004: 509–90).

On the Palestinian front, Barak aimed to reach agreement on the complex final status issues within months even though negotiation of interim measures had taken years. After having tried without success to revive the Syrian track, and having finally withdrawn Israeli forces from the last stretch of Lebanese territory that they held, in early 2000 Barak sought to leap over the remaining loose ends of Oslo II (which concerned promised further "redeployments" of Israeli forces in the West Bank) and go straight for the main prize: a peace treaty ending the conflict. Since there had never before been any serious negotiations between authorized Israeli and Palestinian representatives on these issues, this was indeed a daunting endeavor. But given Barak's strong insistence, President Clinton and (much more reluctantly) Yasir Arafat agreed to a summit meeting at Camp David, in July 2000, dedicated to overcoming all remaining differences.

Explanations for the failure of Camp David, and by extension the collapse of the Oslo process, have become a minor cottage industry. Accounts sensitive to the Palestinian perspective emphasize the feeling among Palestinians that Camp David would not produce a viable Palestinian state – that Israel was not offering a real "two-state" solution. They call attention to Israeli Prime Minister Ehud Barak's "poor management" of the peace process: his peremptory style, his elimination of the remaining interim steps, his presentation of the Israeli position as final and immovable, and – above all – the continued expansion of Israeli settlements in the West Bank and Gaza. To Palestinians, the growth of settlements demonstrated clearly that Israel (even under Labor) had no intention of withdrawing from the occupied territories (Malley and Agha 2001; Sontag 2001; Pundak 2001).

But it was not just the Camp David summit that "went wrong." Underlying this negative assessment of the summit meeting itself is a litany of Palestinian grievances and disappointments that had been accumulating through the period since Oslo I. The litany begins with the perception that since the PLO had made its major concession already in 1993, it had nothing left to give, and that what remained was for Israel to implement its part of the bargain by getting out of the West Bank and Gaza. But as time passed, Palestinians became increasingly doubtful about Israel's intentions. If Israel was ready to withdraw, why did it allow the settlements to continue growing – under both Labor and *Likud* governments? Although no new settlements were established, the growth of existing settlements had nearly doubled the number of settlers since Oslo I. In Palestinian eyes, this was clear evidence that Israel was expanding its presence in order to make it impossible to establish a viable Palestinian state with contiguous territory.

In addition, while Israeli troops were no longer in Palestinian cities, they still controlled 60 percent of the land area in the West Bank and, with the fragmentation of territory in Oslo II, had established checkpoints and other controls that limited Palestinian freedom of movement. In some ways travel was more difficult than before 1993, when the West Bank was treated as an undivided territory. Finally, Israeli promises of safe passage between the West Bank and Gaza, the opening of a Palestinian airport and seaport, and the release of prisoners had not been fulfilled. All in all, after several years of "peace process" the average Palestinian saw few if any benefits.

Accounts more favorable to Israel emphasize the extent of Barak's substantive concessions at Camp David, especially on territorial issues including Jerusalem. They cast doubt on Arafat's commitment to a two-state solution, concluding that because of his identification with the refugee population he was congenitally incapable of accepting a permanent settlement without a sweeping "right of return" that would transform the demography of Israel (Morris 2002; Ben-Ami 2001; Ross 2002). Thus both leaderships accepted partition in principle, but both challenged the sincerity of the other's acceptance.

For Israelis as well as Palestinians the question of "what went wrong" extended to dissatisfaction with the peace process as it had developed in the 1990s. The gains from Oslo were overshadowed for most Israelis by the continuation of violence. Deputy Foreign Minister Yossi Beilin, a key figure in the peace process, later remarked:

> Our most serious mistake was our belief that peace would speak for itself. We assumed that people would automatically associate the peace process with the lifting of the Arab embargo, the boom in investment for Israel, the dramatic fall in unemployment levels, rising living standards, receding prospects of war, and influx of tourists and Israel's emergence from isolation and obloquy into the light of international respect and recognition. Our optimism was misplaced. Instead of associating the peace process with all these indicators of progress, people made the connection between the peace process and the terrorist threat. (Beilin 1999: 270)

The major Israeli demand, an end to Palestinian attacks on Israelis, had been a key provision of every single one of the agreements concluded between the two sides, but attacks had continued with little apparent PLO effort to prevent them. More Israelis were being killed than before the Oslo process began. Most Israelis felt that the PA was at least giving a "green light" to extremist groups to carry out such attacks, in order to increase pressure on Israel. Furthermore, the PA was systematically ignoring the arms limitations of the agreements, and was inciting the Palestinian public rather than preparing it for coexistence with Israel. Arafat, in Israeli eyes, was not truly committed to a two-state solution, but remained intent on the "phased" program for destroying Israel. Why should Israel aid him in this enterprise by providing him with a base of operations?

Because of these vastly different conceptions of the peace process on the two sides, Israel and the Palestinian Authority were still some distance apart at Camp David, despite the agreed framework. Mahmoud Abbas wrote a year later that the Palestinians were unable to make any additional concessions since they had already made the key concession in accepting Resolution 242 in 1988 (Abbas 2001). Gilead Sher, a member of the Israeli team, writes that "even if Camp

David had ended with an agreement, it is highly doubtful that Barak had the political stamina to carry through his ambitious move" (Sher 2001: 239). In fact, neither Israel nor the PA had worked systematically to mobilize public support for the deal that would likely have emerged from Camp David; both would have had great difficulty selling such an agreement to their own publics. According to polls carried out on both sides in late July 2000 – immediately after Camp David – by Jacob Shamir and Khalil Shikaki, 57 percent of Israelis thought that Barak's position was "too much of a compromise," while 68 percent of Palestinians thought Arafat's rejection was "just right," and a solid majority of Palestinians thought Arafat had conceded too much on Jerusalem, Jewish settlements, and security arrangements (Shamir and Shikaki 2002: 190).

In January 2001 representatives of the two sides met again in Taba, the Egyptian resort town on the Gulf of Aqaba, to make one last stab at a final settlement. The Taba talks represented the closest approach to agreement up to that moment; by all accounts, both sides felt the time pressure and made serious efforts to close the remaining gap. A record of the Taba talks was kept by the only outside observer, European Union representative Miguel Moratinos of Spain. Moratinos revised his account in response to comments from both sides until he had a final version confirmed by both. A year after Taba, this document found its way to the pages of the Israeli newspaper *Ha'aretz* (Eldar 2002).

The Taba negotiations were based on proposals (the "Clinton parameters") made by US President Bill Clinton during his last days in office. The establishment of a Palestinian state was taken for granted; the June 4, 1967 lines (i.e. the 1949 armistice lines) would be the "basis" for the border between Israel and Palestine, with agreed land swaps. Israel proposed to annex six percent of the West Bank, incorporating Jewish settlements that reportedly account for 80 percent of the settlers, and to give Palestine the equivalent of three percent of the West Bank in territory elsewhere. Palestinian negotiators proposed a straightforward land swap of three percent of the West Bank for an equivalent piece of land elsewhere that was also contiguous with the rest of Palestine. All of the Gaza Strip would become part of Palestine, with Jewish settlements there evacuated.

In Jerusalem, Arab neighborhoods would be part of Palestine, and Jewish neighborhoods would be part of Israel. This would extend to the Old City, with the Jewish Quarter and the adjacent Western (Wailing) Wall under Israeli jurisdiction, and the Muslim and Christian Quarters under Palestinian rule. There was no agreement on the Temple Mount/Haram al-Sharif, the third holiest site in Islam but also the location of the Jewish First and Second Temples of antiquity. However, since occupying the area in 1967, Israel has not challenged the continuing administration of the site as a Muslim *waqf* (religious trust), and it seemed unlikely that any future arrangement would change this.

On security issues, there was general consensus that Palestine would be subject to arms limitations, but no specifics were agreed upon. The Palestinian team requested an international force to supervise implementation of a peace agreement, and Israel agreed to consider this idea. Less progress was made on the refugee issue, with Palestinians stressing the right of refugees to choose freely between return to their original homes or compensation, and Israel stressing the impossibility of its absorbing more than a small fraction of the four million refugees without threatening the demographic balance and Jewish character of the state. Israel proposed a framework of five choices for refugees, with the return to Israel proper being limited to a relatively small number.

All in all, the Taba negotiations closed the gap between the two sides considerably in some areas, while still leaving many unresolved issues. They indicated the contours of any future negotiations that might take place and were thus useful as a guide. But the negotiations took place under great time pressure, as Israeli elections had been scheduled for early February, and they were also overshadowed by a new convulsion that threatened to reduce all diplomacy to irrelevance.

The Roof Falls In

The Camp David failure evoked bitterness and recrimi-
nations. Some informed observers predicted a return to
violence, but the outbreak of the second Palestinian *intifada* at the end of September 2000 still came as a shock
to most of the Israeli public. Such widespread violent confrontations between Palestinians and Israeli forces seemed
like ghosts from the past, wildly incongruent when 98
percent of the Palestinians in the West Bank and Gaza Strip
(outside East Jerusalem) no longer lived under direct Israeli
occupation.

The PA's posture was to channel any explosion in "useful"
directions – in essence, to ride the wave. Arafat, in the words
of Israeli analyst Ehud Ya'ari, engaged in a "willing suspen-
sion of control" (Ya'ari 2002: 25).

What the *intifada* revealed, however, was not just a chasm
between Israelis and Palestinians on final status issues, but
also diametrically opposed conceptions of the peace process
itself. Surveys indicated that a strong majority of both Israelis
and Palestinians continued to support a negotiated peace
in the abstract, even after months or years of clashes, but
closer examination showed that they associated quite different meanings to the term. For Israelis, the peace process was
a *negotiating model*. In this negotiation, each side trades off
assets that it considers less valuable for more valued concessions from the other side, arriving at a balanced agreement that is better for both. Since the concessions made
are mutually dependent, keeping the bargain is essential; the
agreement becomes a new point of reference that must be
respected. A corollary of the negotiating model is that negotiation and violent confrontations are mutually exclusive, if
not contradictory. Violence, it is felt, undermines the atmosphere of trust necessary for successful bargaining. Adherence
of the Israeli public to this model is seen in survey data from
December 2000, in which 74 percent of respondents favored
negotiations with the Palestinians, 13 percent favored confrontations, and only five percent thought it was possible to

pursue both options simultaneously (Jerusalem Media and Communications Center 2000b).

The Palestinian conception of the peace process was quite different. Palestinian analysts, in various formulations, resisted the idea that negotiations should reflect the "military imbalance of power" between the two sides. Instead, "the Palestinian people view the peace process as a strategic road that is supposed to regain the Palestinian people's national and sovereign rights and secure the return of their territories" (Al-Quds 2000).

This *implementation model* rejects equal concessions on both sides: "Such a policy ignores the fact that the Palestinians are the victims of Israeli aggression and that the land the Israelis are offering to 'give up' is Palestinian land occupied by military force" (Hanieh 2001: 80). The Palestinians therefore tend not to make counteroffers in response to Israeli proposals. At Camp David, Clinton's National Security Advisor Sandy Berger reportedly lashed out at the Palestinians: "We gave you a territorial proposal and you may reject it if you wish, but you have to reply with a methodical counter-proposal" (Ben-Ami 2001). But the Palestinian view is that they do not have to make a counteroffer, as they have nothing left to give: "Rights, by definition, are neither negotiable nor exchangeable" (Palestinian Authority 2000).

Neither the Palestinian leadership nor the Palestinian public accepts the oft-repeated Israeli premise that they must choose between peace and terror. Both negotiations and *intifadas* are seen as legitimate methods for achieving basic rights, and they can be used simultaneously with no contradiction. In Nabil Sha'th's words, "historically many people fought and negotiated at the same time" (Sha'th 2000). Another formulation is "putting the force option on an equal footing with the peace option and placing force into the service of peace" (*Al-Quds* 2001). When asked in a poll whether they favored an intifada with "popular" (i.e. non-military) or military characteristics, 62 percent of Palestinian respondents said they favored both (Jerusalem Media and Communication Center 2001a).

Behind this thinking is a scenario in which Israeli opposition is broken down step by step by a combination of the various pressures, and past history is cited as evidence. In an important speech delivered in March 2001 in Beirut, PA Minister Faysal al-Husayni argued that in the first *intifada* Palestinians had succeeded in breaking important Israeli "taboos" – that there was no Palestinian people, that there would be no Palestinian state – and that in the second *intifada* they had succeeded in breaking taboos regarding Jerusalem and the refugees (*As-Safir* 2001). So long as it does not escalate into war, it is felt, attrition can gradually force Israel to pull back (Schiff 2001; Barel 2001). Meanwhile, the shock of the *intifada* led many Israelis to conclude that Palestinians were aiming for more than an end to the occupation. These perspectives were often reinforced or confirmed by the emphasis on the return of refugees to Israeli territory.

Among establishment figures there was little open reference to "pre-1967" issues. One exception was Faysal al-Husayni, who stated in his 2001 Beirut speech: "We may lose or win [tactically] but our eyes will continue to aspire to the strategic goal, namely, to Palestine from the river to the sea" (As-Safir 2001). Also, PA Minister Yasser Abd Rabbo hinted at an existing ambiguity regarding what might happen after the establishment of a Palestinian state within the 1967 borders: "There is almost a consensus among Palestinians that the direct goal is to reach the establishment of an independent Palestinian state within the June 4, 1967 borders, with Jerusalem as its capital ... [but] regarding the future after that, it is best to leave the issue aside and not to discuss it" (Al-Jazeera 2001).

On the other hand, others deny having any intention and/or aim of destroying Israel. Reflecting the chasms and the ambiguity within the Palestinian community, the poll data show a multifaceted split. In May 2002, 66 percent of Palestinians supported a Saudi proposal based on a two-state solution, but 69 percent also said that they did not think a lasting peace was possible (Jerusalem Media and Communication Center 2002a).

The first pass at peace, in short, produced some changes in the Israeli–Palestinian conflict: mutual recognition, majority consensus on a two-state solution, the sense that a Palestinian state is inevitable, the further disengagement of Arab states. It ended, however, in a quagmire from which neither side seemed able to extricate itself.

The Fourth Stage of the Israeli–Palestinian Conflict

The conflict with Israel is not a matter of land. It's a matter of ideology.

Hamas Leader Sheikh Nayef Rajoub (Remnick 2006: 64)

The End of the Arafat Era

Support for *Hamas* and other Islamic factions grew among Palestinians from 12 percent in June 2000 to 23 percent in December 2000 and to 28.9 percent in October 2003 (Jerusalem Media and Communications Center 2000a, 2000b, 2003). In Israel, Prime Minister Ehud Barak was forced into an early Prime Ministerial election in February 2001, losing to *Likud* leader Ariel Sharon by a 25 percent margin. Sharon, long considered too controversial to reach the Prime Minister's office, was thus swept into office by a wave of anger growing out of renewed *intifada* and violence. Furthermore, when elections for the Knesset were held two years later, in January 2003, the *Likud* doubled its representation, while Labor, and the left generally, were reduced to the lowest level ever.

Sharon's government rejected any negotiation with the Palestinians on final settlement issues until attacks on Israeli civilians ended; this effectively crippled diplomatic activity. The United States and other outside parties made periodic efforts to achieve a cease-fire and get the parties back to the table, but without real success. By early 2002 the violence reached new heights, with 127 Israelis killed by suicide bombers in the month of March alone. In response, the Israeli army reoccupied much of the West Bank, culminating in a prolonged and controversial battle in Jenin in April 2002. Efforts to end the violence broke down under the steady drumbeat of terrorist attacks by Palestinian extremists and contentious "targeted killings" by Israel of militant Palestinian leaders identified as organizers of suicide bombings and other attacks on Israeli civilians.

The peak period of violence in the second *intifada* coincided with the post-9/11 trauma in the United States, contributing to a tendency to bundle all Middle East conflicts into a generalized "war on terror." On September 11, 2001, Islamic extremists of *al-Qa'ida* (The Base), by attacking the World Trade Center and the Pentagon, had shocked all Americans and impelled the Bush administration into a global focus on religiously inspired terrorism. Given this focus, US policymakers were more tolerant of Sharon's harsh measures directed at *Hamas* and *Hizballah*, both understood to be proxies for Iran, which in turn was now a major target in the war on terror. US policy now had, for the first time since the Cold War ended, a clear central theme and a clear list of enemies, most of them in or near the Middle East. As regional hegemon it was faced with a new intricate mission, but also infused with new forcefulness and zeal.

On the other hand, like previous presidents George W. Bush had a clear interest in defusing the Israeli–Palestinian confrontation. Soon after 9/11, he called openly for a Palestinian state. In his address to the United Nations General Assembly on November 10, 2001, he announced that the US government was "working toward a day when two states, Israel and Palestine, live peacefully together within secure and recognized borders as called for by the Security Council resolutions" (United States White House 2001). Support for Palestinian statehood was further affirmed by US support for United Nations Security Council Resolution 1397, of March 12, 2002, which proclaimed "a vision of a region where two

States, Israel and Palestine, live side by side within secure and recognized borders" (United Nations 2002).

But one casualty of the *intifada* was the belief that Yasir Arafat was a credible partner in the peace effort. The Israeli government, under Sharon, refused to deal with the veteran Palestinian leader and openly called for his replacement. President Bush, again breaking with previous US policy, followed suit on June 24, 2002, declaring "I call on the Palestinian people to elect new leaders, leaders not compromised by terror . . ." (United States Department of State 2002). The disillusionment stemmed from Arafat's failure to stop the violent attacks by extremists; whether Arafat was unwilling to move against violent groups, or simply unable to do so, no longer seemed particularly relevant. Palestinians were also very critical of Arafat's leadership and the widespread corruption and lack of democracy within the PA-ruled areas. In a June 2003 poll, 84 percent of Palestinian respondents said that there was corruption in PA institutions (Palestine Center for Policy and Survey Research 2003).

This effort led to a "performance-based roadmap," proposed by the United States, in the name of the "Quartet" of outside parties (United States, European Union, United Nations, and Russia) on April 30, 2003 (United States Department of State 2003). The roadmap envisioned three phases:

1 An end to all violence, Israeli withdrawal from areas occupied during the *intifada,* and a freeze on all settlement activity.
2 Creation of a provisional Palestinian state by the end of 2003.
3 Negotiation by the end of 2005 of a final agreement based on the two-state model that would resolve all outstanding issues and end the conflict.

Consistent with most recent peace proposals, considerable emphasis was placed on building and reforming Palestinian institutions – "nation-building" – in order to ensure a viable and stable Palestinian state capable of suppressing extreme elements.

By tying renewed Arab–Israel diplomacy to "regime change" among the Palestinians, the Bush administration was essentially putting it on the back burner. Israel and the United States were claiming, in essence, that the situation had reverted to the pre-1993 quandary that had stymied diplomatic progress for decades: the lack of a credible Palestinian negotiating partner. US policy evolved further in April 2004 when President Bush declared that there might be changes in the pre-1967 lines: "In light of new realities on the ground, including already existing major Israeli population centers, it is unrealistic to expect that the outcome of final status negotiations will be a full and complete return to the armistice lines of 1949. . . ." (United States White House, 2004).

Palestinians responded by arguing that Israel had shown no inclination to make the concessions necessary for a negotiated two-state solution. Ariel Sharon's career as "godfather of the settlements" established his reputation as a territorial maximalist. Even when Sharon proposed – and in August 2005, carried out – the evacuation of Jewish settlements in the Gaza Strip and four isolated settlements on the West Bank, this did not appear to Palestinians as convincing evidence that Israel would withdraw from the entire West Bank and make a two-state solution possible.

In this context, the death of Yasir Arafat on November 11, 2004, raised the possibility of a change of direction for the Palestinian Authority. Arafat was immediately succeeded as head of the PLO and, following elections, as President of the PA, by Mahmoud Abbas, his long-time associate. Though Abbas was of the same generation and background as Arafat, he had developed a reputation as a political moderate and a critic of the *intifada*: in September 2004 he had said that "I think now that the *intifada* in its entirety was a mistake and it should not have continued . . ." (Abbas 2004). During the same period there was also a distinct shift in Palestinian opinion: in a March 2005 poll, 29 percent approved of a suicide bombing in Tel Aviv carried out in late February, compared to 77 percent approval of a similar bombing in Be'er Sheva in August 2004 (Palestine Center for Policy and Survey Research 2005a). Against this background, Abbas met with

Ariel Sharon in early February 2005 at Sharm Esh-Sheikh, and – with the help of Egyptian President Hosni Mubarak and King Abdallah of Jordan – a cease-fire between the two sides was declared. *Hamas* and *Islamic Jihad* announced that, while they would not sign on to the ceasefire, they would not abrogate it, and in March all Palestinian factions pledged to extend a truce (or "period of calm" in Arabic) until the end of the year.

The critical question was whether Abbas could command the authority and legitimacy to take the PA in a significantly different direction. As noted, support for Islamic militant groups had grown, as *Fatah*'s had dropped, since the onset of the second *intifada*. Abbas was elected as PA President on January 9, 2005, by a 62 percent majority (*Hamas* and *Islamic Jihad* did not participate in the election). But the question was whether Abbas could maintain his dominance in the PA; legislative elections were scheduled for July 2005 (they were eventually held in January 2006), and for the first time *Hamas* was planning to contest seats in the Palestine National Council. More fundamentally, Palestinian society lacked the mechanisms for a relatively smooth and rapid response to new realities. Even at the peak of its effectiveness, the Palestinian Authority was hardly responsive to grass-roots constituencies, and after years of pounding by Israeli forces its governing authority was further shattered.

Israel Turns to Unilateralism

By this time, however, statements by Israeli leaders indicated an important shift in the official line. Ariel Sharon stated publicly that a Palestinian state was inevitable, and that some Jewish settlements would have to be evacuated. Israeli Deputy Prime Minister Ehud Olmert, long a *Likud* party stalwart, in December 2003 advocated an Israeli unilateral withdrawal that would preserve an 80 percent Jewish majority in Israel; in practice, this would necessitate withdrawal from nearly all of the West Bank and Gaza (Barnea 2003). Olmert's position, based primarily on demographic considerations, was almost indistinguishable from arguments long made by dovish advocates of Israeli withdrawal.

For many in Israel, like Olmert, the shift toward acceptance of the two-state model reflected growing awareness of the demographic realities that Israel faced. A Tami Steinmetz Center poll of December 2003 found that 73 percent of Israeli Jews agreed that a *de facto* binational state would emerge if a solution were not found in the near future (Tami Steinmetz Center 2003). A binational state would clearly not be the Jewish state that Zionism had always heralded as its main mission.

Zionists had long relied on "the ingathering of the exiles" to establish a Jewish presence in *Eretz Yisrael* and to preserve it against the much larger Arab population in the region and the higher Arab birthrate. New waves of immigration had, time and again, rescued the Jewish *yishuv* and the state of Israel from the threat of demographic submersion. It took time to adjust to a new reality in which such miracles could no longer be taken for granted. But circumstances had changed. In earlier periods Jewish emigration to Palestine had come in large waves from "distressed" Jewish communities under pressure to flee: from anti-Semitic regimes in Eastern Europe, from the Nazi Holocaust, from the Arab world after 1948. But with the massive influx from the former Soviet Union in the 1990s, these reservoirs were nearly exhausted; future immigration would have to come primarily from Western democratic nations that now accounted for 80 percent of the Jews outside Israel and which had never produced significant flows of immigrants (Della Pergola 1998). As a result, in the new demographic war the higher Arab birthrate was no longer offset by Jewish immigration. It was a war that Israel could not win.

When Israel occupied the West Bank and Gaza in 1967, Jews constituted about a 64 percent majority in Palestine as a whole (Israel, the West Bank, and Gaza). By 2011, according to official estimates there were 5,837,000 Jews and 5,489,000 Arabs in the same area, reducing the Jewish majority to 51.5 percent (Israel Central Bureau of Statistics 2011; Palestinian Central Bureau of Statistics 2011; PCBS figures are reduced by 268,000 to avoid double-counting the

Arab population of East Jerusalem). There are claims that the Palestinian population on the West Bank and Gaza is actually one to one and one-half million fewer than claimed in official figures; if so, there would still be a Jewish majority above 60 percent (Zimmerman et al. 2006). But mainstream Israeli demographers dispute this view, arguing that even if Palestinian figures are too high, the long-term trend is clear and that within little more than a decade there would be more Arabs than Jews in all of Palestine (DellaPergola 2007, 2010). Even with Gaza out of the picture, following the 2005 Israeli withdrawal, the Jewish majority of about two-thirds in Israel and the West Bank together would eventually be offset by faster Palestinian population growth.

In any event the attempt to change the demography of the occupied territories was an abject failure; the total settler population was offset by two years' natural increase of the Palestinian population. In fact, it was nearly offset by the estimated number of Palestinians from the West Bank and Gaza illegally living and working within Israel.

There was also concern about the declining percentage of Jews within Israel proper. If non-Jewish immigrants from the former Soviet Union and foreign workers were added to the 20.5 percent of Israel's population who were Arab or Druze, Jews constituted only 73.3 percent of the Israeli public by 2011 (Israel Central Bureau of Statistics 2011).

A general survey of majority–minority relations in democratic states suggests that states with a minority above about 20 percent generally maintain a stable democracy only by devising power-sharing arrangements with the minority, moving away from strict majoritarian democracy and diluting the ethnic character of the state (Dowty 1998, 2001a: 210–15). The Arab minority in Israel was over 20 percent; the implications were clear. If birthrates could not be changed and no major sources of Jewish immigration remained, and assuming expulsion was unthinkable, then in order to remain both Jewish and democratic, the future borders of Israel would have to remain close to the 1949–67 armistice lines (the "Green Line"), and no significant number of 1948–9 refugees could return to Israel itself. Some also advocated the transfer of contiguous Israeli Arab areas (e.g. Umm El-Fahm, the "Little Triangle"), as well as the Arab areas of East Jerusalem with their 200,000 residents, to a new Palestinian state in the West Bank and Gaza.

Advocates of "The Whole Land of Israel" never offered a convincing answer to this demographic dilemma. Over time, a majority of Israelis came to the conclusion that the costs of occupation outweighed the risks of an independent Palestinian state. A clear majority came to endorse partition in the form of a two-state solution, and an even greater majority (including Ariel Sharon) conceded that a Palestinian state was inevitable.

For many Israelis, there were strong arguments for ending the occupation regime in the West Bank and Gaza without waiting for a formal agreement. Unilaterally ending the occupation, it was argued, would be beneficial to Israel militarily, politically, and diplomatically. Ending occupation, with the evacuation of most of the settlements, would confirm more eloquently than any other action that Israel was committed to the two-state solution. It would give a dramatic boost to moderates on the Palestinian side who sought to end the conflict on the same basis. It would transform Israel's position in the world, where most nations accept the country in its pre-1967 lines but have been increasingly critical of the continued occupation. There was also a strategic case for withdrawing from some or most of the settlements: by some estimates, the Oslo II map, leaving all the settlements under Israeli control, increased tenfold the length of the lines that the army had to defend.

Plans for unilateral withdrawal – or "disengagement" in official language – usually included erection of an effective barrier between Israeli and Palestinian territories in order to reduce infiltration by terrorists and suicide bombers. Plans for such a barrier began to take shape in July 2001, when the Defense Cabinet, in the early days of the second *intifada*, approved the erection of a "security fence" in particular areas vulnerable to infiltration. In June 2002 this was expanded into the idea of a continuous barrier, and the precise route for different segments was approved incrementally during 2002–3.

As projected the entire barrier would be about 440 miles in length, twice the length of the "Green Line" (the 1949 armistice lines). In most places it was built as an electronic fence, with dirt tracks and trenches, along a 200-foot-wide strip; in urban areas (5–10% of the total length) it is a concrete wall 20–25 feet tall.

The idea of a wall or fence – "barrier" is the neutral term – between Israel and Palestinian areas had once been a "dovish" idea, since it implied separation and Israeli withdrawal from the other side. But as adopted by a more hawkish government it took on a different character. The barrier was described as a security measure, not a political line, but as initially projected it would have left about 15 percent of the West Bank on the Israeli side of the line in order to include large settlement blocs inside Israel. In addition, there were many instances in which the projected route would separate Palestinians from their land and pose additional obstacles to free movement, even totally surrounding some towns and villages.

The "separation wall," as Palestinians called it, immediately faced legal challenges. An advisory opinion of the International Court of Justice, in July 2004, ruled that erection of the barrier was a political as well as a security measure and therefore exceeded Israel's powers under the laws of military occupation; Israel refused to recognize the jurisdiction of the court. During the same month, the Israeli Supreme Court accepted the security rationale for the erection of the barrier, but ordered that it be rerouted in order to minimize the impact on Palestinians. Further Supreme Court rulings in 2005 and 2007 ordered additional modifications, reducing the area of the West Bank on the Israeli side to 9.5% according to a 2009 UN report (United Nations 2009; map 7.1). By 2007 about two-thirds of the planned barrier was completed or being built, but construction of remaining portions was halted almost completely because of budgetary constraints and lack of pressing need, as attacks from the West Bank had practically ceased. In addition, the remaining sections involved barriers around three main settlement blocs – Gush Etzion, Ariel, and Ma'aleh Adumim – which raised sensitive political issues.

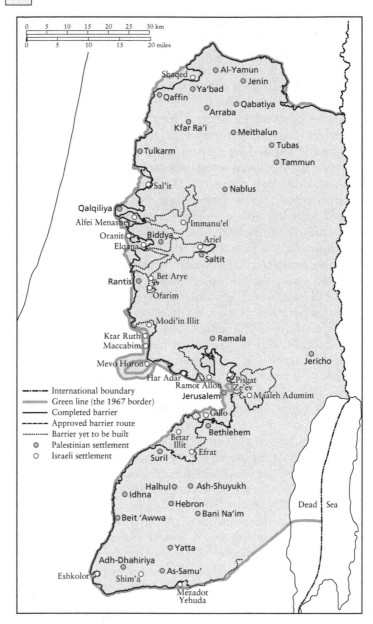

Map 7.1 West Bank Separation Barrier.

The end of the attacks seemed to most Israelis to justify the barrier and it enjoyed overwhelming support in public opinion. Supporters also claimed that it made possible the reduction of checkpoints in Palestinian areas, and that by eliminating terror, it would also help revive the peace process. Others, Israeli and Palestinian, pointed to other reasons for the drop in attacks, particularly changes in Palestinian policies and tactics.

Palestinians, on the other hand, saw the "separation wall," or "apartheid wall," as an indication of Israeli intentions regarding the annexation of West Bank territory, and as a final death-blow to any two-state solution to the conflict. The long, snaky corridors connecting Jewish settlements to Israel, they argued, fragmented Palestinian territory and would make any Palestinian state unviable. Large numbers of Palestinians would be cut off from the land they tilled, from their neighbors, and from the core of their state and society.

The use of the term "apartheid" in Palestinian rhetoric was an indication of an interesting role reversal that had taken place in the relations between the two sides. At one time it had been Israelis who had demanded unfettered contact between the two sides and Arabs who had boycotted Israel; now, with Palestinians dependent in so many ways on Israel for jobs, services, and resources, it was Israelis who stood accused of pursuing separation. While separation was not necessarily "apartheid" on the South African model – so long as the parties on the two sides of the line both governed themselves – the use of the term indicated a very real Palestinian fear of continued Israeli domination despite, or even with the help of, the new barrier being erected.

For many Palestinians, and some Israelis, the goal of an independent Palestinian state alongside Israel no longer seemed relevant or realistic. They concluded that the Israeli presence in the West Bank had already become irreversible, and that it was too late for a two-state solution. The solution would be an undivided state in which (for this school of thought) neither Jews nor Arabs dominated: a binational state. Power would be shared between the two communities through arrangements similar to those in other binational regimes such as Belgium or Canada. This would not be the Jewish state of Zionist dreams, nor would it be the Arab Palestine of Islamic or nationalist ideologues.

Support for the idea of binationalism among Palestinians rose during the second *intifada* to a level of 25–30 percent (with 45–50 percent continuing to support a two-state solution, and 10–15 percent advocating a unitary Palestinian or Islamic state) (Jerusalem Media and Communications Center 2001b, 2002b, 2003, 2004, 2006). Demographic realities explain part of the appeal: since Palestinians would become the overwhelming majority over time, a binational state would inevitably become more Arab and less Jewish. However, it is notable that the binational alternative was not adopted by any of the major Palestinian political groups, and the practical difficulties with this option were daunting (see the critique in chapter 10). Thus the support for binationalism seemed to be more an expression of frustration with the collapse of the peace process than adoption of a carefully considered alternate program (Tamari 2000).

In trying to pursue the two-state option, Abbas had to contend with increasing lawlessness in Palestinian territories and the increasing assertiveness of the militant Islamic groups. His strategy, long declared, was to try to co-opt the radical forces, bringing *Hamas* and *Islamic Jihad* into the political arena in order to curb their military activities. He would not try to disarm the Islamic militias, but create a situation in which they would not flaunt their arms. *Hamas* had agreed to a cease-fire with Israel; from the *Hamas* perspective, this was a logical part of a strategy of sharing power with *Fatah* and Abbas, while building up its support at the grass-roots level, where corruption and widespread disillusionment with the PA played into its hands. As the major alternative to the existing order, *Hamas* was drawing support far beyond its hardcore.

In Israel, unilateral disengagement, originally an idea favored by doves, became a project pushed by hawks. This new alignment was a reminder that most hawks had now come to terms with eventual withdrawal from most of the West Bank and all of Gaza. Growing awareness of the demographic dilemma, and a growing perception that there was no viable Palestinian partner, furnished the backdrop to Prime Minister Sharon's surprising advocacy, in February 2004, of a plan to evacuate Jewish settlements in the Gaza Strip. Though his proposal was defeated in a *Likud* party referendum, Sharon pushed it through his cabinet on June 6. As presented by Sharon, this disengagement was to be seen as a retrenchment, abandoning untenable positions in order to consolidate Israel's hold where it was vital:

> We cannot hold on to Gaza forever. More than a million Palestinians live there and double their number with each generation . . . . It is out of strength and not weakness that we take this step. We tried to reach agreements with the Palestinians that would move both peoples towards a path of peace. These were crushed against a wall of hatred and fanaticism. . . . We are reducing the daily friction and its victims on both sides. (Laqueur and Scheuftan 2016: 516)

Sharon's plan called for total withdrawal from the 21 Jewish settlements in the Gaza Strip, with a total of about 9,000 residents, and dismantling four isolated settlements in the northern part of the West Bank. Knesset approval followed in two stages, in October 2004 and February 2005. Though most *Likud* ministers supported the move, more hawkish cabinet members from smaller parties (National Union and National Religious Party) left the government and forced Sharon to establish, in January 2005, a National Unity Government in which power was shared with the Labor Party.

Most of the Gaza settlers refused to evacuate their homes voluntarily, and as the deadline for withdrawal approached Israeli society was wracked by large-scale marches and protests, and some public disruptions, organized by the settlers and their many supporters within Israel. Support for the disengagement, which had stood as high as 71 percent (with 24 percent opposed) in a May 2004 poll, tended to drop over time: 65 percent in October 2004 and February 2005, and finally only 50 percent (with 37 percent opposed) when the forced evacuation actually began in mid-August 2005 (*Yediot Ahronot* 2004a, 2004b, 2005; Israel Radio 2005).

Nevertheless, the evacuation began on August 15 and was completed a few days later, with the final military withdrawal from Gaza taking place on September 12. Despite dramatic and highly emotional confrontations between the settlers and the 14,000 police and army carrying out the evacuation, there was generally less violence than many had anticipated. For proponents of further unilateral disengagement, the exit from Gaza showed that such a move was thinkable.

The withdrawal did, however, have critics on all sides. Palestinians, though favoring any reduction in Israeli control of their lives, pointed out that Israel remained in control of all access to and from Gaza, including the coastline and the airspace. In addition, Israel still supplied water, electricity, sewage, and communications networks to Gaza, which, together with control of trade (dependent on border crossings), left the Gazan economy still completely tied to Israel. Palestinians still lived in a state of siege, and, in the eyes of some, Gaza was still, legally and factually, under occupation.

Palestinians also objected to the unilateralism of Sharon's move, which implicitly rejected the PA as a negotiating partner and ignored the Palestinian capacity to make the withdrawal more orderly and more successful as a precedent for the future. In fact, the way in which disengagement was carried out only confirmed, for many Palestinians, that leaving Gaza was intended as a substitute for complete withdrawal from the occupied territories, rather than as a first step. At the same time, and somewhat contradictorily, the Gaza withdrawal in August 2005 was credited to *Hamas* and other groups engaged in attacks on Israeli targets; in one poll, 84 percent of Palestinians agreed that the withdrawal was "a victory for Palestinian armed struggle" (Palestine Center for Policy and Survey Research 2005b).

Dovish critics in Israel, for their part, also saw the Gaza disengagement as a way of strengthening the Israeli presence in the West Bank settlement blocs – as indeed Sharon himself had said. Furthermore, the new departure of moving unilaterally in such matters would weaken the position of Mahmoud Abbas just as the new PA President was trying to revive negotiations, and would undercut the chances of any future agreements with moderate Palestinians.

More critically, inherent weaknesses in unilateral disengagement became more evident over time to a wide spectrum of Israeli opinion. For one thing, separation behind fences or walls did not solve the problem of missile attacks over the fence or wall, as the launching of home-made Qassam rockets from Gaza against nearby Israeli targets had demonstrated. While the Qassams did little damage, they seemed to portend a major threat in the future, particularly from West Bank areas close to Israeli population centers. In addition, the use of "liberated" areas for terrorist operations by extreme groups was a major concern; again, Gaza was less of a threat, given the geography, but the potential on the West Bank was much greater. Finally, many Israelis came to give greater weight to how a majority of Palestinians saw unilateral withdrawal: as evidence – correct or not – that armed attacks against Israeli targets were effective in forcing Israeli concessions.

In the immediate aftermath of the Gaza pullout, however, the idea of unilateral disengagement remained at the center of debate in Israel. The matter was put to a test in November 2005 when Amir Peretz, former head of Israel's Labor Federation, defeated Shimon Peres for the leadership of the Labor Party. Peretz immediately pulled his party out of the government, forcing its collapse and the calling of new elections for March 28, 2006. Ariel Sharon, unable to unite a divided *Likud*, formed a new centrist party, *Kadima* (Forward), which was based explicitly on a call for continued disengagement:

> The government shall endeavor, as stated, to conduct negotiations with the Palestinians . . . but if the Palestinians do not behave as stipulated in the near future, the government shall act even in the absence of negotiations . . . The government shall determine the borders of the state. The Israeli settlement in Judea and Samaria must be reduced. (Ha'aretz 2006)

Early polls indicated that Sharon would bring most *Likud* voters, and many centrists, into the new party, and thus radically reshape Israeli politics.

The election campaign was thrown into turmoil, however, when Sharon suffered an incapacitating stroke on January 4, 2006, and was replaced by Deputy Prime Minister Ehud Olmert. Olmert, though from an impeccably revisionist background, had shared Sharon's odyssey from hawkish orthodoxy to separation and unilateralism. As the new leader of *Kadima*, he continued to advocate what was later labeled as a policy of *hitkansut*: literally a "gathering together" or "consolidation" implying withdrawal from untenable positions in order to preserve Israel as both a Jewish and democratic state (in official parlance, the term was misleadingly translated as "convergence" or "realignment"). Though support for Kadima and for unilateral disengagement declined somewhat over the course of the campaign, the election still left it as the largest single party, able to re-establish a unity government with Labor and centrist forces, with *Likud* dropping sharply and cast out of power.

By this time, however, events in the Palestinian camp signaled the emergence of new forces that threatened to reshape the conflict in fundamental ways.

A Turning Point: Ideology Prevails

Historically the clash between Jews and Arabs revolved primarily around land, security, and other concrete interests; religious dimensions were secondary. But the events of 2006 suggested that religious frames of reference, which had undeniably grown in significance over the years, now played a central role. The Arab–Israel conflict now entered a fourth stage in its convoluted historical evolution.

The first stage, from the 1880s to 1948, was a conflict between two communities for land and political control within the historic Land of Israel/Palestine.

The second stage, from 1948 to the early 1990s, was an interstate conflict between Israel and its Arab neighbors, with Palestinians temporarily eclipsed but gradually re-emerging after the 1967 war to reclaim the front ranks of their cause.

The third stage, from the 1990s, though with roots back to the 1960s, put the Israeli–Palestinian relationship, and apparent agreement on a two-state solution, on center stage, with Arab states increasingly disengaged.

During this century and a quarter, nationalism, not religion, was the dominant force. Religious fundamentalists were active and even prominent on both sides, but they were not in charge. As nationalism waned, the chances of closing the gap, by agreement on dividing the land, seemed closer to realization. But in the new reality, religious claims threatened to reverse this closing of the gap. In addition, the intervention of new outside parties – such as Iran and Islamist movements generally – reverses the previous trend toward reduction of the conflict to its core antagonists. This, then, is the fourth stage of the conflict.

These changes in the Israeli–Palestinian conflict did not take place in a vacuum, nor were they superficial or transient. They are were rooted in global tectonic shifts, and in particular the convergence of three major phenomena of our time:

1. The decline of state authority and exclusive control, tied to the rise of non-state actors
2. Changes in the nature of warfare, from classic wars to "irregular" or "asymmetric" warfare.
3. The new tide of religious extremism, redefining the norms in national and international politics

These developments reinforce each other; none is new (they have precedents in antiquity), but they came together to create new realities – with Middle Eastern cases especially prominent.

Regarding the decline of state authority, the World Bank ranked about half of the 196 states in the world as weak or failing, and in more than 20, dissident groups controlled much of the nation's territory (Thomas et al. 2005: 60). These groups, labeled clinically as "non-state actors," are usually impervious to sanctions or outside influences, nor do they recognize international law or obligations. They enjoy the advantages of a disciplined group in an undisciplined setting, and modern technology (the internet, for example) often gives them great access to support and resources. A particularly volatile combination is a non-state actor allied to an outside government, enjoying the advantages of both situations (*Hizballah* in Lebanon, for example, with the support of Iran).

The changed nature of warfare is imparted by the fact that the last major tank battles in the Arab–Israel theatre – or perhaps anywhere – were fought in 1973. Many terms have been applied to the new warfare: irregular, subconventional, counterinsurgent, asymmetric, guerrilla, hybrid. For military analyst Rupert Smith, modern warfare became "war amongst the people" (Smith 2005). There is no battlefield, nor any attempt to conquer and hold territory; fighting drags out over time; the outcomes are fuzzy; and the targets on the insurgent side are very elusive. Decentralized armed cells follow flexible tactics in anarchic conditions. Fighting from weakness is a guiding precept and a point of pride.

Religious extremism needs to be defined; few people describe themselves as "extreme." For this discussion, it is taken to mean all those who claim that their purposes, being sanctified, justify the use of any and all means, including violence and the taking of lives (innocent lives, by conventional standards). The general resurgence of religion throughout the world, not least of all in the Middle East, has produced on its fringes movements that sanctify war and, treat territory as holy ground. On the Israeli side, some religious figures in the settlement movement have ruled that Jews are commanded to conquer and settle the entire Land of Israel, uprooting the present inhabitants. The religious extremist who assassinated Yitzhak Rabin in 1995 acted, in his own mind, on the basis of a religious ruling justifying the killing of a Jew who endangers his own people. Radical Islamic movements among Palestinians also consider the land to be holy and forbid any alienation of it to non-Muslims, justifying indiscriminate attacks on civilians (Reiter 2010).

These three developments began to come together in the Arab–Israel arena in the aftermath of Israel's 1982 war in Lebanon, with the formation of *Hizballah*, a Lebanese *Shi'a* movement inspired and guided by Iran. *Hizballah*'s 1985 program affirmed this link and the place of Israel in the worldwide Islamist movement:

> We are the party of God [*Hizb Allah*] the vanguard of which was made victorious by God in Iran . . . We obey the orders of one leader, wise and just, that of our tutor and ruler . . . Ruhollah Musawi Khomeini . . . We combat abomination and we shall tear out its very roots, its primary roots, which are the US . . . We see in Israel the vanguard of the United States in our Islamic world . . . Our struggle will end only when this entity is obliterated. (*Hizballah* 1985)

The insertion of Iran into the picture added a new dimension to the Arab–Israel conflict. Iran had been a peripheral state in the Arab–Israel arena; it was not an Arab state, and during the Shah's reign had maintained official relations, and even an unofficial alliance of sorts, with the Jewish state. Now the Islamic Republic of Iran was embarked on a "semi-hostile takeover" of the Palestinian cause, contributing an estimated $100 million a year to building up *Hizballah* as a military force on Israel's border (Aversa 2006). Given Iran's military experience and expertise – gained painfully through the long and brutal Iran–Iraq war – and its considerable resources as a state, this was a significant strategic shift. Many in Israel and elsewhere assumed or hoped that Israel's 2000 withdrawal from southern Lebanon would lead *Hizballah* to focus on Lebanon, and thus stabilize that frontier, but subsequent events showed that the anti-Israel agenda of *Hizballah*, and its Iranian sponsor, had not changed.

Iran's power and influence in the region had been boosted, inadvertently but unmistakably, by the US-led overthrow of Saddam Hussein's regime in 2003. Not only Israel, but also Arab states of the Gulf, Saudi Arabia, Jordan, and Egypt felt threatened by the expansion of Iranian influence and its ties to *Shi'a* dissident groups such as *Hizballah*.

Iran's new role gained added significance when its progress in nuclear technology was revealed. Iran had ratified the Nuclear Non-Proliferation Treaty (NPT) under the Shah, putting their nuclear facilities under the safeguards of the International Atomic Energy Agency (IAEA). But in 2002 outside sources revealed that Iran was constructing an as-yet undeclared facility to enrich uranium, one of the two paths to nuclear weapons. A second enrichment facility was discovered, again by outside sources, in 2009. Although both sites were put under safeguards, Iranian non-compliance with IAEA information requests, and refusal to stop uranium enrichment, led to a series of economic and commercial sanctions by the UN Security Council.

Iran-sponsored *Hizballah* was one of the models in the rise of *Hamas*, the Palestinian wing of the fundamentalist Muslim Brotherhood, in the late 1980s. As already recounted in chapter 5, the 1988 *Hamas* Charter defined Palestine as an Islamic trust, every bit of which must be liberated, and condemned all compromise or political solutions as violations of divine law. Jews were charged with responsibility for the two world wars, communism, capitalism, and conspiracy to rule the world (citing the spurious Protocols of the Elders of Zion) (*Hamas* 1988). Though *Hamas* was focused more on Palestine, and was a *Sunni* rather than a *Shi'a* movement, the ideological framework was practically the same (Ya'ari 2006). The fundamental tenets were:

1. Victory will not necessarily come soon; it is a long-term struggle.
2. Cease-fire or truce is permissible when needed, but only temporarily.
3. Fighting out of weakness is a source of strength, and explains setbacks that occur.
4. Do not defend territory; the struggle is over minds, not land.
5. Arab states are corrupt and flawed; only Islamic movements are legitimate.
6. Ultimately, victory is a historical and doctrinal certainty.

Belief in the certainty of victory is an important underpinning in this worldview. Islamists interpret recent history as a series of defeats for those they consider to be the enemies of

Islam: the expulsion of the Soviet Union from Afghanistan, the exit of the United States from Lebanon in the mid-1980s and later from Somalia, Israeli withdrawals from Lebanon in 2000 and Gaza in 2005, attacks on US forces in Iraq and Afghanistan.

In this perspective it is clear that "Islam is winning," that time is on their side. Despite its present strength and assertiveness, Israel's eventual demise is inevitable. Israeli sources are scanned for signs of weakness that confirm this; for example, *Hizballah* leader Sheikh Hasan Nasrallah said in 1999 that "I read Netanyahu's statements that the Israeli people are tired of Zionism and that everybody's interested in their private lives . . . the Zionist society today seems torn apart racially, religiously, and politically . . ." (Nasrallah 1999).

In this context, the Israeli withdrawal from southern Lebanon in 2000 was interpreted as a clear and unambiguous military victory for *Hizballah*. In the words of a leader of *Islamic Jihad*, a Palestinian movement modeled on *Hizballah*, "The shameful defeat that Israel suffered in southern Lebanon and which caused its army to flee it in terror was not made on the negotiations table but on the battlefield and through *jihad* and martyrdom, which achieved a great victory for the Islamic resistance and Lebanese People" (Shallah 2001). As noted, Palestinians overwhelmingly regarded Israel's 2005 pullout from Gaza as a victory for "armed struggle," of which *Hamas* was the leading symbol.

The phenomenon that combined all these elements – new actors, transformed warfare, religious extremism – and stood as an index for them, was the rise of suicide attacks. Suicidal attacks on civilian targets, like terrorism generally, were not new, but their modern revival began in the Middle East. During the course of the Iran–Iraq War, willing sacrifice by Iranian soldiers was seen as martyrdom, and was thus permitted – and celebrated – in this reading of Islamic law and tradition. The first modern suicide attack on a civilian target was the bombing of the US Embassy in Beirut in April 1983, apparently by *Hizballah*, and the tactic was widely used in southern Lebanon in the following years. The first suicide attack within Israel was carried out by *Hamas* in April

1993, during the period in which the ground was being laid for the Oslo peace process (Pape 2003).

At the end of 2005, *Hamas* (though not *Islamic Jihad*) was committed to the cease-fire negotiated by PA President Abbas several months previously. *Hamas* had at this time adopted a political strategy, intending to gain enough power in Palestinian legislative elections (in which it was participating for the first time) to block Abbas's efforts to conclude a final peace agreement with Israel. Portents were good; *Hamas* had been gaining increasing support in polls over the years, actually rivaling *Fatah* in popularity at some points. But given *Fatah*'s institutional advantages, very few foresaw the upset that took place on January 25, 2006, when *Hamas* won a solid majority of 74 of 132 seats in the Palestine National Council.

The victory should not be overstated: *Hamas* received only 44 percent of the direct party vote against 41 percent for *Fatah*, but in a system designed to benefit the largest party and given splits in *Fatah*, this translated into a landslide in terms of seats. Nor did those voting for *Hamas* necessarily agree with all of its program. A large part of the support was a reaction to the corruption, ineptitude, and mismanagement within the PA, run by *Fatah*, and an expression of general economic distress. Also, as noted, *Hamas* was, rightly or wrongly, given much credit for the Israeli pullout from Gaza. Still, the bottom line was that the legislative powers of the PA, and most of its executive powers (apart from the presidency), were now in the hands of a movement that in principle rejected recognition of or permanent agreements with Israel and regarded all attacks on Israeli targets as legitimate.

International donors who had been keeping the Palestinian economy afloat (primarily the United States and the European Union) stopped direct aid to the PA when *Hamas* refused to meet their conditions: recognition of Israel, renunciation of violence, and observance of existing agreements (the latter two conditions being obligations of states in international law). However, other forms of aid, through international humanitarian organizations and direct to individuals, continued to flow, and in fact more than compensated for the lost direct aid (Erlanger 2007). Though the economy remained in dismal shape, the *Hamas* regime under Prime Minister Ismail Haniyeh survived its first year and *Fatah* finally joined it in a unity government at that point, in March 2007, under terms that did not meet the international conditions for resumption of direct aid.

But in the meantime a new kind of war was triggered, revealing how the fundamental structure of the conflict had changed. In late June an Israeli soldier was seized at a Gaza border post by a group that included *Hamas* operatives, and during the fighting that ensued, *Hizballah* carried out a similar operation on the Lebanese border, capturing two Israeli soldiers. Israel launched massive air attacks in Lebanon, followed by a major ground operation, but encountered a well-entrenched *Hizballah* force that, with Iranian support and training, had amassed an arsenal of an estimated 12,000 short-range and medium-range missiles as well as tank weapons and other modern equipment. While Israel was able to inflict heavy losses on *Hizballah* forces, it was unable to destroy them completely, or to stop the launching of hundreds of missiles on Israeli targets throughout the north of the country. In the words of an Israeli military analyst: "Israel finds itself engaged against a substate organization that . . . melts into the populated areas to regroup and renew the fighting. . . . The war in Lebanon cannot, therefore, end in a military victory in the normal sense. . . . " (Brom 2006: 19).

Thus this second Lebanon war was seen by nearly all parties as a *Hizballah* victory, despite its heavier losses, since the organization had survived to fight another day. A poll of Palestinians indicated that 86 percent believed that *Hizballah* had emerged as the winner (Palestine Center for Policy and Survey Research 2006), and the attraction of the *Hizballah* model for *Hamas* and other Palestinian groups caused great concern among Israeli strategists. Would Gaza eventually come to resemble the southern Lebanon of 2006?

Consequently, support for unilateral disengagement or "consolidation" within Israel, already weakening, was now dealt a lethal blow. In the prevailing view, withdrawal from Lebanon and from Gaza had proven to be bad mistakes.

Attacks from both areas had continued, and there seemed to be no immediate solution to the problem of rockets, fired over a separation line or fence, or from sporadic incursions or kidnappings. Above all, unilateral withdrawals were interpreted as victories for the "armed struggle" and were credited to the groups – *Hizballah* and *Hamas* – that Israel had the least interest in helping.

However, the struggle for control of the Palestinian future continued unabated. When President Abbas refused to surrender control of key security agencies, *Hamas* reacted in June by seizing physical control of Gaza in a quick blitz campaign. In response, Abbas dissolved the unity government and appointed a new cabinet headed by the respected economist Salam Fayyad; however, its writ extended only to the West Bank. With the West Bank and Gaza now effectively divided, the prospect of a Palestinian negotiating partner able and willing to deal with Israel on the basis of a two-state solution seemed more distant than ever – despite the frantic efforts of alarmed Arab regimes to breathe new life into the dormant peace process. This de facto partition of Palestine – Hamas in Gaza, Fatah in the West Bank – remained the central reality on the ground in the Israel/Palestine arena, and any initiatives to stabilize the conflict, let alone resolve underlying issues, had to contend with the fact that President Abbas could not speak for or implement any agreement in the Gaza strip – roughly one-third of his theoretical constituency.

Palestinians overwhelmingly favored the restoration of a unity government including both *Hamas* and *Fatah* within the PA framework, and unity talks took place sporadically, usually under Egyptian auspices. But the two sides remained unreconciled: the *Fatah*-dominated PA in the West Bank demanded restoration of PA control of Gaza as a first step, while *Hamas* sought a bigger role in security institutions on the West Bank – the issue that had triggered its total takeover in Gaza. *Hamas* also demanded that, as a condition for joining the PLO, it be granted power proportional to its electoral strength, creating the potential for *Hamas* domination of this key Palestinian organization.

In short, the two parties were engaged in a struggle for pre-eminence in the Palestinian arena, and all negotiations were measured against this reality. There were frequent armed clashes, with each side acting to detain or neutralize activists of the other side operating within territory that it controlled. New legislative and presidential elections, scheduled for January 2010, could not be conducted under these conditions and were postponed indefinitely.

The *Hamas* takeover in Gaza triggered regional and international efforts to squeeze the new regime there by economic pressure and sanctions. International aid donors, a key lifeline of support for the Gaza population, initiated a policy of withholding aid to *Hamas*-controlled institutions and trying to channel it through international governmental and non-governmental organizations. Though direct humanitarian assistance to Gaza residents did not decline as a result of the boycott of Hamas, the overall impact was still a sharp deterioration in living conditions. This was in large measure because of a state of near-siege of Gaza instituted by Israel, which controlled all points of entry into the enclave apart from the Egyptian border. Israel's policy, with much US, European, and Egyptian support, was to bring as much pressure as possible on *Hamas* by allowing only subsistence-level imports into Gaza.

Primitive rocket attacks from Gaza on nearby Israeli cities and towns had been a factor since the second *intifada* began, and their frequency rose sharply after the 2007 *Hamas* takeover, as a form of pressure on Israel to relax its siege of the territory. This led in return to Israeli air strikes and incursions in order to suppress the rocket fire, and also to try to stem the widespread smuggling, of both weapons and consumer goods, that rapidly developed through tunnels under the Gaza–Egypt border.

The moderate Arab regimes – Egypt, Jordan, Saudi Arabia, and the Gulf states – now faced a rising threat from radical Islamist states and non-state movements, and consequently were ready to cooperate with Western powers in efforts to defuse the region's troublespots such as Iraq, Lebanon, and the Israeli–Palestinian impasse. The increased visibility of

Iran under its provocative President Mahmoud Ahmadinejad, fed by controversy over a possible Iranian nuclear weapons program, tied in with concerns about *Hizballah* (a *Shi'a* organization directly tied to Iran) and *Hamas*, also thought to receive support from Iran. Support and pressure from Arab states contributed directly to a new US initiative, in late 2007, to revive peace negotiations on basic ("final status") issues separating Israel and the Palestinians.

The decision to convene a conference to revive negotiations – essentially dormant since the Camp David and Taba talks in 2000–1 – was in some degree a reflection of the degree to which all the major parties felt under great pressure and in need of a dramatic move. The United States, beleaguered in Iraq, needed success elsewhere in the Middle East; the Israeli government, also in a very weak political position following discontent over the second Lebanese War, needed a policy that would pull together the Israeli center; the PA needed to establish that diplomacy, not *Hamas* rejectionism, was the road forward; and Arab states (Egypt, Saudi Arabia, Jordan, the Gulf states) sought to counter the momentum of Iran and its Islamist allies.

Consequently, the Middle East Peace Conference convened in Annapolis on November 27, 2007. Iran, Hamas, and Hizballah were not invited, but some fifty nations (including Syria, a key participant) did attend the formal opening sessions. The intention was to establish a framework for bilateral Israeli–Palestinian and Israeli–Syrian negotiations that would attempt to resolve all outstanding issues in the conflict by the end of 2008. There was general recognition that resolution of these issues – the same ones that are reviewed in detail in chapter 9 – within this time frame, given the hurdles that remain, was a daunting if not foolhardy undertaking. Apart from the huge gaps that remained – in particular, on borders and Israeli settlements, Jerusalem, and above all the Palestinian refugee issue – loomed the central reality, as noted, that one of the two Palestinian territories remained under the control of a political movement that rejected not only the content of any future agreement but the act of an agreement itself. This was underlined by massive demonstrations in Gaza, organized by *Hamas*, denouncing the Annapolis conference in its entirety.

Thus prospects for a breakthrough on the diplomatic front, despite some auspicious circumstances, remained bleak at best. Few international diplomatic initiatives have been accompanied by as many predictions of failure, at the very moment of genesis, as was the Annapolis Conference. But negotiations did resume, behind the scenes, in 2007–8 following the Annapolis Conference. Most of the negotiation took place directly between PA President Mahmoud Abbas and Israeli Prime Minister Ehud Olmert, who met face-to-face 36 times before and during this period; numerous meetings also took place between other officials of the two sides, in particular the respective foreign ministers, Israel's Tzipi Livni and the PA's Ahmed Qurei. The existence of the talks, though not their content, was known at the time.

In early 2011, however, it was revealed that the two leaders had not only made a serious effort to bridge the remaining differences, but had perhaps come as close to doing so as had the negotiators at Taba. The revelations began with a cascade of 1600 documents from the Palestinian side of the talks, published by the Arab media outlet *Al Jazeera* in January 2011 (*Al Jazeera* 2011). These documents, leaked by an advisor to Palestinian negotiators seeking to embarrass the PA, demonstrated some of the far-reaching concessions it had offered.

The Israeli side was filled in a few days later when Olmert, out of office for over two years, published excerpts from his projected memoirs in Israeli's most popular newspaper (YNet News 2011). In this account Israel had also made unprecedented offers, and in the end the two sides had come tantalizingly close to a final deal; in Olmert's words, "We were very close, more than ever in the past, to completing an agreement in principle that would have led to the end of the conflict between us and the Palestinians." Interviews with Olmert and Abbas filled out the picture, presenting reasonably consistent and unchallenged conclusions about what was achieved, and not achieved, in the 2007–8 negotiations (Avishai 2011).

But events on the diplomatic front were soon overshadowed by renewed violence. After a year of low-intensity warfare, in June 2008 Israel and *Hamas* had finally accepted an Egyptian-mediated cease-fire for a period of six months. The cease-fire called for an immediate end to rocket fire and weapons smuggling, and to all smuggling once borders were opened, which in turn depended on progress in negotiations over the release of an Israeli soldier, Gilad Shalit, held since 2006 by Hamas. But negotiations over Shalit stalled, sporadic rocket fire continued, and Israel's blockade was maintained with little change. Though the frequency of rockets dropped from about thirty each week to two or three, the cease-fire remained shaky throughout the rest of the year, with each side blaming the other for not fulfilling its obligations.

When the cease-fire ended officially in December, therefore, the situation reverted to a test of arms. *Hamas* resumed heavy rocket fire on neighboring areas of Israel, reaching further this time with improved missiles, and Israel responded with Operation Cast Lead, an air and ground offensive lasting 23 days that inflicted widespread damage and about 1400 deaths in Gaza, more than half of them civilians (as usual, numbers were hotly disputed). At the end of this period both sides declared a cease-fire unilaterally, meaning that the issues of weapons smuggling into Gaza, the release of Shalit, and the Israeli blockade of Gaza remained unresolved.

The Gaza War of December 2008 to January 2009 illustrated again the features of the new warfare of the fourth stage: no clear battlefield, elusive targets on the insurgent side (resulting in high civilian casualties), and fuzzy outcomes. Again the very definition of victory or defeat was disputed. *Hamas*, simply by surviving the war, could and did claim to be the winner; 47 percent of all Palestinians believed that Hamas had won the war, against only ten percent who believed Israel had won (and 37 percent who said neither) (Jerusalem Media and Communications Center, 2008). Israel, for its part, did reduce the hail of rockets on its bordering areas to sporadic attacks. But the Egyptian border was not sealed to traffic through the tunnels, through which weapons, consumer goods, and even construction materials continued to flow.

The Israeli assault on *Hamas* targets in heavily urbanized areas raised widespread charges of violation of international laws of war. To investigate such charges, United Nations Human Rights Council appointed a Fact Finding Mission on the Gaza Conflict headed by Richard Goldstone, an eminent South African jurist. The Israeli government refused to cooperate with the mission, deeming its mandate to be biased and the Human Rights Council to be a body that had consistently been hostile to Israel.

Based primarily on Palestinian testimony, the "Goldstone Report" therefore reflected the Palestinian case against Israel's conduct of the war. It tied the campaign to Israel's larger strategy of blockading Gaza and to the issue of the occupied territories, finding broad violation of human rights. It condemned the military assault on civilian structures in Gaza, accusing Israel of punishing the Gaza population for its support of *Hamas*. It alleged that the Israeli army had followed a strategy of "zero risk" to its own soldiers, instead of balancing such risks against the destruction of civilian life. Finally it made the damning charge that the civilian losses had been deliberate: "The mission found in every case that the Israeli armed forces had carried out direct intentional strikes against civilians" (United Nations General Assembly 2009).

The Goldstone Report did also condemn the *Hamas* rocket attacks against Israeli civilian centers as violations of international law. *Hamas* and its supporters argued that such attacks were the legitimate response of a weaker party, with no other recourse, facing an illegitimate and illegal blockade; they also emphasized how little actual damage such attacks inflicted, making military ineffectiveness into a legal argument.

Critics of the Goldstone Report from the Israeli side argued that it focused almost entirely on international law on the conduct of war *(jus in bello)* to the neglect of law justifying the resort to force in the first place *(jus ad bellum)*, thus overlooking Israel's right to self-defense. But even in this restricted sphere, they noted that international law had not kept up with the shift from conventional war to "war amongst the people" where insurgents try deliberately to erase the distinction, basic to international law, between combatant and non-combatant. What is the answer when a warring party deliberately uses civilian populations as a shield? In Gaza, Hamas reputedly used schools, ambulances, hospitals and mosques to house military bases and actions; some charged they were intentionally trying to cause civilian deaths, among their own people, in order to gain international support. Finally, the conclusion that Israel was *deliberately* targeting civilians was dismissed as unproved; had this been the case, it was argued, civilian deaths would have been incomparably greater. Goldstone himself later retracted this particular conclusion (Goldstone 2011).

In summary: by the beginning of 2009 the forces undermining what remained of the Oslo peace process – the new realities of the fourth stage – had at least for the moment gained the upper hand. This remained the case in the period that followed.

8 | The Downward Spiral

Now, every single terrible act of violence, every new settlement announcement, takes us not closer to peace; they take us closer to a one-state solution. That is no solution. It is an invitation to perpetual conflict. . . . It will bring one war, not one state.

US Secretary of State John Kerry, Sept. 19, 2016
(Ravid 2016)

Palestinian Unilateralism

The Gaza War was not the only untoward event derailing Israeli–Palestinian diplomacy; political instability in Israel also played a part. By midway in 2008, Israeli Prime Minister Olmert was facing no fewer than five ongoing investigations of alleged corruption, forcing him finally to call a new leadership election in *Kadima* on September 17. Foreign Minister Tzipi Livni emerged as the new *Kadima* leader, but was unable to reconstitute the existing government, forcing the calling of new general elections for February 10, 2009. With changes of administration pending both in Israel and in the United States, Middle East diplomacy in the latter half of the year was reduced to going through the motions, even before the war.

The Israeli election of 2009 confirmed that a significant shift to the right, first seen in 2003, had taken place in reaction to new realities of the fourth stage. In essence, the 2009 election erased the impact of the 2006 election that followed Ariel Sharon's establishment of the new centrist party *Kadima*. It affirmed the result in 2003, when the second *intifada* produced the most hawkish Knesset ever. This turn to the right was set in motion by the second *intifada*, the rise of *Hamas* as a pivotal Palestinian player, the intrusion of Iran, and what was seen by many Israelis as the failure of unilateral disengagement in Lebanon in 2000 and Gaza in 2005.

Following the election, *Likud* leader Benjamin Netanyahu formed a government based on four right-wing or religious parties together with the Labor Party; Kadima moved into opposition. Israel's turn to the right did not necessarily mean the end of the two-state solution as the dominant model for resolving the Israeli–Palestinian conflict. *Likud*'s platform neither endorsed nor ruled out a two-state solution, but simply condemned any further unilateral withdrawals on the model of Lebanon in 2000 or Gaza in 2005. *Yisrael Beitenu*, the other major right-wing party, actually did not oppose establishment of a Palestinian state, and was ready not only to surrender Arab population centers on the West Bank and Gaza, but even to cede Arab-inhabited areas of Israel itself. In fact, in the 2009 election only two small parties, which together won seven seats, presented platforms of uncompromising opposition to any Palestinian state.

The willingness of a right-wing Israeli party to part with areas of Israel itself was testimony to the impact of a new assertiveness among Palestinians in Israel. Building on the earlier movement toward challenging the Jewish character of Israel, leading figures in this community now articulated a call for a deJudaized Israel that would be "a state of all its citizens." In 2006–7 they issued an interlocking set of four documents, labeled "the Vision Documents" after the title of the key paper: The Future Vision of the Palestinian Arabs in Israel (National Committee 2006). The documents adopted the general Palestinian narrative as that also of Palestinians in Israel, defining themselves as the indigenous national community and Zionism as a colonial intrusion. In this view the inequality experienced by the minority in Israel was an unavoidable consequence of the Jewish character of the state, and the only solution was to remove this character, including such symbols as the flag and anthem (Peleg and Waxman 2011).

The reaction to these ideas in Israel ranged from alarmed to hostile, and in more hawkish circles it led to such proposals as the above-mentioned transfer of contiguous Arab-inhabited areas of Israel to the new state of Palestine, whenever it is created. This in turn met a hostile reception in the areas concerned, where such proposals were denounced as racism. But in the new Knesset elected in 2009 a number of laws aimed at Arabs in Israel were proposed. Among those passed was a proposal that government funding be denied to groups commemorating *Nakba* Day – marking Israel's independence Day as a "disaster" – and that smaller communities be allowed to establish "Acceptance Committees" that could exclude would-be residents.

Returning to the two-state issue: since the two-state solution was the only agreed framework for further diplomacy, Netanyahu came under intense pressure internationally (especially from the United States) and domestically to take the final step in this direction. This he did conditionally, in an address on June 14, 2009. Emphasizing that a Palestinian state must be demilitarized and that there must be unambiguous acceptance of Israel as a Jewish state, Netanyahu said that "if we receive this guarantee regarding demilitarization and Israel's security needs, and if the Palestinians recognize Israel as the State of the Jewish people, then we will be ready in a future peace agreement to reach a solution where a demilitarized Palestinian state exists alongside the Jewish state." He also stressed the importance of defensible borders and of Jerusalem remaining the united capital of Israel, but promised no building of new settlements in the West Bank or expropriation of additional land for existing settlements (Israel Ministry of Foreign Affairs, 2009).

The commitment to no new settlements was not novel, actually going back to Rabin's government in the early 1990s; what was critical to Palestinians was expansion of existing settlements on land already expropriated. Thus Netanyahu's acceptance of the two-state model did not produce a renewal of talks on a final agreement, since the PA insisted on a total freeze on all new settlement construction as a precondition for negotiations on final status issues. The insistence that Palestinians recognize Israel as a Jewish state presented yet another hurdle to renewal of talks, and one that was new to the mix. For Israelis this was more than a verbal formula; it would signify the genuine acceptance by Palestinians of Israel's legitimacy, without which there could not be complete trust. Palestinian leaders countered that they had already recognized Israel as a state, that this was normally adequate in interstate relations, that Israel's self-definition was not their business, and that such a declaration might harm the interests of Arab citizens of Israel.

In the meantime, Israel's attention was significantly diverted by two strategic threats that had developed in recent years: the proliferation of increasingly sophisticated medium- and short-range missiles in the hands of *Hizballah* in Lebanon and *Hamas* in Gaza, and the apparent nuclear weapons program in Iran. As noted, support for unilateral Israeli withdrawal from occupied territories evaporated when rockets and missiles began to fall in Israel from territories evacuated in southern Lebanon and Gaza. What Israeli government would allow the West Bank to become a launching pad for rocket fire into Israel's major cities? As it was, reports of up to 50,000 short- and medium-range missiles with ranges of up to 120 miles in Hizballah's arsenals, and of improved Hamas rockets possibly able to hit Tel Aviv, raised the same spectre.

For lack of a better answer, Israel turned to technological fixes on the missile problem. Following the Scud attacks from Iraq in 1991, development had begun on the Arrow, a joint US–Israel anti-missile system against ballistic missiles with a range greater than 120 miles. The first Arrows were deployed in 2000. In response to the threat of shorter-range missiles with less warning time, a multi-layered defense has been developed: David's Sling, also a joint US–Israel project, against missiles with a 25–180 mile range (the *Hizballah* threat); and the Iron Dome, an Israeli system designed to intercept missiles with a 3–45 mile range. Israel has also reportedly bought one US Vulcan-Phalanx system to test as a defense against the shortest-range rockets and mortars fired from Gaza. The Iron Dome missiles were deployed, and used successfully, in April 2011; David's Sling was deployed during 2016. A successful shield against missile attack would presumably lessen opposition to further Israeli withdrawal from the West Bank.

The threat of an Iranian nuclear bomb cast a more ominous shadow. In defiance of international pressure and UN sanctions, Iran continued to enrich uranium to a level useful as fuel for medical isotopes, for which they claimed a need (International Atomic Energy Agency, 2011). Further enrichment to weapon-grade level would be detected by IAEA inspectors, but the question was how long such a process would take, should Iran withdraw from the NPT (as legally entitled) and expel the IAEA. Estimates ranged from a few months to a few years. In late 2007 a US National Intelligence Estimate concluded that Iran had stopped work on actual weapons design in 2003 after the revelation of the first enrichment site. Not all intelligence sources agreed with this assessment, but in any event the acquisition of weapon-grade material, and not actual weaponization, is the key to a nuclear weapons capacity.

The dominant view in Israel was that an Iranian bomb would be an existential threat, in light of the apocalyptic vision of the end of days expressed in extreme Shi'a beliefs. Accordingly the bomb must be prevented by all means. Diplomacy and sanctions would be preferred if they worked, and US military action would be preferable to an Israeli military operation. But Israel would act as a last resort; the main constraint would be the question of military feasibility, on which opinions both in Israel and elsewhere were divided. An attack on Iran would also exact a high price in retaliation: massive missile attacks, closure of the Persian Gulf, crippling the world's oil supply, the unleashing of *Hizballah* and *Hamas*, and possibly world-wide terror attacks against Israeli and Western targets; and at best such an attack would only delay the Iranian program by a few years. In mid-2011 Meir Dagan, the just-retired head of Israel's foreign intelligence agency (Mossad), declared that a military attack on Iran would be "the stupidest thing I have ever heard" and hinted that covert action was more effective (bringing to mind a reported computer worm that had created havoc in the Iranian program) (Melman 2011a). But the issue remained on the top of the Israeli agenda.

For Palestinians on the West Bank, the disruption of the Gaza War and the turn to the right in Israel only added to existing frustration. The new Israeli government was likely to favor expansion of Jewish settlements on the West Bank, and with the end of the Olmert-Abbas talks, renewal of serious negotiation over final status issues was unlikely. In November 2009 Israeli Prime Minister Netanyahu did announce a ten-month freeze on new residential housing starts on the West Bank, exempting houses already under construction, public buildings, and East Jerusalem. The PA found this inadequate as a basis for renewing final status talks, insisting that only a total halt in all settlement construction would show that Israel was negotiating in good faith. In March 2010 the PA agreed to renew indirect ("proximity") with the help of US special envoy George Mitchell, and after several months of intense US diplomatic efforts direct talks resumed on September 2, 2010 – only to be cut short by the expiration of the Israeli settlement freeze at the end of the month. At this point Netanyahu, under heavy pressure from settlers and unable to hold his coalition together otherwise, allowed new construction to resume on existing settlements, and Abbas withdrew from the barely resumed negotiations. The new US administration of President Barack Obama, like its predecessor, was focused on the renewal of these talks. Obama began his term with an ambitious effort to totally recast the prevailing mood between the West and the Islamic world. Speaking in Cairo on June 4, 2009, he reiterated US criticism of Jewish settlements in the West Bank, called for easing the humanitarian crisis in Gaza, and reaffirmed support for the roadmap and a two-state solution. None of this was new; what was different was the drama of the occasion. On May

19, 2011, he made another important policy statement on the conflict, calling for two states based "on the 1967 lines with mutually agreed [land] swaps." Though the mention of 1967 lines occasioned a minor tempest, this also was nothing new; since Camp David in 2000 the idea of the 1967 lines with land swaps had been the basis of all Israeli–Palestinian negotiation. In any event, the Obama administration also was unable to overcome the settlement freeze issue and matters remained at an impasse.

Most Palestinians supported the PA's refusal to negotiate without a settlement freeze, but were divided on the best course of action in the absence of negotiations; only a minority (39%) supported the idea of a return to armed *intifada* (Palestine Center for Policy and Survey Research 2009). But with the continuing expansion of Jewish settlements as time passed, and the constant threat of settler violence against neighboring Arab residents and property, continuation of the *status quo* was not an option in the eyes of West Bank inhabitants.

Given the impasse, the PA leadership embarked on a new strategy of Palestinian unilateralism. Building on *de facto* separation between Israel and the West Bank that had been re-established by the intifada and Israel's security barrier, PA Prime Minister Fayyad – a US-trained economist – focused on a program of nation-building on the West Bank that would culminate in a demarche to the UN to demand international recognition of Palestinian statehood. PA President Abbas noted that "we have been negotiating with the State of Israel for twenty years without coming any closer to realizing a state of our own," and that Palestinian admission to the UN would "pave the way for us to pursue claims against Israel at the United Nations, human rights treaty bodies and the International Court of Justice" (Abbas 2011).

The nation-building program – labeled by some as "Fayyadism" – did for a time change life on the West Bank. Law and order was largely restored while the economy grew by an estimated 8.5% in 2009 and 9% in 2010. In the same period some 120 new schools and 50 health clinics were built, over 1,000 miles of road paved, and unemployment reduced by a third. By the end of the decade GDP per capita and life expectancy in the West Bank were higher than in many neighboring Middle Eastern states. In early 2011 both the International Monetary Fund and the World Bank confirmed that the West Bank was, in fact, ready for statehood in economic terms. PA success on the West Bank was reflected in polls taken in both the West Bank and Gaza in June 2011, which favored Abbas over *Hamas* leader Ismail Haniyeh, in a vote for President, by 54–38%, and support for *Fatah* over *Hamas* by 39–17% (even in Gaza, *Fatah* had a 2–1 edge) (Palestine Center for Survey and Policy Research 2011; Jerusalem Media and Communications Center 2011a).

Conditions in Gaza did not keep pace with the West Bank, given the siege on its borders and the devastation of the 2008–9 war. This clearly fit the preferences of Israel, Egypt, the United States, and European nations, all of whom welcomed the weakening of *Hamas* rule in Gaza. Only in 2010 did the Gaza economy show signs of significant recovery, testifying to success in overcoming blockade through the widespread use of smuggling tunnels under the frontier with Egypt. Pro-Palestinian supporters in other countries also sought to challenge the blockade by organizing flotillas to transport aid to Gaza; in May 2010 this led to a confrontation between the Israeli navy and the Turkish-owned ship *Mavi Marmara* in which nine Turkish citizens were killed. Relations between Israel and Turkey, already in bad repair as the Islamist government of Tayyip Erdogan took a more pro-Palestinian line, entered into crisis mode.

The PA under Abbas proceeded with its unilateral initiative for international recognition when the UN convened in mid-September 2011. In this arena, Palestinians were playing to their strength – international support – while Israel was on the defensive. Once recognized within the 1967 borders by the United Nations, PA leaders claimed, there would be no need for further negotiations with Israel, but only for Israel to withdraw from the territory of a fellow UN member. And since over 130 nations had recognized Palestinian statehood in one form or another since it was formally declared in 1988, winning UN support would not be a problem.

One obvious obstacle to recognition of the PA as "Palestine" was the divided rule over Palestinian territories. This hurdle was in theory overcome in May, when *Fatah* and *Hamas* signed an agreement calling for a unity government of non-partisan "experts" and new presidential and legislative elections, in both the West Bank and Gaza, within a year. Negotiations over the composition of the new government stalled, and there was widespread skepticism that the agreement could be implemented in its entirety (would *Hamas*, in view of recent polls, permit itself to be voted out of power in Gaza?). But for the purpose of the UN exercise in September 2011, Palestinians would appear as a united front.

Feeling that peace talks were dead and that he was impelled to find a new approach, PA President Abbas proceeded to pursue the UN bid. In response to the argument that Palestine was not under one government, Abbas reinforced the (as yet unimplemented) May agreement on unity with *Hamas* with further agreement in November for a unified government and elections in May, 2012. In the meantime, he submitted the Palestinian application for UN membership on September 23, 2011, in a widely broadcast speech at the United Nations. The Security Council, under US pressure not to act hastily, referred the question to a committee of the whole. In early November the PA (as Palestine) achieved full membership in the United Nations Educational, Scientific, and Cultural Organization (UNESCO), which could be added to full membership already achieved in the Non-Aligned Movement, the Organization of the Islamic Conference, and the Group of 77 (an international organization of developing nations).

Israel's response to this initiative was that Palestinian statehood could only be determined by negotiation, and that the bid for UN membership was also a violation of the Oslo prohibition of any moves that would alter the status of the territories being negotiated. (Palestinians had long argued that the expansion of Jewish settlements in these territories was a violation of the Oslo accords.) The United States and major

European states also opposed the PA's move, on grounds that it undermined chances for negotiation and that statehood requires a government in control of a defined territory, while Palestine's borders were not yet determined and *Hamas* controlled Gaza. Furthermore, since *Hamas* refused to renounce terrorism, violence, or its stated aim of destroying Israel, it was not seen as a "peace-loving" party as stipulated by the UN Charter.

The PA lacked the support of nine Security Council members, the number needed to force a vote – which, if favorable, would in any case be subject to a US veto. In the meantime, the US Congress reacted to the UN bid by freezing aid transfers to the PA for the current fiscal year (amounting to about $200 million). After the admission of Palestine to UNESCO, Israel began withholding tax and custom transfers which were a part of the Oslo structure.

Given this impasse, Abbas turned instead to the upgrading of the PA's status in the UN General Assembly. The plan, in this case, was to change the observer status of "Palestine" from that of an "entity" – a status held only by Palestine – to that of a non-member state, a status then held only by the Holy See (the Vatican). This would give Palestinians better footing to claim full membership in other international organizations, including international legal bodies where they could submit claims against Israel. Although only states can recognize states, the General Assembly could also recommend that UN members extend full recognition to Palestine. The campaign culminated on November 29, 2012, when "Palestine" was in fact recognized as a non-member observer state in a vote of 138 to 9, with 41 abstentions.

Another dimension of Palestinian unilateralism was the "Boycott, Divestment, and Sanctions" (BDS) campaign that had been initiated by 170 Palestinian non-governmental organizations in 2005. Inspired in large part by the sanctions movement against *apartheid*-era South Africa, BDS organizers sought to encourage governments, international organizations, financial and commercial interests, religious movements, academic institutions, labor unions and other civic bodies to boycott Israeli products and institutions, withdraw all investments in Israel, and impose punitive sanctions on Israel in the United Nations and elsewhere.

The BDS movement formulated three demands as the goals of their campaign: an end to the post-1967 occupation including the dismantling of the security wall; full equality for Arab citizens of Israel; and implementation of the right of return for 1948–9 refugees. Palestinian and other supporters of BDS argued that since the original Arab boycott of Israel had languished during the days of the peace process, it was important to develop new forms of pressure on Israel to adhere to international law. Israeli and other opponents of BDS condemned it as a double standard, since states with incomparably worse human rights records were not targeted by such movements. BDS was actually, they argued, a cover for the delegitimization of Israel; for example, the unlimited right of return for refugees would clearly end the existence of Israel as a Jewish state.

By all indications BDS did not have, and was not likely to have, a significant impact on Israel's economy or international connections. It did have, however, some successes in academic and religious circles and among political groups on the left. A variant version of BDS, focusing on the boycott of Israeli settlements on the West Bank only, had somewhat broader success. The European Union, for example, in November 2015 began requiring that West Bank products be labeled to distinguish them from other Israeli imports, which enjoy privileged trade status.

The Arab Spring

As Palestinian unilateralism moved into the critical phase, the entire Middle East context was shifting with the advent of the "Arab Spring." After four decades of relative stability, long-established authoritarian rulers were shunted aside, beginning with Tunisia, moving on to Mubarak's ouster in Egypt in early 2011, disintegration in Libya, civil war in Syria, and challenges to almost every Arab regime. What impact would this have on the Israeli–Palestinian conflict?

At first glance it might seem that the impact would be minimal. Public opinion in the Arab world had been moving in a moderate direction: by 2010, 86% of those surveyed in six states were ready for Arab–Israel peace if Israel withdrew to the pre-1967 lines – up from 73% two years earlier (Telhami 2010). Moreover, the Arab uprisings centered almost entirely on domestic issues – human rights, brutality, corruption – and very little on foreign concerns, including the Palestinian issue. But to the extent that domestic reforms might influence foreign policy, it had always seemed that greater democracy within states would encourage greater moderation in external conflicts.

But this is not an iron law of history. Regimes that are threatened could use the Palestinian issue to deflect anger to the usual target elsewhere, as Saddam Hussein did in 1991. More fundamentally, stronger democracy in the Middle East has often led to more radical, anti-Western or anti-Israel policies, as seen in Algeria and Turkey and in the victory of Hamas in 2006. Arab public opinion has been more sympathetic to the Palestinians than Arab governments that had to deal with realities. Greater democracy has also benefited Islamist parties that had been suppressed. In short, both Israelis and Palestinians had good reason to be apprehensive about what the Arab Spring might bring. Israelis feared the rise of radical Islamism and the sheer chaos of failed states on their borders. Palestinians already faced the challenge of radical Islam, and now added to this the prospect that prolonged unrest in the Arab world would greatly reduce interest in and support for their own struggle.

The threat of radical Islam seemed to be realized with a vengeance when Presidential elections in Egypt, in June 2012, brought to power Muhammad Morsi, leader of the Muslim Brotherhood, of which *Hamas* was formally the Palestinian branch. Despite fears for the survival of the peace treaty between Israel and Egypt, during his year in office Morsi was too preoccupied by immediate problems within Egypt to open up a new conflict on the country's borders. While relations with Israel became strained, the treaty remained in force and there was little change on the border. When Morsi was removed from office by the Egyptian army in July 2013, relations between the two countries returned to their former state and even improved after General Abdel Fattah as-Sisi's new government faced a challenge from Islamic militants in Sinai, close to the Gaza border.

The civil war in Syria, beginning in 2011 and intensifying in the years following, had a number of implications for Israelis and Palestinians. For Israel, Syrian President Bashar al-Assad was an implacable enemy and whatever weakened his regime seemed welcome, but on the other hand Assad was a known quantity and under his tight control the Israel-Syria border had been stable. Whatever followed Assad could conceivably be worse. Thus when the war in Syria was radicalized, with the participation of *Hizballah* forces from Lebanon in support of Assad, and the emergence of the militant Islamic State (ISIS, ISIL, Da'esh) in control of much of northern Syria, alarm bells sounded. The immediate concern was *Hizballah*, and Israeli forces carried out a number of attacks on *Hizballah* weapons convoys and other targets in Syria. Islamic State was not seen as an immediate military threat, but there was concern over its importance as inspiration for other extremists, especially after its triumphant conquest of Mosul in Iraq in June 2014. Cells of adherents appeared throughout the area, including Jordan, Sinai, the West Bank and Gaza, and even within Israel itself.

Palestinians found themselves torn between the opposed forces in Syria. While the Assad regime had supported their cause, Palestinian Islamists were drawn to the Islamist rebels fighting the secularist government. *Hamas* withdrew its headquarters from Damascus and generally supported the anti-Assad movement. *Fatah*, on the other hand, tried to remain neutral in the Syrian struggle in order to maintain strong relations with all parties and maintain unified Arab support for Palestine. Another key component was the presence in Syria of over half a million Palestinian refugees, caught up in the war and also torn between the opposed parties. Whether willing participants or not, many became refugees a second time.

The turmoil of the Arab Spring came on top of the developing divide between *Shi'a*-dominated states and movements, led by Iran, and an axis of Sunni-majority nations including Egypt, Saudi Arabia, Jordan, and the Gulf states. Strategic considerations brought about a measure of convergence between Israel and the Sunni states in dealing with the threat both of Iran and radical Islam (whether *Shi'a* or *Sunni*). Israeli security coordination with Jordan and Egypt reached new levels, according to knowledgeable observers; for obvious reasons, most of this cooperation took place quietly and with minimal publicity. But following the establishment of the Sisi regime in Egypt, there was in particular close cooperation in closing tunnels between Sinai and Gaza, given Egyptian hostility to *Hamas* as an affiliate of the Muslim Brotherhood.

The Second Round in Gaza

Tension between Israel and *Hamas*-controlled Gaza did not subside after the 2008–2009 conflict. A tenuous cease-fire held but did not end sporadic rocket attacks from Gaza on nearby Israeli towns and cities, if not by *Hamas* then by other radical groups. In response Israeli forces tried to hit the launch sites and other military targets, mostly by air strikes, with inevitable civilian casualties and damage in the densely populated urban setting. As *Hamas* (and other Palestinians) saw it, Israel was still occupying Gaza since it still controlled its land and sea frontiers as well as its air space. In this perspective, attacks on nearby Israeli targets were a legitimate response against the occupation in general, but even more pointedly against the illegal blockade that Israel had imposed on all movement in and out of Gaza. Israel's response was that the blockade was a legitimate sanction against a regime that had seized power illegally – in fact the UN report on the Mavi Marmora incident had affirmed as much – and that the rocket attacks were a clear violation of the laws of war since they deliberately targeted civilians.

By early November 2012 the clashes had instensified to the point that over 100 rockets were launched on Israeli targets within a single day. On November 14 Israeli forces targeted and killed Ahmed Jabari, head of the military wing of *Hamas*, and announced the launching of Operation Pillar of Defense, an air campaign that hit more than 1,500 launchpads, weapon depots, command centers and other military targets. In retaliation *Hamas* and other groups in Gaza launched over 1,400 rockets and mortars into Israeli territory. Since they had managed to either smuggle in or copy Iranian missiles, these weapons were more effective than in the previous round of fighting, reaching a number of Israeli cities and as far as Tel Aviv. But as many as 400 were reportedly intercepted by the new Israeli Iron Dome missile defense, while many others fell in uninhabited areas.

After eight days of intense exchanges, a cease-fire was reached through the mediation of the Egyptian government (then under President Morsi's short-lived regime). Despite the demands of both sides for far-reaching conditions for such a cessation of arms, both settled in the end for a simple end of the hostilities with no guarantees that any of these demands would be met. *Hamas* was forced to come to terms with a continued Israeli blockade, while Israel was unable to achieve any changes in the *Hamas* control of Gaza or tighter control on the Egyptian border where the blockade was breached on a massive scale. Both sides nevertheless claimed victory, as is often the case in modern asymmetric ("fuzzy") wars. The Netanyahu government claimed to have substantially crippled the rocket-launching capability of *Hamas*, while *Hamas* leaders could point out that their control of Gaza remained intact and that they had faced down the threat of another Israeli invasion.

The UN estimate for Palestinian casualties was 174, while six Israelis were killed. The low number of Israeli casualties reflected the effectiveness of shelters and alarm systems against rocket fire, success in pre-emptive attacks on launching sites, and the success of the Iron Dome anti-missile system. There was the usual controversy over the number of civilians, as opposed to active fighters, among the Palestinian casualties, with *Hamas* claiming that most of those killed were civilians and Israel asserting that the majority were combatants engaged in acts of war. Part of the difficulty lay, once more, in the nature of such warfare, where the distinction between civilians and soldiers is obscured, sometimes by design. *Hamas* also pointed to the extensive destruction of mosques, hospitals, schools, and other public institutions, while Israeli spokesmen blamed *Hamas* for deliberately locating fighters and launch pads near such buildings in order to discourage attack. Israel also pointed to its efforts to warn civilians to flee an area about to be bombed, in contrast to *Hamas* rocket attacks that deliberately targeted civilians.

The continuing clashes with *Hamas* and the lack of progress on the diplomatic front contributed to a hawkish trend in Israeli opinion. Elections were called in January 2013, shortly after the 2012 Gaza war; the immediate issue was actually a long-simmering battle over the exemption of *yeshiva* (religious seminary) students from military service. In the election a new centrist political party, *Yesh Atid* (There is a Future), exploited the military exemption issue successfully enough to emerge as the second largest party in the Knesset.

Nevertheless, right-wing and religious parties together were able once again to secure a majority, as they had in 2009. Prime Minister Netanyahu's *Likud* ran in an alliance with *Yisrael Beitenu*, a hawkish party supported primarily by immigrants from the former Soviet Union, and remained the largest party. Netanyahu was able to form a government together with centrist parties, for once excluding the religious parties because of commitment to restrict the exemption of religious students from military service. Though this government was potentially more open to peace initiatives, it was in fact still dominated by Netanyahu and his hawkish allies.

The Kerry Initiative

John Kerry, the incoming US Secretary of State in President Barack Obama's second administration, took as one of his first priorities the pursuit of Israeli-Palestinian peace. Kerry made the argument, increasingly heard from other observers as well, that time was limited for a two-state solution. If current trends continued, it was feared, within a very short time it would be impossible to devise a feasible division of the territory between Israel and Palestine. Netanyahu's more centrist coalition could conceivably be more receptive to the concessions needed to get talks started. The key issue was the continuing expansion of Jewish settlements in the West Bank; though formally no entirely new settlements had been established since the early 1990s, new construction in or near existing settlements had proceeded during the years of *Likud* governments and the settler population had grown apace.

Palestinians therefore refused to participate in renewed negotiations until Israel froze new settlement construction; they also stipulated that any negotiation must be based on the pre-1967 armistice lines. This impasse was what had led PA President Abbas to turn to the United Nations and other international bodies in order to gain international recognition and intensify pressure on Israel. But this new Palestinian initiative also furnished the basis for a deal to get negotiations started: the Palestinians would for the moment put off their international campaign, in return for Israeli concessions on settlement building – and, for good measure, the release of a number of Palestinian prisoners held by Israel.

The Israeli government had serious concerns about potential sanctions by international bodies such as the European Union, where the BDS campaign had had some success. Kerry was able, therefore, to secure agreement in July 2013 to renewed negotiations with a compromise along the lines outlined. Israel would not initiate new settlement construction, though it excluded from the bargain construction projects already underway – an exception that invited much dispute later on. The prisoners were to be released in groups over the anticipated nine months that was allotted for the completion of a final settlement. Setting a tight deadline for completion of the talks was at the demand of the Palestinians, who feared Israel would simply drag out the talks. The gradual release of the prisoners was at the insistence of Israeli negotiators, who feared that the PA would simply pocket the prisoner release and abandon serious negotiations.

The talks were carried out over several months in meetings between representatives of the two parties and active US involvement. Leading the Israeli team was Justice Minister Tzipi Livni, leader of the centrist *HaTnu'ah* (The Movement) party and a moderate in the governing coalition. The PA negotiators were led by Sa'eb Erekat, a veteran *Fatah* leader and experienced negotiator in previous talks. As time passed, however, it became apparent that the conclusion of a detailed final settlement in nine months – by April 2014 – was entirely unrealistic. Kerry therefore turned to the idea of a "framework agreement" that would establish the outline of a settlement by that date, leaving the details to be filled in later. The basic outline of this framework seemed clear: two states, 1967 borders with agreed land swaps, Jewish Jerusalem to Israel and Arab Jerusalem to Palestine, an international role for the holy sites, demilitarization of Palestine, most of the refugees to be resettled in Palestine or elsewhere outside Israel. But in truth neither leader completely supported all these points as generally understood, and both remained highly constrained by more radical elements within their own camps (Birnbaum and Tibon 2014).

Netanyahu did reportedly accept the formula of pre-1967 lines with agreed land swaps, as well as unprecedented concessions on the number of refugees to be admitted to Israel. But he had to face vociferous opposition from a party within his coalition, *HaBayit HaYehudi* (The Jewish Home), which represented the interests of Jewish settlers in the West Bank. When Netanyahu seemed to suggest in a public statement that settlers could remain in territory that became part of Palestine, the leader of *HaBayit HaYehudi* – Naftali Bennett – went public with a vicious attack on Netanyahu and the negotiations.

Another thorny issue was the Israeli insistence on having a troop presence in the Jordan Valley over an extended period of time, given fears of Islamic extremists crossing into the West Bank as a base of operations against Israeli targets. Palestinians were inevitably opposed to having Israeli control over their only non-Israeli international border. U.S. proposals to replace a troop presence in the Jordan Valley with sophisticated warning systems encountered the strong opposition of Israeli Defense Minister Moshe Ya'alon, and the problem remained unresolved.

As in previous final status talks, the two sides also remained far apart on arrangements for Jerusalem and on the refugee issue, where the Palestinians had to consider the demand of over five million refugees for an unrestricted "right of return" to their original homes in the state of Israel. As the nine months came to a close, and a snag developed on the release of the final batch of prisoners, the PA demonstrated its distrust of the entire process by dramatically signing all of the UN conventions that it had agreed to put off joining. Efforts to salvage the process were upset by the surprise announcement of a new unity government of *Fatah* and *Hamas*, which clearly would not be an eligible negotiating partner for either Israel or the United States.

Third Round in Gaza: The Gap Widens

Attempts to restore a unified Palestinian government in the West Bank and Gaza had continued sporadically since the *Hamas* take-over of Gaza in 2007. The Cairo "Reconciliation Pact" of May 2011 and the Doha agreement in February 2012 both revolved around promised elections to be held in May 2012. But these agreements, like all other attempted unification efforts, foundered over disagreement about the modalities and control of promised elections that were to be the basis of the unfied government. Neither *Fatah* in the West Bank, nor *Hamas* in Gaza, was ready to risk losing control over its own domain. There was also continuing conflict over the demand of *Hamas* to be incorporated into the PLO – still the recognized representative of all Palestinians – in a position proportional to its numerical strength.

The agreement announced on April 23, 2014, called for a unity government to be established within five weeks and for elections to be held by December. The unity government was duly established with *Fatah*'s Rami Hamdallah continuing as Prime Minister (Salam Fayyad had been forced out in 2013 over policy differences with Abbas). Most of the members of the new cabinet were "technocrats" unaffiliated formally with any party; none were identified with *Hamas*. Nevertheless, the formal partnership with *Hamas* had immediate repercussions for the peace process. The United States and other involved parties expressed concern about the role of *Hamas*, while Prime Minister Netanyahu broke off peace talks with the PA and instituted punitive measures such as halting the transfer of tax revenues collected on behalf of the PA.

In the meantime, little actually changed on the ground. The unity government, although it convened once in Gaza, did not exercise any meaningful authority there, where *Hamas* continued to rule. The planned elections, as before, did not take place as the two sides could not agree on how such elections would be organized and supervised. In November 2014 *Hamas* stated that it no longer recognized the unity government, whose six-month term had expired; nevertheless, the government continued to operate, with periodical reshuffling of cabinet posts, also not recognized by *Hamas*. Negotiations continued in the framework of the 2014 agreement, still considered valid by both sides, but by the end of 2016 had not yet achieved any breakthrough.

In the meantime, the end of the Kerry initiative in 2014 was followed by a quick escalation of violence and a third round of fighting between Israel and *Hamas*. The cease-fire that had ended the previous round in November 2012 held tenuously for about twenty months. There were occasional rocket launches from Gaza into Israel and Israeli responses, but on a low level, and the rocket fire was attributed to more extreme elements in Gaza that *Hamas* could not control. In June 2014, however, three Israeli teenagers were kidnapped and murdered in the West Bank. Israel accused *Hamas* operatives of the crime and carried out a massive operation in the West Bank, arresting several hundred *Hamas* personnel. *Hamas* then openly resumed rocket attacks from Gaza, launching 40 missiles in a single day. The attacks would only end, they announced, when Israel released *Hamas* prisoners and ended the blockade of Gaza.

On July 8 Israel launched Operation Protective Edge, beginning with air and artillery strikes aimed at launch sites and weapon depots. On July 16 Israeli ground troops began a ground offensive, mainly in order to locate and destroy tunnels that *Hamas* had dug under the frontier in order to carry out surprise attacks on Israeli towns and settlements. On August 3 the ground forces were withdrawn, having reportedly destroyed 32 tunnels. Rocket launches and air and artillery fire continued, however, until August 26 when a cease-fire was finally accepted by both sides. As before, the cease-fire did not meet the broader demands of either; there was no end to the Israeli blockade, and the grip of *Hamas* in Gaza was not weakened. While Israel claimed to have destroyed most of the *Hamas* rocket inventory and tunnels, nothing stood in the way of another rebuilding for yet another round in the future.

Since the fighting lasted longer than in the previous two rounds, casualties were also higher. UN figures estimated 2,251 Palestinians killed, 70 percent of them civilians; Israel estimated that no more than half were civilians, illustrating the ambiguities of defining "combatants" in such warfare. On the Israeli side 72 were killed, 66 of them soldiers in the ground campaign. Although *Hamas* and other forces in Gaza launched an estimated 4,500 rocket and mortar attacks during the fighting, only six Israeli civilians were killed as the Iron Dome missile system and other defensive measures again proved effective.

The damage in Gaza was very extensive, with UNRWA estimating that about 30 percent of the population was at least temporarily displaced from their homes. Israeli forces hit over 5,000 targets, many of them located in or near schools, hospitals, public institutions, and residential neighborhoods. Israel accused *Hamas*, as before, of intentionally using such locations as shields for their launch sites, weapon depots, and command centers.

Each side accused the other of war crimes. *Hamas* was charged first of all with the illegal targeting of Israeli civilians, but also with the use of Gaza civilians and civilian structures as shields, forcing civilians to stay in their homes, military use of UN facilities, intimidation of journalists, and killing of protestors and accused collaborators. Given the number of civilian deaths and extensive destruction of homes, Israel was generally accused of disproportionate and undiscriminating use of force, as well as particular attacks on public institutions, UN facilities, and infrastructure, and also the use of human shields. Once again, the waging of "asymmetric war" created challenges to traditional international law that engendered vociferous verbal battles after the guns had fallen silent.

And once again, both sides claimed victory. A poll among Palestinians on both the West Bank and Gaza showed that 79 percent believed that *Hamas*, despite its heavy losses, had won the battle; interestingly, this figure was only 70 percent in Gaza. *Hamas* leader Ismail Haniyeh became the preferred Presidental candidate of 61 percent of those responding, compared to 41 percent in the previous poll (Palestine Center for Policy and Survey Research 2014). An Israeli opinion poll in August, during the war, showed that 92 percent of Israeli Jews believed that the campaign was justified (Tami Steinmetz Center for Peace Research 2014).

Another test of Israeli opinion came in elections called for March 17, 2015, following rising tensions between Prime Minister Netanyahu and his centrist partners in the governing coalition. Netanyahu's *Likud*, through the electoral campaign, trailed a new alliance (the Zionist Union) of Labor with the centrist party *HaTnu'ah*. But by playing to apprehension of a new unified Arab party, Netanyahu was able to pull in voters from other right-wing parties, and *Likud* emerged as the single largest party. Accordingly, the Prime Minister was able to stitch together a narrow right/religious coalition by a tight margin, leaving the centrists in opposition and giving greater influence to the supporters of Jewish settlements in the West Bank.

The new government, with several Ministries headed by leaders of far-right parties, seemed unlikely to pursue actively any diplomatic opening based on the two-state model. Moreover, there were a number of initiatives aimed at delegitimizing the left in Israeli politics. For example, a "Non-Governmental Organizations Transparency Law," after months of vigorous debate, was finally passed in July 2016. The law stipulated that if an NGO operating in Israel received more than half of its funding from foreign sources, it must state this fact in its publications and correspondence. The law was aimed at liberal and dovish civic groups, which tend to be dependent on foreign donations.

Israel's move to the right was reinforced by a wave of violent attacks, mostly within Israel itself, in late 2015 and early 2016. The trigger was tension over the Temple Mount/ Noble Sanctuary, when rumors of impending Jewish designs to change existing arrangements circulated in October 2015. This wave of violence differed considerably from earlier waves, consisting primarily of attacks by individuals wielding knives or other home-made weapons, or driving vehicles into crowds (the "Loners' *intifada*"). Anger mounted at the senselessness of the attacks, in which the assailant was almost always killed or captured on the spot. Palestinians saw the phenomenon as a natural expression of frustration and outrage that could find no other outlet, even though the attacks achieved little beyond creating fear and hostility on the other side. Israelis, however, tended to believe that Palestinian leaders were ultimately responsible for the attacks; 61 percent of Israeli Jews blamed them for the violence in a November 2015 poll (Tami Steinmetz Center for Peace Research 2015).

Various efforts to revive the peace process during 2016 – primarily a French effort to bring the parties together – all fell short. The downward spiral that had begun with the fourth stage of the conflict seemed to be still playing itself out. Waves of violence, and rounds of fighting between Israel and *Hamas*, shared the stage along with announcements of new Jewish settlement construction in the West Bank – presented as merely expansion of existing settlements, but making the demarcation of a border between two states increasingly difficult.

Supporters of the West Bank settlements, enjoying a strong position in the Netanyahu government, also tried to make settlement expansion as irreversible as possible. In February 2017 they pushed through the Israeli Knesset a controversial proposal that would retroactively legalize settlements built on private Palestinian land. This stood in opposition to decisions of the Israeli Supreme Court, which had declared appropriation of private land to be illegal, and had ordered the evacuation of such a settlement. A PA spokesman described the projected law as an attempt to bury the prospect for peace.

At this point the outlook for an end to the downward spiral, in the near future, is grim. But there are many elements in the situation that make a return to negotiation over basic issues seem the most likely outcome – eventually.

First, Oslo is not totally dead. Clearly the Oslo process is moribund for now, and what remains of its vital organs are on critical life support. But it is premature to pronounce eulogies over its corpse. Oslo produced the first mutual recognition between established Israeli and Palestinian leadership. Oslo introduced the first Palestinian self-governance on Palestinian soil. Oslo enabled the second peace treaty between Israel and an Arab neighbor, Jordan, stabilizing the longest international border in the conflict. Oslo led to Israeli withdrawal from southern Lebanon, even if it did not completely stabilize that border. Oslo created ongoing Israel–Palestinian interaction on official and unofficial levels that has continued through all the ups and downs. Oslo shaped a majority on both sides for a two-state solution. And even in its ultimate failure, Oslo engendered the first serious direct negotiations over the basic issues of the conflict.

None of this has been reversed, nor is likely to be. Oslo deserves better than to be treated as the worst four-letter word in Middle East diplomacy.

Second, the common historical pattern is that ideological movements tend to lose their intensity over time. This has been the experience with both religious revivals and secular movements, including Palestinian national movements and, for that matter, Zionism. It seems especially true of movements that succeed in coming to power and then face the realities and pressures of actually governing. Ironically, the goal of non-state actors is precisely to become a state. So will the responsibility of governing serve to moderate *Hamas* over time? Like all such organizations, *Hamas* includes different factions and tendencies: insiders (those living in the West Bank and Gaza) vs. outsiders, political and military wings, pragmatists and ideologues. As with the PLO earlier, the "insiders" on the front line tend to be more pragmatic than the outsiders sitting safely at a distance. Perhaps, as with the PLO, power will shift over time from the outsiders to the insiders.

Subsequent *Hamas* emphasis on Israeli withdrawal from lands occupied in 1967 reminds us of the PLO strategy of "stages" enunciated in 1974, when that organization was midway in its evolution from total rejection to acceptance of a two-state solution. Will *Hamas* follow the path of other actors in the conflict and eventually seek a political, not a military, solution? It has not yet altered its Charter, or even debated doing so – but who would have imagined in 1974 that the PLO would ever do so?

Third, although support has slipped in recent years, half of both Palestinians and Israelis continue to support a two-state solution in principle. In a joint poll conducted by Palestinian and Israeli pollsters in August 2016, 51 percent of Palestinians and 53 percent of Israeli Jews continued to support the two-state framework, even while expressing disbelief that such a solution could be achieved in the near future (Palestine Center for Policy and Survey Research 2016b).

How can this be? We have just seen that Hamas won an election and that Israeli politics has moved to the right. Can people be both more hawkish and more dovish at the same time? The answer is yes. When there is a mutually painful stalemate, the two sides will look for a "way out," even while adopting more hawkish poses. In the Israeli case, greater support for rightist parties, on one level, is offset by the move of the entire political spectrum toward greater acceptance of political options that were anathema in an earlier period. There was a time when recognition of the PLO, or acceptance of a Palestinian state, were supported by a tiny minority of Israelis – just as there was a time when the PLO rejected the idea of a Jewish state alongside a Palestinian state.

9

The Impasse that Remains

We were very close, more than ever in the past, to completing an agreement in principle that would have led to the end of the conflict between us and the Palestinians.

Former Israeli Prime Minister Ehud Olmert, January 28, 2011 (YNet News 2011)

The End of the Two-State Solution?

In his annual address before the UN General Assembly in September 2015, PA President Mahmoud Abbas announced that so long as Israel did not observe the Oslo agreements, the PA would no longer be bound by them. As it turned out this did not involve any actual changes in arrangements between the two parties, which continued as before.

But it recalled the many sages and soothsayers who had proclaimed "the death of Oslo," even though the two sides roughly observed these arrangements and accused each other of violating them. But even if the specific terms of Oslo were to become irrelevant, did this mean that the two-state concept was also outmoded?

Increasingly, some observers, particularly on the Palestinian side, argued that the two-state solution was no longer feasible. The expansion of Jewish settlements in the West Bank, the territorial closure of the West Bank and Gaza, the fragmentation of Palestinian-ruled territory, and the *de facto* control over much of Palestinian life by Israel, had reached the point that creation of a truly independent and viable Palestinian state was, in this view, now impossible. Like it or not, the reality of one state was emerging and becoming irreversible. This was of course the acknowledged aim of some on the right in Israel, who seemed to believe that some form of autonomy for Arab residents, together with greatly improved living conditions, would make incorporation of the territories into Israel a viable solution. Needless to say, the vision of a one-state solution in the eyes of Palestinians was diametrically different. Also, most Israelis did not agree; when asked whether they favoured control of the West Bank if it led to a single state without a Jewish majority, 64 percent opposed the idea (Tami Steinmetz Center for Peace Research, 2012).

As noted in Chapter 4, a one-state solution would either be one in which one side dominated the other, or a "binational" state in which power was shared. The prospect of a binational solution will be addressed in Chapter 10. For the moment, it is enough to note that neither side will willingly allow itself to be dominated by the other. Palestinian Arabs will soon, by most projections, constitute a growing majority within Mandatory Palestine (Israel, the West Bank, and Gaza). If so, why would they agree to a subordinate role in a unified state called Israel and defined as a Jewish state?

This very same demographic reality explains why Palestinians might favor the one-state solution, but with a dominant Arab role.

How long would the Jewish state remain Jewish? Edward Said, the prominent Palestinian intellectual, told an Israeli interviewer that "you're going to be a minority anyway . . . The Jews are a minority everywhere . . . They can certainly be a minority in Israel" (Shavit 2000a). This image of demographic submersion seemsed to inspire Palestinian advocacy of a one-state solution, as well as a two-state solution with the right of return to Israel itself for six million refugees, and also the binational model that Said favored.

However, the state of Israel is not going to be submerged or fade away. In fact, by the early twenty-first century Israel had emerged as a success story by most standards. Its Jewish population had increased tenfold since its founding, and it was set to become the home of a majority of the world's Jews within a generation. It was ranked eighteenth in the world on the 2015 Human Development Index, which measures social and economic well-being, and also eighteenth in life expectancy (United Nations 2015). It was first in the world in the percentage of the population with university degrees and in scientists and scientific papers *per capita*, and had more mobile telephones than people – reflecting the fact that half of its exports were in high technology. Clearly Israel was here to stay – as were the Palestinians, whose population growth was higher and whose economy was beginning to surpass others in the region. Only a two-state solution, it can be argued, can adequately encompass the reality of two societies pursuing successful but separate paths of development. It is not by chance that all serious diplomacy on Israeli-Palestinian issues, in the last three decades, has been based on the two-state model.

References to demographic submersion reinforce existing Israeli apprehensions about any settlement concluded on a "land for peace" basis. Israel would be surrendering tangible assets in return for intangible commitments regarding future behavior. This is the problem of "the day after": What happens after a Palestinian state is established in the West Bank and Gaza? Will it in fact be "the end of the conflict," or will the Palestinian state serve as a base for further demands and threats? The post-1967 focus on the issue of Israeli occupation obscured the fact that for Palestinians there were two sets of issues: the "1967 file," of primary relevance to non-refugee Palestinians in the West Bank and Gaza, and the "1948 file," still the primary focus of Palestinian refugees everywhere. Historically, the PLO's base of support was in the refugee camps, particularly in Syria and Lebanon, where the focus was on the 1948 file, and the aim was defined as the destruction of Israel. Only the elimination of Israel, it was reasoned, would enable refugees to exercise their unqualified right of return. But for the residents of the West Bank and Gaza, getting rid of the occupation was a more immediate concern, and the two-state solution was therefore a more thinkable option. As the "insiders" gained ground within the Palestinian community and in the PLO – they were, after all, the ones on the front lines – their agenda came to dominate, and support for a negotiated solution grew. Even during the angriest days of the second *intifada*, this constituency remained fairly intact.

Criticisms of the "militarization" of the *intifada*, and of suicide attacks on Israeli civilians in particular, were voiced by some Palestinian leaders almost from the outset. At the same time, most of the Palestinian public voiced support for these attacks. Rashid Khalidi, editor of the *Journal of Palestine Studies*, explained such support as a result of "the absence of any voices positing an alternative strategy, combined with popular anger over the deaths of more than 1,500 Palestinians, most of them civilians, since the *intifada* began, and the unending intensification of Israeli settlement activity and of its evil twin, the Israeli military occupation, over the entire eleven-year period of the Madrid–Oslo 'peace process'." However, as Khalidi explained to a West Bank audience in mid-2002, this did not mean that attacks on civilians within Israel was in the Palestinian interest:

> It is hard to explain how such attacks could be seen as furthering the achievement of the national objectives that a majority of Palestinians still support, notably the creation of a Palestinian state alongside Israel. What is clear, however, is that they led directly to Israel's invasion of West Bank cities and towns in March and April 2002, making the creation of such a state more distant . . .
>
> However, revenge is not a strategy, and anger is no substitute for a rational calculation of the balance of forces. (R. Khalidi 2002: 7)

Sooner or later, the interests of Israelis and Palestinians, majority public support for negotiations on both sides, pressures from outside parties, and the realities on the ground were bound to bring the two sides to the table. When negotiation resumed, the experience of previous talks would inevitably serve as a point of reference. While it was avowed repeatedly that proposals or concessions made during these transactions were not binding, concessions once made are difficult to retrieve and unfailingly shape expectations on the other side. Furthermore, neither the basic world view nor the bargaining leverage of either side would be significantly different, and therefore previous experience remained a good predictor of how future talks would proceed.

With the help of these accounts, and building on the earlier negotiating experiences, we now turn to an examination of where Israelis and Palestinians stand on the basic issues of the conflict. Can we see, even if dimly, the likely contours of a future agreement?

Territory and Settlements

The dominant model for resolution of the conflict between Jews and Arabs over *Eretz Yisrael/Filastin* is the model of two states within the borders set by the British Mandate: Israel and Palestine, each sovereign and serving as a homeland for its respective people, with a clear border between them – in other words, partition. Partition accords with the dominant paradigm of the nation-state in today's international system; it gives each people a place to call its own and a haven to which its persecuted brethren can retreat; and it puts squarely on each party the responsibility for governing or misgoverning itself. But it requires, as a first step, a territorial definition: is it possible to draw a line between the two sides that will meet the minimal requirements of justice and will not itself become a source of instability?

Despite strong support for partition, there remains strong opposition to it on both sides. In Israel, opponents of partition include settlers, religious nationalists, and secular nationalists motivated by religious visions, nationalist ideologies, historical arguments, security concerns, and simple distrust of Palestinians. Often these motivations are mixed together, although over time security issues and distrust of Palestinian intentions have come to dominate. As indicated in the polling data, some 30–40 percent of the Israeli public share these views.

Among Palestinians, Islamic fundamentalists clearly oppose partition, since they oppose the existence of a Jewish state in the center of the Islamic world. There are likewise factions on the left who continue to espouse a "secular, democratic Palestinian state" in all of Palestine. But the most notable recent trend is the revival of support for a binational state, now favored by as many as 30 percent, making it the second favorite solution behind the two-state, partition model (favored by some 45–55 percent, with most of those remaining presumably advocating an undivided Islamic or Arab state).

What this tells us is that any final territorial division will face entrenched opposition on both sides, and that a final settlement based on partition will have to be accompanied by a strategy for dealing with, and if necessary neutralizing, the extremists who will try to sabotage it. But assuming that a majority on both sides continue to support partition of historic Palestine as a framework for ending the conflict, what line of division is likely? And what will happen to the Jewish settlements in the West Bank and Gaza?

The 1949 armistice agreements between Israel and its neighbors emphasized that the post-war lines between Israel and the West Bank/Gaza were not political borders, but only armistice lines. Nevertheless, these lines – the "Green Line," the "pre-1967 borders" – became the basic territorial point of reference, and over time acquired legitimacy as the likely basis for any final territorial settlement. When Israel took over the rest of Palestine in 1967, it was the areas beyond these lines, and only those areas, that were defined as "occupied territories" by most observers, including most Arabs and Palestinians. And when Israel and the PLO agreed on a territorial framework at the Taba talks, it was that the June 4, 1967, lines would be the "basis" for the border. This also held true in the 2007–8 talks and in the Kerry Initiative of 2013–14.

At Camp David, Israel proposed that it annex about 12 percent, later reduced to nine percent, of the West Bank in order to incorporate most of the Jewish settlers. At Taba, the final Israeli plan asked for six percent of the West Bank, with half of that annexation offset by a land swap. This would have given the Palestinian state the equivalent of 97 percent of the West Bank (and 100 percent of the Gaza Strip); the gap between the two sides was only three percent. Israel would have needed to dismantle most of the Jewish settlements in the West Bank and all of them in Gaza, but the six percent annexation would presumably put 80 percent of the settlers on the Israeli side of the line, since the suburban-style settlements close to the Green Line actually contain the bulk of the West Bank settlers. Only 20 percent of the settlers (about 63,800) would have to be relocated (Makovsky and Benedek 2003). With a bypass road around Jerusalem, the Palestinian state would have territorial contiguity in the West Bank, which would be connected to the Gaza Strip by a "safe passage."

Some Israeli observers concerned with demography have suggested that any territorial swap might include some of the Israeli Arab communities located near the Green Line. This would reduce the number of Palestinians forced to live as a minority in Israel, but without any actual physical relocation. The areas most often mentioned are the "Little Triangle" and Umm al-Fahm regions on the west and northwest borders of the West Bank. It is not clear that the residents of these areas would actually favor being annexed to the Palestinian state, but proponents argue that they could at least be given the option in an open and free referendum.

Regarding territorial issues, Palestinians point out once again that in joining the Oslo process they conceded the existence of Israel within the 78 percent of Palestine bounded by the 1949 armistice lines. Consequently, they should not be expected to accept less than the full 22 percent remaining to them in a West Bank/Gaza state. Since Jewish settlements in the occupied territories are and always have been illegal under the Geneva Conventions to which Israel is a party, these settlements should be dismantled in any event, and without being traded off for other assets. If there are to be any agreed changes in the lines of June 4, 1967, they should be exchanges of territory of equal size and value. In addition, such changes must not further break up the contiguity of the new Palestine, which is already broken into two pieces (Israeli proposals at Camp David would have further divided the West Bank into four separate enclaves). Finally, Israeli territorial demands based on supposed security needs are largely fallacious; with the change in warfare to threats of terrorism or missile attack, the security value of a few kilometers of land in the West Bank or Gaza is nil.

When negotiations resumed in 2007–8, Olmert eliminated the "three percent gap" between West Bank territory that Israel sought to annex and the extent of land offered in exchange. For 6.3 percent of the West Bank, Israel offered the equivalent of 5.8 percent in land contiguous to it or to the Gaza strip, plus a 25-mile tunnel to connect the West Bank and Gaza. Furthermore, there were hints that the 6.3 percent might be reduced to 5.9 percent. The PA countered with an offer of an equal land swap of 1.9 percent, adequate in its view to bring 60 percent of the settlers within Israeli territory. The gap now was over the absolute size of the land swap, not net gain or loss, and the difference involved three of the larger Israeli settlements that, Palestinians said, would seriously interfere with their territorial contiguity: Ariel in the center, Ma'aleh Adumim east of Jerusalem, and Efrat south of Jerusalem, with Ariel as the main sticking point. And here matters remained; at their last meeting on September 16, 2008, Abbas copied Olmert's map on a napkin, but there were no further negotiations. Abbas apparently expected bridging proposals from the United States, but matters were overtaken by Israel's political crisis.

Subsequent efforts at a Washington think tank have produced maps with land swaps in the 4–5 percent range that would put up to 80 percent of Jewish settlers on the Israeli side of the new border (Makovsky et al. 2011). Negotiations since that time, including the Kerry initiative, have according to available evidence played out along these lines (Birnbaum and Tibon 2014). Putting 80 percent of the Jewish settlers inside Israel would require the inclusion of the major settlement blocs around Ariel, Ma'aleh Adumin, and Efrat, something very hard for Palestinians to accept.

The territorial issue is dominated, as this shows, by the question of Israeli settlements: Israel's efforts to include as many as possible on the Israeli side of the border, and the question of what happens to those that, for all that, end up on the Palestinian side.

Israeli settlements in the West Bank and Gaza developed in three different phases, each with its own motivations and ethos. In the first years after the 1967 war, Israel's Labor government sponsored or authorized settlements of two sorts: (1) where Jewish settlements had existed before 1948 but had been conquered and destroyed, such as the Jewish Quarter in Jerusalem and the Etzion bloc south of Jerusalem; and (2) where strategic considerations dominated, as on the Golan Heights, in the Jordan Valley, and on the Egyptian border in Gaza. During the decade ending in the Labor defeat in 1977, the total number of such settlers was about 4,000.

The second phase of settlement began on a small scale under Labor rule, and often in conflict with it. It consisted of settlers with strong ideological and religious commitments to resettling the land, typically in the heart of the West Bank, where it would be more difficult to "disentangle" the two populations and reverse the settlement process. These settlements included Kiryat Arba adjacent to Hebron and Jewish enclaves near the major Palestinian cities of Ramallah, Nablus, and Jenin. After 1977 the new *Likud* government gave strong support to such committed groups, and by 1982 there were over 21,000 settlers. The third phase began in the 1980s, as the number of ideologically motivated settlers dwindled and the government began building "bedroom communities" just across the Green Line, within easy commuting distance of Tel Aviv and Jerusalem. By offering suburban-style homes at a heavily subsidized price, the enterprise attracted larger numbers of settlers, and the total grew to 115,000 by 1993 and approximately 296,000 in 2010 in the West Bank alone (not including new neighborhoods within the Jerusalem municipal borders). The "quality of life" settlers, those in the third category, probably account for about three-quarters of this total, against roughly 20–25 percent who cite religious or ideological motives for living in the West Bank and Gaza (Ha'aretz 2003). At the end of 2015 the number of Jewish settlers in the West Bank had grown to 406,302, not including East Jerusalem neighborhoods, according to the Population Registry of Israel's Ministry of the Interior (Inside Israel 2016).

Since the early 1990s there has been a freeze on the creation of new settlements, but this has not stopped the "natural growth" of existing settlements. In fact, the number of settlers doubled during this period, despite the peace process and the freeze on new settlements. For Palestinians, this was evidence of an Israeli intention – even under Labor governments – to consolidate the Israeli presence in the occupied territories and prevent the emergence of a Palestinian state. It led to the cantonization of the West Bank and the creation of limits to Palestinian movement in order to guarantee the safe movement of the growing settler population. It was also a violation of the basic principle of equality before the law, since Israeli settlers in the territories were still Israeli citizens and fell under Israeli law, while the Palestinians were still subject to military rule.

In response, Israeli defenders of the settlements argued that they were not illegal since Israel was (so far) the only successor state to Mandatory Palestine, that Jewish settlement developed at a time when Arabs refused to negotiate, that Jews should not be barred from living in any area of their historic homeland, and that just as there were Arabs in Israel, there could be Jews living in a Palestinian state (Halkin 2002). This last argument hypothesized that if a two-state solution were implemented, many Jewish settlers would be willing to live under Palestinian authority and would be able to do so peacefully; the troubled relationship of many settlers with their Arab neighbors raised doubts about this scenario.

Looking more closely at geographical patterns, one survey divided the settlements into eight categories (Remez 2000):

1 Settlements in the Gaza Strip, in the heart of a densely populated Palestinian area (evacuated in 2005).
2 Settlements in the West Bank that are in the heart of a densely populated Palestinian area or close to it.
3 Settlements surrounded by Palestinian towns.
4 Settlements deep within the West Bank.
5 Jordan Valley settlements.
6 Settlements that break the contiguity of Palestinian areas.
7 Gush Etzion (south of Jerusalem).
8 Settlements adjacent to the Green Line.

Projecting from past negotiations, it is categories (7) and (8) – Gush Etzion and the settlements adjacent to the Green Line – that will constitute the minimal territorial change that any Israeli government is likely to push for. To this most Israeli proposals have added the Ariel and Ma'aleh Adumim blocs.

The other settlements in the first six categories, to judge from the course of negotiations, would revert to the Palestinian state. Assuming that most settlers in these categories choose to relocate rather than live in Palestine, this would make available to the new Palestinian state a large number of homes that could be used to resettle 1948 refugees. But could the evacuation of settlers be carried out peacefully? The majority of settlers who moved across the Green Line for "quality of life" reasons would presumably be open to compensation and equivalent housing elsewhere. But the more ideologically committed settlers, who also tend to be those in the heart of the West Bank who would clearly not be annexed to Israel, represent a different problem. Pessimists have evoked images of widespread violence, and even civil war, should forced evacuation be attempted.

Surveys of the settlers themselves suggest that the problem may not be that severe. Similar threats were heard when the settlement of Yamit, in Sinai, was forcibly evacuated with the return of the territory to Egypt in 1982 and when Gaza was evacuated in August 2005; in the end, both evacuations were carried out quickly and without casualties. In a 2002 survey sponsored by the dovish movement Peace Now – but carried out by neutral survey institutes – 68 percent of the settlers said they would respect a democratic decision to withdraw; 26 percent said they would fight such a decision by legal means but would comply in the end; six percent said they would fight the decision by extralegal means; but only two percent said that they would resort to arms in order to fight evacuation. In the final analysis, "the settlers, with the exception of a very small extremist minority, will not be an obstacle to a peace agreement" (Shragai 2002).

Jerusalem

Jerusalem seems to encapsulate all of the ethereal dimensions that give the Arab–Israel conflict an aura of enigma and intractability. It is a territorial issue, but it is not just about territory. The city is holy to the three Abrahamic faiths, and therefore attracts international interest as other Arab–Israeli issues do not. Given the passions that religion can arouse, many assume that Jerusalem is the hardest nut to crack among the final status issues, and will fall into place only after all other issues have been settled. Negotiators do not always have the luxury, however, of indefinitely postponing hard issues, and in the final status talks they actually made progress in demystifying the concrete issues involved.

After all, Jerusalem is not a religious museum, but a living city of about three-quarters of a million people. Most of this growth is relatively recent; only 150 years ago, Jerusalem was only the walled Old City – today about one percent of the city – with some 15,000–20,000 inhabitants. The British made Jerusalem the capital of Mandatory Palestine, and it grew from about 65,000 to 165,000 during the Mandate. In 1948 the city was divided between Israeli forces and the Arab Legion of Transjordan, which captured the Old City. Transjordan annexed the West Bank, including East Jerusalem and the Old City, and renamed itself Jordan, though only Britain and Pakistan recognized the annexation. Israel reunified the city in the 1967 war, and greatly expanded its borders; the population was then about 263,000, three-quarters Jewish.

The Temple Mount, *Haram ash-Sharif* or Noble Sanctuary to Muslims, might be described as the focal point of the Arab–Israel conflict. It is a rectangular platform of about 45 acres, occupying the southeast corner of the Old City. For Jews it is the site of the First and Second Temples, while today it holds two of the most important mosques in Islam, *Al-Aqsa* and the Dome of the Rock. In Arabic, Jerusalem is known as *al-Quds*, the Holy City, and only Mecca and Medina are considered more sacred. The area of the Noble Sanctuary has been administered by a Muslim religious trust, or *waqf*; Israel made no change in this arrangement after 1967. Jews have traditionally prayed at the Western Wall, on the outside of one of the retaining walls of the compound; after 1967 this area was cleared and made into a major religious site. Friction was minimized by the fact that religious Jews obeyed a rabbinical injunction not to enter the Temple Mount.

Also within the Old City, the Jewish Quarter, which had been evacuated in 1948, was rebuilt and reoccupied. New Jewish neighborhoods were built to the north, east, and south of Arab neighborhoods in East Jerusalem, as part of the policy of incorporating an undivided Jerusalem into Israel. But Arab Jerusalem is also the logical capital of any Palestinian state that might be created, making the city into a focal point, if not the focal point, of the conflict. All Israeli governments, Labor or *Likud*, vowed that Jerusalem within its post-1967 borders, which included most Arab neighborhoods, would remain the undivided capital of Israel, and that the Temple Mount would remain under Israeli rule. Palestinians were equally insistent that Arab Jerusalem, and above all the Noble Sanctuary, could not be ceded to Israel. The future of the city was deemed to be the most difficult and intractable of all the final status issues.

Israelis stressed the historical uniqueness of Jerusalem to Jews: for 3,000 years it has been the only capital that Jews have ever had. They also pointed out that the city had had a Jewish majority since the middle of the nineteenth century, according to available records. Furthermore, Israeli rule promised free access to all holy sites, in contrast to the exclusion of Jews from the Old City and the Western Wall when Jordan ruled there. Undivided Jerusalem since 1967, they argued, had undeniably flourished and expanded, as seen in the population figures. Arabs in Jerusalem would receive the same full civil rights as other Arab citizens of Israel, and Arab neighborhoods in Jerusalem could also be given considerable autonomy.

In the Taba talks, there was agreement that Arab neighborhoods, including the Muslim and Christian Quarters of the Old City, would become part of Palestine. The Jewish Quarter and the Western Wall would be Israeli. The fate of the Temple Mount/Haram ash-Sharif was not resolved, but the clear tendency was to accept President Clinton's proposal for continued Islamic administration of the area, with some recognition of the Jewish historical link. (Various suggestions were floated on the knotty issue of sovereignty over the site: either giving Palestinians sovereignty over the area above ground and Israel over that below – or, more sublimely, assigning sovereignty to God.)

The Clinton parameters – Arab neighborhoods to Palestine, Jewish neighborhoods to Israel – also served as the point of departure in the 2007–8 talks. Abbas balked, however, at conceding the newest Jewish neighborhood, *Har Homa*, overlooking the main road south from Jerusalem to Bethlehem. Negotiators also wrestled with the novel concept of a "Holy Basin," an area encompassing the historical core of the city that would be put under joint custody of Israel, Palestine, the United States, Jordan, Saudi Arabia and possibly one or two other parties. The holy sites within this area would remain under the control of the respective religious bodies, in accord with the prevailing *status quo*. But the two sides disagreed in delineating the Holy Basin: the PA sought to limit this internationalized administration to the Old City, while Israel proposed a broader area including the Mount of Olives (site of an ancient Jewish cemetery) and the "City of David," the original site of ancient Jerusalem outside present-day city walls. This broader definition would have removed sizeable

Arab neighborhoods from Palestinian jurisdiction, and therefore PA negotiators opposed it.

Given the fact that Israel has not challenged Muslim administration on the Temple Mount/Noble Sanctuary since gaining physical control in 1967, it seems unlikely that it would get the other side's consent to dilute this control as part of final status talks. The recognition of a Jewish link, to judge from proposals being discussed, might take the form of identifying an area on the Mount where Jews would be permitted to pray. But any formal surrender of Jewish claims to the site will arouse strong opposition within Israel, primarily but not exclusively from the religious public. It is not clear that Barak could have gained majority approval of the agreement on Jerusalem towards which the Taba talks seemed headed, or that Olmert's agreement to joint administration of the Old City would have been accepted back home. In any future talks, considerable care will have to be taken in dealing with the symbolic and formalistic issues of sovereignty and rights of access.

Palestinians, on the other hand, point out that Jerusalem has been a dominantly Arab and Muslim city since the seventh century, with the exception of the Crusader interlude. It is also, in modern terms, the natural linchpin of a Palestinian state, at its geographic center and dominating its economic and cultural life; without Jerusalem, there could be no viable Palestinian state. Recent Israeli efforts to separate Arab Jerusalem from the West Bank, by repeated closures and other measures, only underscore this point; they have inflicted tremendous hardships on both Jerusalemites and non-Jerusalemites. Israeli opinion also understands this connection, clearly regarding Arab East Jerusalem as a part of the West Bank (R. Khalidi 2001; Segal 1997).

By accepting eleven new Jewish neighborhoods built in territory conquered by Israel in 1967, Palestinians feel that they have conceded all that could reasonably be expected. The intertwining of Jewish and Arab neighborhoods on the post-1967 map will make the drawing of new lines of division a very tricky proposition, but it is one that will have to be faced sooner or later. With enough geographic and geometric imagination, it should be possible to connect the enclaves on both sides so as to secure reasonable contiguity. To this can be added the concept of an "open city," which would make normal life possible despite the intricate lines between the two communities.

During the 2013–14 talks of the Kerry initiative, Jerusalem was apparently discussed only in general terms. Palestinians again made it clear that the capital of a Palestinian state could only be East Jerusalem; Israeli negotiators resisted, willing at that stage only to refer to Palestinians' "aspirations" for a capital in Jerusalem (Lehrs 2016).

Security Issues

Given the absence of trust or mutual confidence between the parties, much of the negotiation over an Israeli–Palestinian settlement will inevitably revolve around its military and strategic impact on the ground. Ideally, each side will feel more secure than it did before the agreement; otherwise, what is the incentive to negotiate? If the new arrangement at best provides the existing level of security, why not stay with the *status quo*, which is more familiar and less unpredictable? Israelis often point out that they are being asked to surrender tangible advantages (usually land) in return for intangible commitments (a pledge of peaceful behavior), with very little in the way of guarantee or enforcement. Since they tend to be risk-averse, and since they see the entire Arab world as a potential threat, they push for strong security provisions in any agreement.

Palestinians challenge the Israeli perspective, pointing to their own weakness and vulnerability against Israeli military might. Palestine, not Israel, is the threatened party in their view. With a total armed force of more than 700,000 troops (including reserves), with state-of-the-art weaponry and one of the world's finest air forces, Israel ranks at least as a regional power and, soldier for soldier, as one of the most effective fighting forces anywhere. Palestinians have no army, no heavy weapons, no tanks, no air force, and no real defense against Israeli forces and weapons; they have only a lightly armed police force. Israel can act in Palestinian areas at will, as it has done. It is Palestinians who need protection.

Palestinian forces are not even adequate, it is argued, for keeping internal order in Palestinian areas – something that Israel wants these forces to do, in theory. But while Israel constantly condemns the Palestinian Authority for not preventing hostile actions by extremists against Israeli targets, it also attacked the infrastructure of the PA throughout the second *intifada* and weakened its ability to act.

Palestinians contend that in order to be viable, a Palestinian state must be able to fulfill the basic function of any sovereign state: to ensure domestic order and to defend itself. It must have control of its own borders and airspace. It must be free from the arbitrary intervention of the Israeli army. All this is, after all, an inseparable part of the basic right of selfdetermination. Such a state would not be a threat to Israel; there is simply no way that a Palestinian state could match Israel. In any event, Palestine would be focused on the many problems of building a new nation, not on quixotic campaigns against a more powerful Israel. Israeli concern about security threats from a Palestinian state are so overdrawn that they can only be an excuse for continued domination.

Furthermore, Palestinian spokesmen argue, the tremendous gap in conventional military capability is reinforced by the elephant in the living room whose presence is not mentioned in polite society. Israel has possessed nuclear weapons since the 1970s, and clearly has by now accumulated a significant stockpile (Cohen 1998, 2010). Experts believe that it also possesses chemical, and possibly biological, weapons. The official Israeli policy is that "Israel will not be the first to introduce nuclear weapons into the Middle East." Such a stance is consistent with a policy of reserving such weapons for "last resort" circumstances, in the unlikely contingency that Israel was losing a conventional war and was in imminent danger of being destroyed. In the final analysis, no Arab government would push Israel to this point, even if it could; in the last major Arab–Israeli war, 1973, for example, the war aims of Egypt and Syria were strictly limited. The threat of weapons of mass destruction (WMD) is one reason, and probably a sufficient reason, that Arab governments and most

Palestinians have *de facto* abandoned any thought of eliminating Israel as an operational objective.

In fact, as the threat of defeat in a conventional war with Arab states receded, the strategic rationale of Israel's nuclear deterrent shifted dramatically – a development that occasioned surprisingly little discussion, given the muted character of public debate on the topic. It is no longer imminent invasion by a conquering army that Israel's nuclear force serves to block, but rather the threat of unconventional weapons – nuclear, chemical, or biological – in the hands of a hostile (and suicidal?) enemy. This is what nuclear strategists have termed minimal deterrence: using WMD to deter the threat of the other side's WMD, a deterrence in kind rather than the threat of a nuclear response ("first use") to a conventional threat. In theory minimal deterrence makes for a more stable balance, provided neither side fears a surprise attack ("first strike") that would wipe out its own weapons of mass destruction. It could also furnish a better foundation for arms control or disarmament agreements, since the weapons are there only to block similar weapons elsewhere.

The proliferation of weapons of mass destruction in the Middle East has been a reality for some time; it is assumed that several states in the region possess chemical weapons. Such weapons were already a part of the equation between Israel and Syria, for example, and in 1991 Israelis feared that Scud missiles launched on its cities from Iraq might carry chemical warheads. That they did not may have been because of Iraqi fear of Israeli nuclear retaliation. In other words, a Middle East "balance of terror" already exists.

The focus now is, of course, on the threatened development of an Iranian bomb. This has put pressure on Israel to guarantee the "second-strike capability" of its nuclear force: the capacity to survive a surprise attack and strike back at the attacker. One way of achieving this capability is by deploying nuclear-armed missiles on submarines. Israel has five German-built Dolphin submarines, with a sixth on order, each equipped to launch eight missiles. At any given time one or more of these submarines could be deployed south of Suez, in the Persian Gulf region.

How can the security needs of Palestinians be met? Many Palestinians favor the deployment of an international peace-keeping force to stabilize any agreement, and more particularly to discourage arbitrary Israeli intervention in Palestinian territory. The fact that Israel has often opposed such measures is taken by Palestinians as the natural desire of a stronger party to maintain its freedom to intervene. In the Palestinian view, the international community should show more determination in backing up its own decisions, as embodied in UN resolutions, that call for a two-state solution. An international presence between the two sides would deter Israeli violations of an agreement and give Palestinians a chance to build their own state and society.

The Israeli view is of course quite different. Israelis do not see themselves as being so powerful, but still feel quite vulnerable. For one thing, they remind the outside world, they face not only Palestinians but, potentially, the entire Arab world (outnumbering Israelis by about 50 to 1) or even the entire Muslim world (roughly 250 to one in population). The neighboring states alone possess armed forces about eight times as large as Israel's forces, with a three-to-one advantage in airplanes and tanks. Israel is also vulnerable geographically, with most of its population in the coastal plain area, which at one point is only about nine miles wide from the Green Line to the Mediterranean. In any agreement Israel would be surrendering very real and concrete military advantages for promises of future behavior; if there were to be another general war, obviously Israelis would prefer to fight it from current positions.

But security is more than a question of winning full-scale wars. Israelis emphasize the importance of "current" or "personal" security: being able to go about one's daily life without fear of assault or attack. Few Israelis have this sense of security; in 2003, 83 percent expressed worry that they or a member of their family would fall victim to a terrorist attack (Arian 2003: 19). In relation to population size, the killing of 60 Israelis in terrorist attacks is the equivalent of the September 11, 2001, World Trade Center in the United States; in one month alone during the second *intifada*

(March 2002), Israel suffered the equivalent of two World Trade Center attacks. So long as extremists are allowed to operate, the problem of terrorism will remain a major, and perhaps insuperable, problem. Restoration of the Green Line, or something close to it, as the border between Israel and Palestine, would add to the difficulty of preventing terror across the border by providing bases close to Israeli population centers. In addition, this border is about 15 miles from the center of Tel Aviv and less than one mile from the center of Jewish Jerusalem; roughly 75 percent of Israel's population are within artillery range from the Palestinian side.

Furthermore, Israelis argue, the PA has not demonstrated the ability or the will to suppress attacks from its territory. To the contrary, PA violation of arms limitations seems to indicate an intention to build as much military capability as possible. It is the basic responsibility of any sovereign state to prevent attacks on neighbors from its own territory; Egypt, Jordan, and even Syria have in recent years met this standard. If the PA aspires to the privileges of statehood, it is reasonable to expect that it would also fulfill this responsibility.

In the meantime, for Israel the key security measure is a demilitarization of the Palestinian state being created. If this state is indeed no longer planning for the ultimate elimination of Israel, then its military forces should be limited to those arms necessary to maintain internal order, including the suppression of violent extremists. Major offensive weapons systems are not required for this purpose, and should be voluntarily relinquished. As for this being a negation of Palestinian sovereignty, a number of states in the modern world have agreed to measures of demilitarization without loss of status or prestige: Germany, Austria, Japan, and – closer to home – Egypt in the demilitarization of Sinai. Demilitarization would include a commitment not to allow the entry of forces from other states, as in the Israel–Jordan treaty.

Israel has also asked for early warning stations on Palestinian territory, at least for a specified period of time, and for use of Palestinian airspace for training and reconnaissance. These issues remain to be worked out. As for the stationing of international forces, Israel has agreed to the presence of peacekeeping forces on its borders with Syria and Egypt, where these forces have performed a useful monitoring and verification role in the context of agreements that both sides have a strong interest in observing. In the case of an equally credible Israeli–Palestinian treaty, Israelis would tend to favor an international presence – both forces and formal guarantees – that would reinforce the agreement. What Israelis see as less than useless, in their view, is an international force that shields the covert actions of terrorists while inhibiting overt Israeli responses (as happened in the past, for example, in Lebanon).

In light of the differing perspectives, it is remarkable that in the 2007–8 negotiations between Abbas and Olmert the two sides came closer to final agreement on security issues than in any other area. Abbas accepted the principle of a demilitarized Palestinian state, with a strong police force but no army or air force. No foreign army would be allowed to enter Palestinian territory, and the Palestinian-Jordanian border would be patroled by an international force, probably from NATO, under US command. All in all, "the file on security was closed" (Avishai 2011). However, it was opened again during the Kerry initiative talks, when Israel pressed a demand for the stationing of Israeli forces in the Jordan Valley, as a defense against infiltration, and PA negotiators refused to accept the loss of control over their major non-Israeli border (Birnbaum and Tibon 2014).

Refugees

The most difficult remaining issue in Israeli–Palestinian peace negotiations is probably not Jerusalem, as difficult as that is, but rather the perennial question of the Palestinian refugees of 1947–9 and their descendants. A close look at the three sets of peace talks indicates that less progress was made on this front than any other. The refugees themselves, opposing any compromise of their absolute right of return to pre-1948 homes in Israel, express fear that Palestinian negotiators, focused on 1967 occupation issues, might trade away their rights (Kifner 2000). In some ways, the initial positions of the two sides were frozen in time, having been set in absolutist terms soon after 1949, then seldom examined and never negotiated in the years since. After 50 or more years of immobility, it was fanciful to imagine that a few months of face-to-face talks would bridge the gap.

The causes of the refugee flight were discussed in chapter 4: among Arabs in areas captured or threatened by Israeli forces, some fled, some were expelled, and some remained (the present Arab citizens of Israel). Those who fled or were expelled gathered in refugee camps in the West Bank, Gaza Strip, Lebanon, Syria, and Jordan (then Transjordan), and the United Nations Relief and Works Agency (UNRWA) was established to provide for their basic needs. Unlike the United Nations High Commissioner for Refugees, who deals with all other refugees in the world, UNRWA is not mandated to find solutions other than repatriation, since Palestinian refugees rejected any solution other than a return to their homes.

The original refugee population of an estimated 700,000–750,000 has grown to 5,266,603 refugees registered with UNRWA in 2015 (United Nations Relief and Works Agency 2015). About 41 percent of the refugees live in Jordan, where they comprise about a third of the population; another 40 percent are in the West Bank and Gaza, 11 percent are in Syria, and 9 percent in Lebanon. In the West Bank refugees constitute about one-third of the population, and in Gaza over 80 percent, far outnumbering the original Gazan residents. Palestinians assert that there are another 1–2 million unregistered refugees in locations not served by UNRWA; Israelis claim that all of these figures are inflated for political and practical reasons.

In the Palestinian view, the right to return to one's country is a basic principle of international law, and therefore the refugees have this right regardless of what the UN does or doesn't do. However, in this case the UN has also added its affirmation of the specific right of Palestinians to return to their homes, in the framework of UN General Assembly Resolution 194 of December 11, 1949, which states that refugees wishing to return to their homes and live at peace with their neighbours should be permitted to do so at the earliest practicable date, and that compensation should be paid for the property of those choosing not to return and for loss of or damage to property which, under principles of international law or in equity, should be made good by the Governments or authorities responsible.

Palestinians stress that in this resolution it is the refugees who are to choose between return or compensation, not the state of Israel. Furthermore, in their view, the mention of "the earliest practicable date" makes it clear that this repatriation is not dependent on other events; it should be implemented independently and quickly.

The refugees, and particularly those in the squalid refugee camps, were the historic base of support for the PLO. Thus the PLO always put the refugee issue high on its agenda, and – since the return of all refugees was hardly possible otherwise – remained committed until recently to the destruction of Israel. Focus on the occupation of the West Bank and Gaza, after 1967, tended to obscure this commitment to the absolute right of return. As Palestinians turned to a two-state solution, implications for the refugee issue were not spelled out openly. Palestinian statements ignored the fact that Israelis see a mass return of refugees to Israel as a threat to the existence of the state. In the words of Khalil Shikaki, the leading expert on Palestinian opinion, "the Palestinian national movement never seriously debated the implications [of adopting a two-state program] for . . . the 'right of return' as understood up to that time by the refugees," because it "did not want to lose the support of its largest constituency" (Shikaki 2001).

The opinion of this constituency has always seemed very clear: in a 2001 survey of West Bank and Gaza refugees conducted by the Israel Palestine Center for Research and Information (IPCRI), 99.8 percent agreed with the statement that "return must be to exact places of original residence," 96.7 percent said that if given the chance they will return to their original homes, and 64.5 percent would forcefully resist an unsatisfactory solution (IPCRI 2001). However, a later survey by Shikaki himself suggests that these opinions may not be quite as rigid as would appear. By presenting the question in the framework of the five options suggested at the Taba talks (see table 9.1), the insistence on a return to original homes – within the present boundaries of Israel – is less monolithic.

In this survey, more than 70 percent of those polled indicated that they would accept compensation and either remain where they were or, in most cases, move to territory that is or would be Palestinian. Only ten percent indicated that they would choose to return to their original homes within Israel. This suggests that the problem lies in the clash between the absolute right to choose, meaning theoretically the right of 5 million refugees to transform totally the demography of Israel, and the reality that only a relative few would choose to live in a Jewish state rather than a Palestinian state; this conclusion is confirmed in some journalistic accounts (see Fattah 2007).

Israeli arguments on this issue begin with the reminder that if Palestinians and Arab states had accepted the UN partition plan in 1947, there would be no refugees. The refugees were, after all, the result of a war that was explicitly declared as an attempt to eradicate Israel completely. Furthermore, in the few cases where Arab armies occupied Jewish settlements, inhabitants who survived were without exception expelled. Arabs were, therefore, in a weak position to appeal to morality or legality on the issue.

As for UN Resolution 194, the Israeli position is that the single clause dealing with the refugee issue cannot be ripped from its context. The resolution as a whole deals with the establishment of a Palestine Conciliation Commission charged with resolving all issues of the conflict, and not just the refugee question. Furthermore, the Arab states voted against this resolution, which again puts them in a poor position to argue for the implementation of any part of it.

Israelis also point out that in the years following the 1948–9 war, Israel absorbed several hundred thousand Jewish refugees from Arab states, many of whom were also forced out of their native lands. There had been a *de facto* exchange of populations between Israel and the Arab world, and the usual

Table 9.1 Refugees' first choice (for the exercise of the right of return)

	WBGS (percent)	Jordan (percent)	Lebanon (percent)	Total (percent of total population in the three areas)
1 Return to Israel and become (or not become) an Israeli citizen	12	5	23	10
2 Stay in the Palestinian state that will be established in the West Bank and Gaza Strip and receive a fair compensation for the property taken over by Israel and for other losses and suffering	38	27	19	31
3 Receive Palestinian citizenship and return to designated areas inside Israel that would be swapped later on with Palestinian areas as part of a territorial exchange and receive any deserved compensation	37	10	21	23
4 Receive fair compensation for the property, losses, and suffering and stay in host country receiving its citizenship or Palestinian citizenship	–	33	11	17
5 Receive fair compensation for the property, losses, and suffering and emigrate to a European country or the US, Australia, or Canada and obtain citizenship of that country or Palestinian citizenship	1	2	9	2
6 Refuse all options	9	16	17	13
7 No opinion	2	8	0	5

Source: Palestine Center for Policy and Survey Research 2003

historical outcome of such situations is the absorption of the refugees among their ethnic brethren. Israel did proceed to integrate the Jewish refugees, with much cost and effort, and today they constitute a vital and integral part of the Israeli public. But only in Jordan were Palestinian refugees given citizenship and equal rights.

In any event, Israelis say, after more than half a century the return of refugees to their original homes is no longer even feasible. Abandoned Arab towns and villages have been destroyed or swallowed up in urban growth, and the houses that remain would certainly not provide for more than a small fraction of a population that has grown more than sixfold in the interim. For that matter, how many refugees, the single most hostile group toward Israel, are really willing and able to live as Arab citizens of a Jewish state? Clearly they would be better off as Palestinian citizens of a Palestinian state – and in fact 40 percent of them are already living in the West Bank and Gaza.

With this gap between perspectives at the beginning of the negotiations, it is no surprise that the two sides made less progress on this issue than on others. Nevertheless, the Moratinos document on the Taba talks does report that serious efforts were made, including the delineation of the five options for refugees that were laid out in the survey above. The two sides reportedly also made some progress in agreeing on a "narrative" that would frame agreement on the issue, which would include Israeli acceptance of partial responsibility for finding a solution. It seemed likely that the five options would be posed in such a way as to encourage choice of options other than a return to Israel, and that some upper limit on return to Israel would be imposed. Despite the lack of final agreement, there was a sense among some of the negotiators that even on this issue, with the greatest difficulties and the least preparation, progress was possible.

The negotiations between Abbas and Olmert in 2007–8, and the Kerry initiative of 2013–4, did not advance far beyond this. Again Israel indicated willingness to express its sensitivity to the plight of the refugees and to contribute generously to a solution. But again the two sides remained far apart on the number who would be allowed to return to their (or their parents' or their grandparents') original homes in what is now Israel. Olmert suggested permitting the "symbolic" return to Israel itself of 1,000 a year for five years, and in any event no more than 15,000 total. Basically Israel was adamant that the problem be solved through the other options: return to Palestine, settlement in place, or relocation to a third country. Abbas, with over five million refugees to consider, did not regard the number returning to Israel itself as a serious offer. And there matters stand.

A General Prognosis

The degree of convergence on an agreed framework is reflected in the remarkable fact that it is easier to predict the likely content of a final agreement than it is to figure out how the parties will get there. The negotiators in 2000–1, 2007–8, and 2013–14 produced a clear outline of the settlement that can be expected given the respective interests, priorities, and leverage of the two parties. Even with the retreat from Taba after Sharon's election as Prime Minister, and from the Olmert-Abbas talks after Netanyahu's return to power, the gap remains smaller than at any previous time in the conflict. It is generally conceded that there will be a Palestinian state alongside the Jewish state; that its borders will be based on the 1949–67 armistice lines with minor changes; that the status quo on holy sites (the *Haram ash-Sharif* under Muslim control, the Western Wall under Jewish control) will be maintained and formal sovereignty left vague; that Palestine will have forces to maintain law and order but not to threaten Israel; that an international presence may be needed to guarantee the agreement; and that the number of refugees returning to Israel will be severely limited.

Close observers of the peace process narrow this down to two "red lines" that comprise the ultimate trade-off that must be made in order for a final deal to be concluded. Israelis must concede that the *Haram ash-Sharif*, the third holiest site of Islam, will remain under Muslim administration as it has, in fact, since 1967 under even the most hawkish of Israeli governments – even though it is also the site of the ancient First and Second Jewish Temples. Palestinians must come to terms with the reality that the vast majority of refugees will not be exercising their right of return to homes and villages that are now a part of Israel – even though they believe this to be a choice they should have according to elemental justice. Each side will have to make a concession that fundamentally runs against the grain, and which neither has yet been forced to even contemplate. But without this final hard bargain, respecting the other side's red line in return for the same in return, there will be no resolution.

The potentially explosive nature of the Temple Mount/ Noble Sanctuary issue is only too obvious. With 1.5 billion Muslims in the world, and religious extremism emerging as the major contemporary threat to peace, any attempt to alter existing arrangements is playing with fire. Even suggestions for very limited Jewish prayer and worship in the vicinity have met with vehement resistance; pushing beyond this is simply not in the cards.

The refugee issue is key because it touches on what is for Israel a fundamental question of greater consequence than the details of a final agreement. Will the founding of a Palestinian state complete the two-state solution, as Israel and Palestine embark on stable, and hopefully peaceful, coexistence? Or will it simply be a stage in the conflict, with Palestine as a base for future challenges to a Jewish state whose legitimacy is still rejected by many? There is going to be a Palestinian state; the issue, in Ehud Ya'ari's formulation, is "whether the Palestinian state is going to be born in peace and for peace, or whether it will be some sort of runaway state that is allowed to come into being without resolving the conflict with Israel, in order to maintain a state of fluctuating hostility." Demands for the return of Palestinian refugees to Israel are seen as indicating intent to continue the conflict through the tactic of demographic submersion: "The Palestinian national movement is about the right of return; it is not about the West Bank and Gaza" (Ya'ari 2002).

At this point a cynic might well ask: could the leadership

of either side actually bring their own public aboard on the far-reaching concessions that are so easily tossed back and forth between would-be statesmen behind closed doors? It is one thing to throw out sweeping proposals in the glow of intimate diplomacy, but it is another to sell the resulting package back home to a distrustful constituency that has not experienced the glow and in fact dislikes the entire process. The specific concessions made in the negotiations would have encountered hostile receptions by home audiences. Following the revelations of the 2007–8 talks, only 34 percent of Israelis supported, and 60 percent opposed, evacuating the West Bank except for the large settlement blocs in return for a permanent peace treaty – the very basis of the deal being consummated (Israel Democracy Institute 2011). A Palestinian poll in December 2010 asked about specific concessions similar to those being considered in the talks; 74 percent opposed the demilitarization of Palestine, 63 percent were against dividing Jerusalem along ethnic lines, 57 percent rejected the five-option refugee framework, and 58 percent disagreed with the package as a whole even though it called for a Palestinian state in the equivalent of 100 percent of Gaza and the West Bank (Palestine Center for Policy and Survey Research 2010b). Does this contradict the previous report that a majority of both Israelis and Palestinians favor a two-state solution (pp. 218–19)? Not necessarily; as has often been remarked, God (or the devil, depending on one's perspective) is in the details.

But astute leaders also read polls, and are surely aware of the task of gaining acceptance that awaits them after the euphoria of the signing ceremony. They believe that when the public has the chance to look at the agreement as a whole and see what they are gaining, rather than reacting to specific points they dislike, opinion will shift. In the case of the 2007–8 talks, there was also a game plan to create international momentum behind a settlement. The leaders would get the unanimous support of the UN Security Council and the near-unanimous backing of the General Assembly, as well as votes of support from the European Parliament, US Congress, and other bodies. Regional leaders would be invited to a massive ceremony on the White House lawn, and world leaders would descend on Jerusalem in suitably dramatic style. With all this at their backs, Israelis and Palestinians would go to elections to overwhelm the skeptics (Avishai 2011: 50).

But apart from theatrics, when the time comes again for negotiation on final status issues, will either side have a strategy for dealing with fundamental distrust? Because of historic circumstances, strategic thinking in this conflict has been severely circumscribed. Military considerations have ruled, while diplomatic and political dimensions have been ignored. Emphasis has been on the use of force to compel or deter, with little room to consider other ways of influencing the other side's intentions, motivation, or level of hostility (Merom 2003; R. Khalidi 2002). The lack of attention to one's own impact on the politics, society, and public attitudes of the other side seems to be a fixed attribute of Middle East conflicts. Perhaps the "winner" in the Arab–Israeli conflict will be the first party to realize how much power it has to influence the internal dynamics of the other side and to use this power effectively.

And in this vein, perhaps the most significant survey numbers in this conflict, of the many cited, are those regarding what each side believes about the ultimate aspirations of the other. Over two decades after mutual recognition and an agreed framework between mainstream leadership of both parties, 81 percent of Palestinians in an August 2016 survey still believed that Israel's aspirations, in the long run, were to extend the borders of the state of Israel to cover all the area between the Jordan River and the Mediterranean Sea and expel its Arab citizens (54 percent) or deny them their rights (27 percent). In the same joint survey, 54 percent of Israelis believed that the main aspiration of Palestinians was to conquer the state of Israel; 35 percent believed that Palestinians would destroy its Jewish population if they could (Palestine Center for Policy and Survey Research 2016).

This analysis has focused on the core Israeli–Palestinian confrontation, and only secondarily on the role of Arab states. We have seen that the Arab states became major players in this drama only a little over half a century ago, and that during the latter half of this period they gradually disengaged themselves from front-line duty in what was less and less an "Arab–Israel" conflict. In a less ideological climate, they gave greater weight to their own particular interests. The core conflict re-emerged: a struggle between Jews and Arabs in *Filastin/Eretz Yisrael*. This was for Israel, at least, a favorable trend. The Palestinians are not an existential threat to Israel; only when the Arab and/or Muslim world is mobilized against it does one ask if Israel can survive. The greatest threat to Israel came from the elevation of the conflict to the interstate level in 1948–9; the greatest boon came from the post-1967 trend to reduce it back to its core (a process that Israel, somewhat shortsightedly, tried in many ways to resist). The question raised in the fourth stage of the conflict, beginning in the middle of the first decade of the twenty-first century, was whether this trend would again be reversed, with Islamist movements – Palestinian, Arab, and non-Arab – playing the role once played by Arab states.

A number of regional and international developments have helped to entrench Israel in the Middle East (Inbar 2000). Efforts to eliminate Israel by force failed; there has been no general war since 1973. The orientation of Arab countries changed with the decline of pan-Arabism and the rise of particular state interests. Within the PLO, "insiders" living under Israeli occupation pushed for greater focus on the 1967 file, and with the *intifada* in the late 1980s they gained center stage. Arab states were also distracted by other threats in the region, such as the Iran–Iraq War. In many cases domestic pressures and plain war-weariness forced rethinking of national agendas. And finally, the end of the Cold War and the decline of oil power cut off outside sources of military and economic assistance.

Building on these developments, Israel has of course tried to encourage Arab states to drop out of the conflict, primarily by offering separate peace treaties based on the "land for peace" formula. But a full-blown strategy for detaching the neighboring states would also include lowering the profile of the Israeli–Palestinian conflict so that Arab governments – and now Islamic militant forces – would be less inclined to become involved. Israeli governments in the 1970s and 1980s, however, tried to wish the Palestinian dimension out of existence rather than address it directly, often acting as though the Arab–Israeli conflict could be resolved with the Arab states alone, leaving out the Palestinians. In order better to disengage the Arab states, Israel actually needed to engage the Palestinians. But instead of trying to find a viable Palestinian negotiating partner, the "Jordanian option" was pursued until the very last possible moment, when the Jordanians themselves abandoned it.

An Israeli–Palestinian relationship not only gives Arab states greater slack to drop out as belligerents (possibly even becoming useful intermediaries instead); it also opens up a channel for Israel to try to influence perceptions and attitudes among Palestinians. But this requires a clear view of the objective. What kind of Palestine should Israel favor? In particular, does Israel really want a functioning, effective, democratic Palestinian government? Wouldn't more Palestinian democracy mean more hostility to Israel, given the depth of violent emotions stirred up by recent events? In systematically attacking PA institutions and infrastructure during recent military campaigns, Israeli governments gave the impression that they viewed any Palestinian government as a threat. But a two-state solution cannot be realized until there is a credible Palestinian regime with a base of support broad enough to promise stability and to enforce the law. The view that Palestinian anarchy serves Israeli interests can be argued only if the Israeli government is pursuing future visions that do not include a Palestinian state, and is even less tenable in the light of the rise of *Hamas*.

In the end, only an effective, legitimate Palestinian government can control the extremists in its own territory and reduce terrorism to a negligible threat. The Israeli army can, through renewed attacks and occupation, disrupt terrorism and reduce its incidence, but there is no purely military solution. As numerous other cases in today's world illustrate, control of terrorism requires the building of a civic order that provides no sanctuary and a government that, acting in accord with its obligations as a sovereign state, prevents attacks on others from its own territory. Furthermore, the idea that this can be done (at least in the Palestinian case) only by a regime that ignores democratic limits and the rule of law is patent nonsense. In fact, it is done best, or perhaps only, by a government that enjoys broad support from its own public.

Israel's clear interest is in encouraging the emergence of an effective Palestinian government with an incentive to prevent attacks on Israeli targets. This is not unrealistic; the government of Syria, while still quite hostile, enforced quiet on its border with Israel (before civil war erupted). And Israeli policy toward the Palestinians can also stress the positive inducements as well as the negative sanctions, making a reasonable life alongside Israel possible and showing that options exist between destruction of Israel and occupation by Israel.

Such a credible Palestinian interlocutor can emerge only through the reform of the current PA. Past criticism of the PA focused on the role of Yasir Arafat, and indeed his record confirmed the observation that historically the Palestinians have been cursed by catastrophic leadership. Arafat was rooted in the old PLO, in the world view of the 1948–9 refugees in camps outside Palestine, and he never appeared to internalize the two-state solution in his thinking and actions. Did he ever intend to establish a Palestinian mini-state, in 22 percent of Palestine, as an end of the conflict? His contradictory indications on this subject were grist for boundless debate. Even the most fervent supporters of a two-state solution had to recognize "the disquieting signals about the Palestinian leader's intentions" (Ross 2002; Ya'ari 2002).

These questions are even more critical with *Hamas* as a key, if not dominant, player in Palestinian politics. *Hamas* has announced that it will abide by any peace agreement that is approved in a global referendum of all Palestinians, but this condition would be difficult if not impossible to meet.

Even with a reformed and effective Palestinian partner, there is no guarantee of total agreement on an "end of conflict." There may be no treaty, but only formal or informal arrangements that secure an armed peace without genuine reconciliation. Any accommodation, whether by treaty or not, will be opposed by some on both sides. The "end of conflict" is a particularly unrealistic expectation for Palestinian refugees whose core identity is tied up with the right of return. In any likely settlement the refugee issue will persist. The assumption that the 1967 occupation was the center of the conflict, and that when the occupation ends the conflict will as well, does not withstand critical scrutiny in the new realities of the fourth stage of the conflict.

10

The Perfect Conflict ————

↓

> During our last visit to the region, we met with the families
> of Palestinian and Israeli victims. These individual accounts
> of grief were heart-rending and indescribably sad. Israeli and
> Palestinian families used virtually the same words to describe
> their grief.
>
> Report of the Sharm El-Sheikh Fact-Finding Committee
> (United States Department of State 2001)

Right against Right?

This book began with accounts of the historical perspectives
and claims of Jews and Arabs. These perspectives and claims
are important to an understanding of the Arab–Israel conflict,
since they are the source of many of the concepts and much of
the vocabulary with which it is waged. Throughout the text,
the conflicting claims have been presented in juxtaposition
to each other, challenging the reader to make his or her own
judgment. In many if not most places, both sides probably
seemed quite reasonable in their own terms, before the juxtaposition. This may help explain why the Arab–Israel conflict,
more than most, generates heated partisanship among outside
observers; those who are exposed primarily to one side find
that side's arguments utterly compelling – as they are, when
taken without reference to the other side's perspective.

Let us take first the Jewish claims. Jews point to a unique historic tie to the Land of Israel, extending over at least 3,200 years, with a continuing (if sometimes small) physical presence throughout that time. Such a bond between a land and a people is unique in human history. It has been formally recognized in the modern period by those institutions with the best claim to speak for the international community – the League of Nations, the United Nations – and by most national governments. Jews who returned to their ancestral homeland have built a dynamic society that will, within the next generation, be home to over half of the world's Jews – fulfilling Theodor Herzl's vision of a Jewish state as the ultimate answer to anti-Semitism.

To those who argue that ancient history cannot shape modern territorial dispensations, the Jewish answer is that there is no recognized statute of limitations on the restoration of historical rights or the rectification of past injustice for an entire people. Jews were exiled from their homeland and have always prayed for return to it; only in the last century and a quarter did this become possible. Return to a homeland after generations or centuries is not uncommon; there have been numerous cases in the post-World War II and post-colonial world: Greeks, Turks, Germans, European colonists in Asia and Africa (British from East Africa, French from Algeria; Dutch from Indonesia). Is the Jewish claim weaker simply because it is more ancient than other claims?

All in all, could a fair-minded observer deny any historical connection whatsoever between Jews and the Land of Israel – a connection that is even recognized in the Holy Qur'an (for example, in "The Night Journey," 17:104)? The case is very strong – considered in isolation from other claims.

But now consider the Palestinian case, which rests on one basic incontrovertible fact: Palestinians were the indigenous population of Palestine 125 years ago, and did not invite European Jews to enter their homeland and transform it into an alien state and society. Had the native citizens of Palestine possessed the right of self-determination at the time, they would certainly have acted to block this challenge to their culture, society, and basic identity. Furthermore, this resistance to forced demographic change is in perfect accord with the norms that now prevail in today's world, norms that have₁ stigmatized the displacement (or "ethnic cleansing") of one people by another.

Palestinians are the descendants of all the indigenous peoples who lived in Palestine over the centuries; since the seventh century, they have been predominantly Muslim in religion and almost completely Arab in language and culture. For the last two centuries they have, however, been subjected to an onslaught of Western military, cultural, and economic imperialism, of which Zionist colonialism was an integral part. But the indigenous peoples of the Middle East are no longer in thrall to Western imperialism, and Palestinians are engaged in a national revival for the restoration of their dignity and basic rights.

Could a fair-minded observer ignore the claims of a people who were, after all, in actual possession of Palestine for centuries before Zionism arose? Palestinians also have a very strong case – considered in isolation from other claims.

But of course one cannot consider the two claims in isolation from each other: there is only one Palestine. The most common response, probably, is to pronounce that if one side is right, the other must be wrong; the rights and wrongs must match each other, like the wins and losses in a zero-sum game. But life seldom mimics a zero-sum game. There are clashes of right with right, in which history offers no easy answer about which right is superior to the other. Does the most ancient claim take precedence, or the most recent? Which course best serves justice, or at least creates the least injustice? Tragedy, it has been said, is the clash of right with right. The Arab–Israel conflict certainly fits this definition.

In addition, both Israelis and Palestinians have good reason to think of themselves as victims. Jewish history, as noted in chapter 2, is a chronicle of persecution, culminating in the most horrific genocide in history. Only part of this victimization came at the hands of Muslims or Arabs, but the past left a frame of reference in which Arab attacks today are seen as a continuation of the same unreasoning hatred of Jews. For Palestinians, the image of suffering at the hands of the Jews has been central to their history and very identity; as a people they are defined by victimization. In both cases the suffering was real, creating a deep sense of grievance that complicates any effort to transcend the violence. Victims often do not see the "other" at all, save as a victimizer; nor do they see that how their own acts of righteous anger may be creating new victims. There is a sense that their suffering releases them from constraints and entitles them to act with impunity to secure their rights (Meister 2002). This sense of victimhood on both sides, on top of a strong belief that one is in the right, is what has made this into a "perfect conflict," in the sense of a "perfect storm." It would be difficult to design a conflict with more self-generating power for continued confrontation and collision.

A Practical Solution

It should be clear by now that the Arab–Israel conflict will not be solved by arguments over historical rights or claims of victimhood. This is not to say that such subjects are irrelevant or unimportant. But few if any international or ethnic conflicts are resolved by agreement over rights and wrongs; the issues are too complex and the actors too self-centered to reach a common conclusion. And in the Arab–Israeli conflict, these issues are particularly complex, and the actors particularly self-absorbed. In the end, rights must be balanced against each other and against reality, and the most relevant yardstick is how to ensure the least future suffering.

On both moral and practical grounds, the best and perhaps only path out of this tangle is the two-state solution: partition of historic Palestine between Israel and a Palestinian state. Some Palestinians still cling to the phased solution, relying on the model of *Hizballah* in Lebanon for forcing Israel out of the occupied territories, and on demographic submersion for the eventual Arabization of Israel. This represents, however, a complete misjudgment of the strength, determination, and intelligence of Israelis, who will hardly allow themselves to follow this scenario blindly (hence the strong support for separation). Some Israelis also cling to outdated fantasies, believing, for example, that Palestinians will accept less self-governance than other peoples have demanded.

Many features of a final settlement appear more distinct today than they did a few years ago; the final status talks have illuminated the basic contours of the landscape, showing what is plausible and what is not. The likely elements of a final agreement were identified in chapter 9; what is much more difficult to predict is how long it will take to get there. How many more ups and downs on the roller-coaster will it take? There is no way to know.

There is another school of thought that needs to be considered, and which was introduced in chapter 7: the idea of a binational state. The vision of Israelis and Palestinians living together cooperatively in a neutralized state, with neither side dominating the other, is undeniably attractive when set against renewed violence. The question of whether such a design is workable in intense ethnic conflicts, however, is seldom examined by the proponents. Binational states have a very poor track record; apart from Belgium, Canada, and Switzerland (a trinational state), stable models are few and far between. More numerous are the cases in which power sharing has broken down, as in Cyprus, Lebanon, Sri Lanka, Pakistan, Yugoslavia, and a number of African states. The "successes," clearly, have been limited to Western liberal democracies in which the ethnic conflict has been muted and largely nonviolent. Conspicuously missing are any examples of power sharing successfully implemented between parties still at war.

Also conspicuously missing is support for the binational alternative from major political groups on either side. Among Jewish Israelis it is limited to the anti-Zionist left and a few idealistic ideologues on the right; some Palestinian citizens of Israel understandably support the idea, since it would remove them from minority status (Jerusalem Media and Communications Center 1999). Palestinians in the West Bank and Gaza support binationalism in larger numbers, between 20–30 percent, but, as noted, this appears to be an expression of frustration with the collapse of the peace process more than adoption of a carefully considered alternative program. Furthermore, the prospect of demographic submersion clearly puts a different spin on the idea among Palestinians; since Palestinians would become the overwhelming majority over time, a binational state would inevitably become more Arab and less Jewish. But Israelis can also count, and the same prospect makes binationalism much less appealing to them – even should they miraculously be coaxed into foregoing the basic Zionist dream of a Jewish state.

The separation of a two-state solution certainly faces many obstacles, such as Jewish settlements in the West Bank and Gaza, shared resources such as water, environmental issues, and economic interdependence. But living together does not make these obstacles easier to overcome. The same problems would remain, but would have to be dealt with daily rather than in one decisive denouement. A binational state would be vastly more complicated, requiring intricate cooperation in every area of public life – and all this from two parties that so far have seldom been able to forge a common consensus on if and when to talk to each other. It is a gigantic leap of faith to believe that warring enemies who are having trouble agreeing on terms of separation will suddenly be able to cooperate on everything.

In the end, a binational state would give neither side the sense of self-determination and national identity that both have defined as the *sine qua non* of their respective struggles over the last century. This helps to explain the lack of organizational support for the idea; individuals may in sheer frustration turn to binationalism as a slogan, but political parties and movements have to face the explicit conflict with sacrosanct nationalist dogmas. Take just one question that would be raised at a very early stage: What would the immigration policy be? Would the binational state continue to welcome all Jews? Would it be open to all of the over five million registered Palestinian refugees? For both Israelis and Palestinians, the "right of return" is enshrined in basic scripture; without it, the new homeland would have no legitimacy. But if the door were open to all, the resulting demographic war would make previous demographic conflict look idyllic in comparison. In the end, a difficult divorce is better than hostile cohabitation.

Building Foundations: Extremists and Illusions

The road to peace through separation is difficult enough, and there are no magical shortcuts. There are forces that are pushing both sides along this road: realistic recognition of limits, exhaustion of other options, outside pressures, and above all growing fatigue over a stalemate that inflicts constant pain with no promise of ultimate victory. There are also obstacles and illusions along this road that need to be recognized.

One of the major obstacles is extremism, defined as the belief that one's own cause is so righteous that it justifies (or even demands) the use of any means, no matter how violent or how immoral by ordinary standards. Extremists have had a disproportionate influence on the course of the Arab–Israel conflict. The fact that both sides see themselves as victims has helped to foster extremism, since the absolute conviction in one's own victimhood makes moral restraints seem irrelevant. In addition, it is easier to disrupt the peace process than it is to nurture it; a few activists – even a single person – can in one violent act set in motion a cycle of responses that changes the entire diplomatic and political climate. The assassin of Yitzhak Rabin, for example, could feel with some justification that he had brought about Labor's defeat in the 1996 elections.

Extremists are not "crazy" on the tactical level; their actions are generally calculated to produce an intended effect, which may depend on the reactions of extremists on the other side. Extremists on the two sides are, in a very real sense, allies. Not only are they united in the goal of defeating negotiated or compromise solutions, but they count on each other for the violent actions that, they claim, are the "true face" of the enemy. They serve to validate each other. Moderates in the Arab–Israel conflict, on the other hand, have not yet figured out how to influence the internal dynamics of the other side. Cooperation is still at an early stage, and the idea that the other side is responsive to moderate, as well as violent, actions has not really taken root.

Related to this are illusions that prevail among wide sectors on both sides. Palestinian attitudes toward the violent factions in their own community, for example, are colored by the stubborn notion that the option of "armed struggle" is still a useful and viable option that will push Israeli opinion in a moderate direction. This is of course related to the popular gospel, in all conflicts, that "the only language they [the enemy] understand is force." Despite overwhelming evidence that this was not the case in the second *intifada* (unlike the first, which was much less violent), large majorities of Palestinians favored "military" attacks, including suicide bombings, and believed such tactics would force Israelis to back down.

Palestinians can indeed make Israelis live in fear of terror attacks, but this will not defeat Israel or bring any benefits to Palestinians. In theory, Palestinians surrendered all military options in the Oslo accords; the obligation to refrain from the use of force, and to prevent attacks from Palestinian territory, was written into each agreement, ultimately in the most inclusive language ever devised for such commitments (see the 1998 Wye Accord). For Israelis, the promise of an end to violence was the major incentive in the Oslo process; when violence did not end, the motivation for making further concessions was undermined. The PLO could sell its commitment to end violence for a high price once, or maybe twice, but not repeatedly. By the end of the decade there was no taker; the second *intifada* brought about the election of the most martial Prime Minister in Israeli history, the end of negotiations, and military incursions into West Bank cities.

In a sense, Palestinian thinking was not keeping pace with the changes on the ground. Palestinians moved toward becoming a proto-state, as the PA, but clung to the major weapon that had served them as a revolutionary movement: low-level violence. The PA was an aspiring state, but it did not take on the basic responsibility of a sovereign state to prevent its citizens from attacking neighbor states, or to prevent the use of its territory for such attacks – a responsibility that Jordan, Egypt, and Syria have generally met. The accession to power of *Hamas* sharpened this dilemma, since *Hamas* refused to surrender "the right of resistance" as a matter of principle. But at some point, if only to preserve its own future bargaining power in negotiations, the PA would have to respect its own commitments to give up violence as a weapon and to move on to the more acceptable weapons of influence among states. One of these weapons, still almost entirely unexploited, is potential Palestinian influence on Israeli opinion. For example, a credible campaign to make it clear that most Palestinians accept, or would accept, a two-state solution as an end to the conflict, and can control those among them who do not, would conceivably revolutionize opinion in Israel. As shown in the impact of Sadat's 1977 trip to Jerusalem, Israeli opinion can be very responsive to dramatic moderate gestures.

But illusions persist on both sides. Israelis also cling to military solutions in situations that call for more than force alone, as seen in the "get tough" responses to Palestinian violence. Though it is commonly stated that "there is no military solution" to the *intifada*, official policy focuses on the military dimension with little or no attention to possible political or diplomatic moves. The major thrust was to convince Palestinians that continued violence would bring no gains, forcing them to return to negotiation with reduced expectations. With Israelis, as with Palestinians, the possibiliity of influencing the other side's thinking by employing the carrot as well as the stick has not been exploited. If the Israeli government is committed to a two-state solution, there are many ways in which Israel could be acting to make this outcome more appealing to Palestinians and underlining the fact that there is "a way out" of the current impasse. As with the Palestinians, simply making a clear and credible repeated public commitment to a two-state solution would spark some happy confusion on the other side.

Another illusion that needs to be challenged on the Israeli side is the notion that Palestinian self-determination is a bargaining chip that can be held for final negotiations. Self-determination is a universal norm and an almost universal practice; neither the international community nor the Palestinians feel the need to compensate Israel for recognizing what is inevitable. Attempts to rouse international support against Palestinian violations of signed agreements fell flat, according to former Israeli Foreign Minister Shlomo Ben-Ami, because even friendly governments considered it normal for people under occupation to resort to violence: "Accusations made by a well-established society about how a people it is oppressing is breaking rules to attain its rights do not have much credence" (Siegman 2001). At this point the remnants of the occupation are a burden, not an asset, for Israel. But as the case for unilateral disengagement is weakened by the "lessons" of the Lebanese and Gaza withdrawals, the difficulties of a negotiated separation between the two parties are again the central reality of the conflict.

Reflections

In its origins, as stated at the outset, the Arab–Israel conflict was a struggle between two peoples fighting over the same land: an objective conflict, as theorists would put it. Yet, in the course of time this core has been enlarged by other dimensions that have developed, some of them also objective (territorial disputes) but many of them belonging to the "subjective" realm: emotions and passions, ideological justifications, religious intolerance, demonization of the enemy, misunderstanding and prejudice, ethnic hatred, etc. It could even be argued, perhaps, that the subjective factors have become, if not the core of the conflict, then at least the major obstacles to its resolution. At Taba, for example, Israelis and Palestinians came close to agreement on the core "objective" issues of the conflict, yet distrust and dislike intervened and led to an explosion that defied all rational justifications. The increased influence of religious dogmatism has only intensified this impasse.

In a sense, I have argued, the conflict was being reduced to its core geographically as Arab states dropped out of the front line and Palestinians emerged to speak for themselves. This was, all things considered, a positive development. Recent trends have in part reversed this process; restoring it – discouraging the interlopers – is thus a top priority. Perhaps we then need to focus on reducing the confrontation to its core causally as well, stripping away the layers of accumulated anger and alienation so that a resolution of the basic issues can be achieved. Otherwise, this "perfect conflict" could outlive the *de facto* resolution of the issues that triggered it in the first place.

Chronology ————————————————————

c. 2000 BCE	Approximate era of Abraham, traditional father of Jews and Arabs
c. 1500–1300 BCE	Approximate date of Hebrew Exodus from Egypt
c. 1220 BCE	First non-biblical reference to Israel, Merneptah Stele (Egypt)
c. 1000–900 BCE	United monarchy under David and Solomon, building of First Temple
853 BCE	First historical reference to Arabs, in Assyrian inscription
722 BCE	Assyria conquers northern kingdom (Israel)
586 BCE	Babylonia conquers southern kingdom (Judea), beginning of Babylonian exile
539–140 BCE	Persian and Greek rule, return from Babylon, building of Second Temple
63 BCE–638 CE	Roman and Byzantine rule; Palestine Christianized, center of Jewish life passes to Babylonia
622	Beginning of Muslim era
636–40	Muslims conquer Palestine, beginning of Islamization and Arabization
661–750	Rule of Umayyad Caliphate from Damascus

750–1258	Rule of Abbasid Caliphate from Baghdad
c. 800–1300	Center of Jewish life passes to Muslim Spain
1096–1291	Crusades seek to reconquer Holy Land for Christianity; massive persecution and expulsion of Jews in Europe
1250–1516	Palestine ruled by Turkish Mamluk dynasties in Damascus and Cairo
1453	Ottoman Turks conquer Constantinople
1492	Following Christian reconquest, Jews are expelled from Spain; center of Jewish life passes to Eastern Europe
1517–1918	Ottoman Empire, based in Constantinople, rules Palestine
1771, 1793, 1795	Partition of Poland; Russia becomes home to half of world Jewish population
1798	Napoleon invades Egypt; beginning of European colonialism in the Middle East
1881	Assassination of Russian Tsar Alexander II; pogroms in Russia, beginning of immigration to Eretz Yisrael (first aliyah)
1882	British occupation of Egypt
1888	Ottoman government establishes Jerusalem and southern Palestine as a special district under direct control from Constantinople
1891	Arab notables petition the Ottoman government to halt all Jewish immigration and land purchases
1896	Theodor Herzl publishes *Der Judenstaat*, calling for creation of a Jewish state

1897	Under Herzl's leadership, First Zionist Congress convenes in Basel and establishes the World Zionist Organization
1904	Death of Theodor Herzl
1905	First Russian Revolution; beginning of new wave (second aliyah) of Jewish immigrants to Eretz Yisrael. Najib Azuri publishes *Le Réveil de la Nation Arabe*, first major treatise of Arab nationalism
1907	Yitzhak Epstein publishes "A Hidden Question," first Zionist analysis to argue that relations with Arabs were the movement's greatest problem
1908	Young Turk Revolution in Constantinople, leading to greater visibility of Arab nationalism
1915	In context of World War I, Great Britain supports an "Arab Revolt" within the territory of the enemy Ottoman Empire, promising to secure the establishment of an Arab state in the Middle East
November 2, 1917	Great Britain issues Balfour Declaration supporting the establishment in Palestine of a national home for the Jewish people
December 9, 1917	British army captures Jerusalem
April 1920, May 1921	Arab anti-Zionist riots in Palestine
1922–48	British govern Palestine as a League of Nations Mandate
1929	Arab anti-Zionist riots in Jerusalem and Hebron
1936–9	General Arab insurrection against British rule and Jewish presence

July 1937	Peel Commission recommends partition of Palestine into Arab and Jewish states
May 1939	British White Paper rejects partition, calls for Arab-majority state in ten years
1942–5	Killing of six million Jews in Holocaust transforms context of the Palestine question
May 1942	At Biltmore Conference in New York, World Zionist Organization calls for creation of a Jewish state in all of Mandatory Palestine
February 1947	Britain refers Palestine question to United Nations
November 29, 1947	UN General Assembly passes Resolution 181 calling for partition with economic union and internationalization of Jerusalem
November 1947	Beginning of first Arab–Israeli war, with fighting between Jewish and Arab communities in Palestine
May 15, 1948	State of Israel established; Arab states invade Palestine
January–July 1949	Arab–Israel war ends with armistice agreements between Israel and the four bordering Arab states
July 1952	Revolution in Egypt, ascent of Gamal Abdul Nasser to power
September 1955	Egyptian arms deal with Soviet bloc shatters Western control of weapon levels in region
October–November 1956	Suez Crisis: Israel invades Sinai peninsula in coordination with British and French efforts to regain control of Suez Canal
March 1957	Israel completes withdrawal from Sinai; Israeli passage through Strait

	of Tiran secured by UN Emergency Force (UNEF)
October 1957	Creation of *Fatah*, the Palestine Liberation Movement, under leadership of Yasir Arafat and others
January 1964	Palestine Liberation Organization (PLO) founded under auspices of Arab League
June 5–10, 1967	Six Day or June War, following renewed Egyptian closure of Strait of Tiran to Israel; Israel occupies West Bank, Gaza Strip, Sinai peninsula, and Syrian Golan Heights
August 1967	Arab summit meeting in Khartoum rejects direct talks with Israel, leaves door open to indirect political and diplomatic solutions
November 22, 1967	UN Security Council adopts Resolution 242 calling for a comprehensive Arab–Israeli settlement based on the principle of land for peace
February 1969	Yasir Arafat's *Fatah* movement takes control of PLO
March 1969– August 1970	Egypt and Israel fight a "war of attrition" along Suez Canal
September 1970	Jordan expels PLO fighting groups from its territory
October 6–22, 1973	Yom Kippur/Ramadan War; Egypt and Syria attack Israeli forces in Sinai and Golan Heights
January 1974	Egypt and Israel reach agreement on disengagement of forces
May 1974	Syria and Israel reach agreement on disengagement of forces
November 1974	Arab states in summit meeting recognize PLO as "sole legitimate representative of the Palestinian people"

November 1977	Egyptian President Anwar Sadat travels to Israel and speaks before the Israeli Knesset
September 1978	With US President Jimmy Carter as mediator, Egypt and Israel reach agreement at Camp David on a framework for peace
March 1979	Egypt and Israel conclude a bilateral peace treaty
June 1982	Israel invades Lebanon in order to eliminate PLO military presence there
September 1982	Lebanese Christian forces, operating in Israeli-controlled territory, massacre Palestinians in Sabra and Shatilla refugee camps
1982, 1983, 1985	Israel withdraws in stages from all Lebanese territory except a "security zone" on the Israeli–Lebanese border
July 1988	King Husayn withdraws Jordanian claims to the West Bank, leaving PLO as Israel's only bargaining partner
November 1988	PLO accepts UN Resolution 242 and calls for Palestinian state alongside Israel
October 1991	Following first Gulf War, first peace conference with all parties represented convenes in Madrid
September 13, 1993	Mutual recognition between Israel and the PLO; Declaration of Principles establishes a framework for comprehensive peace including Palestinian self-government in West Bank and Gaza
May 1994	Signing of Gaza–Jericho Agreement; Palestinian Authority (PA) takes control of most of Gaza Strip and Jericho area on the West Bank

October 1994	Signing of Jordan–Israel treaty
September 1995	Signing of Palestinian–Israeli Interim Agreement (Oslo II) enlarges area of PA authority to include most Arab cities and villages in West Bank
November 1995	Assassination of Yitzhak Rabin
May 1996	Benjamin Netanyahu elected Israeli Prime Minister
September 1996	Palestinian riots following opening of tunnel near Temple Mount
January 1997	Agreement on Israeli redeployment from most of Hebron
September 1998	Wye Accord for further Israeli withdrawals from West Bank
May 1999	Ehud Barak elected Israeli Prime Minister
September 1999	Sharm Esh-Sheikh Agreement to complete Israeli withdrawal from a total of 40 percent of West Bank
July 2000	Camp David talks fail to bring agreement on final settlement of remaining Israeli–Palestinian issues
September 2000	Beginning of Al-Aqsa intifada, collapse of peace process
January 2001	At Taba, Israeli and Palestinian negotiators try but fail to reach comprehensive settlement before Israeli elections
February 2001	Ariel Sharon elected Israeli Prime Minister, refuses to negotiate with Palestinians until violence ends, forms National Unity Government with opposition Labor Party
March 2002	In response to a wave of suicide bombings, Israel launches Operation Defensive Shield and reoccupies all the major Palestinian cities in the West Bank

June 24, 2002	US President George W. Bush calls for new Palestinian leadership, halts direct dealings with Yasir Arafat, and outlines "roadmap" for peace designed by "Quartet" of outside powers (United States, United Nations, European Union, and Russia)
January 2003	Ariel Sharon re-elected Israeli Prime Minister in landslide victory for his *Likud* Party, forms narrow government without Labor Party
June 29, 2003	Islamic militant groups and Fatah announce three-month cease-fire
August 2003	Following Hamas suicide attack in Jerusalem, cease-fire breaks down; Israel speeds construction of security barrier in West Bank
February 2004	Sharon announces intention of unilaterally evacuating Israeli settlements in the Gaza Strip
March 2004	Following a suicide attack in the port of Ashdod, Israel targets and kills two top Hamas leaders
June 6, 2004	Israeli government decides in principle to dismantle all Jewish settlements in the Gaza Strip and four settlements in the West Bank by the end of 2005.
July 1, 2004	Israeli Supreme Court orders rerouting of security barrier to minimize impact on Palestinians
November 11, 2004	Death of Yasir Arafat; Mahmoud Abbas emerges as immediate successor
January 9, 2005	Mahmoud Abbas elected PA President with 62 percent of vote; calls for immediate peace talks

January 10, 2005	Sharon forms unity government with Labor Party in order to implement unilateral disengagement plan
February 8, 2005	Agreement on cease-fire in talks at Sharm Esh-Sheikh; Hamas and Islamic Jihad promise not to abrogate
May 5, 2005	Hamas wins 33 percent of the vote in Palestinian municipal elections
August 17–23, 2005	Israel evacuates Jewish settlements in Gaza and four isolated outposts in West Bank
November 11, 2005	Amir Peretz wins leadership of Israel Labor Party, initiates withdrawal from government coalition
November 21, 2005	Sharon calls for new elections, announces formation of new centrist *Kadima* party.
January 4, 2006	Sharon incapacitated by stroke; Deputy Prime Minister Ehud Olmert becomes Acting Prime Minister and head of *Kadima* list in elections
January 25, 2006	In PA legislative elections Hamas captures 74 of 132 seats, taking control of PA institutions apart from the presidency
March 28, 2006	*Kadima* emerges in Israeli elections as largest single party, forms center-left government with Labor and other parties
June 25, 2006	Israeli soldier captured in attack, with *Hamas* participation, on Gaza border post; beginning of extensive fighting
July–August, 2006	*Hizballah* attack on Israeli post, and capture of two soldiers, broadens fighting to Lebanon; massive Israeli air and ground attacks in southern Lebanon, *Hizballah* rocket attacks throughout northern Israel

August 14, 2006	UN resolution imposes cease-fire in Lebanon; *Hizballah* forces on Israel border replaced with Lebanese army and international forces, but Hizballah gains prestige for forcing stand-off
November 25, 2006	Israel and PA President Abbas agree on renewed cease-fire, with *Hamas* acquiescence
February 8, 2007	*Fatah* and *Hamas* reach agreement in Mecca, under Saudi Arabian sponsorship, on a PA unity government led by Hamas
June 2007	*Hamas* takes total control of Gaza; Abbas dismisses unity government and appoints new government under Independent Prime Minister Salam Fayyad, in control of West Bank; Israel initiates partial blockade of Gaza
November 27, 2007	US-sponsored conference of 40 nations convenes at Annapolis; sets goal of agreement on two-state solution by end of 2008; beginning of offstage negotiations between Abbas and Israeli Prime Minister Olmert
June 17, 2008	Beginning of six-month cease-fire agreement between Israel and *Hamas* forces in Gaza
September 17, 2008	Tzipi Livni elected new leader of Israel's *Kadima* party as Olmert forced to resign as Prime Minister, leading to calling of new elections in February 2009
December 19, 2008	Expiration of Israel–*Hamas* cease-fire agreement, resumption of *Hamas* rocket attacks from Gaza and Israeli retaliatory attacks

December 27, 2008	Israel launches Operation Cast Lead, attacking *Hamas* forces in Gaza by air and by land
January 18, 2009	Operation Cast Lead ends with unilateral cease-fires declared by Israel and by Hamas
February 10, 2009	Elections in Israel marked by turn to the right; *Likud* under Benjamin Netanyahu forms new government
June 14, 2009	Prime Minister Netanyahu announces his government's conditional acceptance of a Palestinian state and a two-state solution
November 25, 2009	Israeli government announces ten-month freeze on new residential housing starts in Israeli settlements in West Bank, not including East Jerusalem; PA considers move inadequate for renewal of direct peace talks
March 8, 2010	Israel and PA agree on indirect "proximity" talks with US special envoy George Mitchell as go-between
March 31, 2010	Israel stops flotilla of ships challenging naval blockade of Gaza; nine Turkish activists killed in boarding of *Mavi Marmara*
September 2010	Direct talks between Israel and PA resume under US sponsorship, but are halted at end of month after Israeli settlement freeze expires; PA also rejects renewal of indirect talks
January 23, 2011	Arab media outlet *Al Jazeera* publishes 1600 leaked documents on Israeli–Palestinian negotiations, revealing much of 2007–8 Abbas-Olmert talks

February 11, 2011	Abdication of Egyptian President Hosni Mubarak raises key issue of impact of "Arab Spring" on Israeli–Palestinian conflict
May 3, 2011	*Fatah* and *Hamas* announce agreement to unify West Bank and Gaza; agreement fails over differences regarding the conduct of new elections.
September 23, 2011	In speech at UN, Abbas calls for admission of Palestine as member state.
November 2012	Breakdown of Gaza cease-fire; Israel launches Operation Pillar of Defense; eight days of fighting ends in Egyptian-sponsored cease-fire
November 2012	Palestine is recognized as non-member observer state at United Nations
January 22, 2013	Elections in Israel; Benjamin Netanyahu continues as Prime Minister with a center-right coalition
July 2013–April 2014	US Secretary of State John Kerry pushes diplomatic initiative to reach framework agreement between Israel and the Palestinian Authority; effort fails among mutual recriminations
April 2014	PA and *Hamas* announce formation of unity government; PA signs 18 international conventions
July–September 2014	Renewed fighting between Israel and *Hamas* in Gaza; Israel launches Operation Protective Edge, fifty days of air and ground campaigns ends in cease-fire.
March 17, 2015	Early elections held in Israel following collapse of center-right

coalition; *Likud* emerges again as largest party, Netanyahu forms narrow right-religious government

October 2015   Beginning of wave of stabbings, vehicular assaults, and other attacks by lone Palestinians against Israeli civilians

February 2017   Israeli Knesset adopts law retroactively legalizing many West Bank Jewish settlements built on private Palestinian land.

Further Reading

Mahmoud Abbas (Abu Mazen), *Through Secret Channels*. Garnet Publishing, 1995.

George Antonius, *The Arab Awakening*. Capricorn Books, 1946.

Myron J. Aronoff, *Israeli Visions and Divisions: Cultural Change and Political Conflict*. Transaction, 1989.

Shlomo Avineri, *The Making of Modern Zionism: The Intellectual Origins of the Jewish State*. Basic Books, 1981.

—— *Herzl's Vision: Theodor Herzl and the Foundation of the Jewish State*. BlueBridge, 2013.

Yossi Beilin, *Touching Peace: From the Oslo Accord to a Final Agreement*. Weidenfeld and Nicolson, 1999.

Neil Caplan, *The Israel–Palestine Conflict: Contested Histories*. Wiley-Blackwell, 2010.

Avner Cohen, *Israel and the Bomb*. Columbia University Press, 1998.

—— *The Worst-Kept Secret: Israel's Bargain with the Bomb*, Columbia University Press, 2010.

Alan Dowty, *The Jewish State: A Century Later*. University of California Press, 1998, 2001.

Martin Gilbert, *The Routledge Atlas of the Arab-Israeli Conflict*. 10th edn. Routledge, 2012.

Yosef Gorny, *Zionism and the Arabs, 1882–1948: A Study of Ideology*. Clarendon Press, 1987.

Yehoshafat Harkabi, *Arab Attitudes to Israel*. Keter Publishing House, 1972.

Theodor Herzl, *The Jews' State: A Critical English Translation*. Jason Aronson, 1997.

Albert Hourani, *A History of the Arab Peoples*. Harvard University Press, 1991.

Rashid Khalidi, *Palestinian Identity: The Construction of Modern National Consciousness*. Columbia University Press, 1997.

—— *Sowing Crisis: The Cold War and American Dominance in the Middle East*, Beacon Press, 2009.

Walid Khalidi (ed.), *From Haven to Conquest: Readings in Zionism and the Palestine Problem until 1948*. Institute for Palestine Studies, 1987.

Baruch Kimmerling and Joel Migdal, *The Palestinian People: A History*. Harvard University Press, 2003.

P. R. Kumaraswamy, *Historical Dictionary of the Arab–Israel Conflict*. The Scarecrow Press, 2006.

Walter Laqueur and Dan Schueftan (eds), *The Israel–Arab Reader: A Documentary History of the Middle East Conflict*, 8th edn. Penguin Books, 2016.

Matthew Levitt, *Hamas: Politics, Charity, and Terrorism in the Service of Jihad*. Yale University Press, 2006.

Bernard Lewis, *The Arabs in History*, new edn. Oxford University Press, 1993.

—— *What Went Wrong: Western Impact and Middle Eastern Response*. Oxford University Press, 2002.

Neville Mandel, *The Arabs and Zionism before World War I*. University of California Press, 1976.

Benny Morris, *The Birth of the Palestinian Refugee Problem Revisited*. Cambridge University Press, 2004.

—— *Righteous Victims: A History of the Zionist–Arab Conflict 1881–2001*. Vintage Books, 2001.

Marwan Muasher, *The Arab Center: The Promise of Moderation*. Yale University Press, 2008.

Muhammad Y. Muslih, *The Origins of Palestinian Nationalism*. Columbia University Press, 1988.

Michael B. Oren, *Six Days of War: June 1967 and the Making of the Modern Middle East*. Oxford University Press, 2002.

—— *Power, Faith, and Fantasy: America in the Middle East 1776 to the Present*. W. W. Norton, 2007.

Ami Pedahzur, *The Triumph of Israel's Radical Right*. Oxford University Press, 2012.

Ilan Peleg and Dov Waxman, *Israel's Palestinians: The Conflict Within*. Cambridge University Press, 2011.

Derek J. Penslar, *Israel in History: The Jewish State in Comparative Perspective*. Routledge, 2007.

Dennis Ross, *The Missing Peace: The Inside Story of the Fight for Middle East Peace*. Farrar, Straus and Giroux, 2004.

Scham, Paul, Benjamin Pogrund, and As'ad Ghanem, Special Issue: Shared Narratives – A Palestinian-Israeli Dialogue. *Israel Studies* 18:2 (Summer 2013).

Tom Segev, *One Palestine, Complete*. Metropolitan Books, 2000.

Anita Shapira, *Israel: A History.* Brandeis University Press, 2012.

Kenneth Stein, ed., *History, Politics and Diplomacy of the Arab-Israeli Conflict*. Center for Israel Education, Israeled.org/Product/Arab-Israeli-Conflict, 2015.

Mark Tessler, *A History of the Israeli–Palestinian Conflict*. 2nd edn. Indiana University Press, 2009.

Shabtai Teveth, *Ben-Gurion and the Palestinian Arabs, from Peace to War*. Oxford University Press, 1985.

David Vital, *The Origins of Zionism*. Clarendon Press, 1975.

—— *Zionism: The Formative Years*. Clarendon Press, 1982.

—— *Zionism: The Crucial Phase*. Clarendon Press, 1987.

Bernard Wasserstein, *Israelis and Palestinians*. Yale University Press, 2003.

Dov Waxman, *The Pursuit of Peace and the Crisis of Israeli Identity: Defending/Defining the Nation*. Palgrave Macmillan, 2006.

Internet Links ─────────────────────────────

ISRAEL

Israel Ministry of Foreign Affairs: www.mfa.gov.il/MFA
Ha'aretz (daily newspaper): www.haaretzdaily.com
Jerusalem Post (daily newspaper): www.jpost.com
YNet News (daily newspaper): www.ynetnews.com
Jerusalem Report (biweekly): https://thejerusalemreport.
 wordpress.com
Begin-Sadat Center for Strategic Studies: http://besacenter.org
Leonard Davis Institute for International Relations: http://
 en.davis.huji.ac.il
Institute for National Security Studies: www.inss.org.il
Harry S. Truman Research Institute for the Advancement of
 Peace: www.truman.huji.ac.il
Tami Steinmetz Center for Peace Research: peace.tau.ac.il
Middle East Review of International Affairs (electronic
 journal): www.rubincenter.org/about-**meria**
Arutz 7 (right-wing radio): www.israelnationalnews.com
B'tselem (human rights organization): www.btselem.org
Israel Resource Review: www.israelbehindthenews.com
Middle East Media and Research Institute (MEMRI): www.
 memri.org
Palestinian Media Watch: www.palwatch.org

PALESTINIAN

Palestinian National Authority Official Website: minfo. gov. ps/English.ps

Palestine Central Bureau of Statistics: www.pcbs.gov.ps

Palestinian Center for Policy and Survey Research: www. pcpsr.org

Palestinian Academic Society for Study of International Affairs (PASSIA): www.passia.org

Institute for Palestine Studies: www.palestine-studies.org

Jerusalem Media and Communications Center: www. jmcc.org

Jerusalem Times (weekly): www.jerusalem-times.net

Al-Haq – Law in the Service of Man: www.alhaq.org

Palestinian Human Rights Monitoring Group: www.ngo-monitor.org/ngos/palestinian_human_rights_monitoring_group_phrmg

Ezzedeen Al-Qassam Brigades (Hamas): www.qassam.ps

The Electronic Intifada: http://electronicintifada.net

Palestinian Information Center: www.palestine-info.co.uk/en

OTHERS

Israel–Palestine Center for Research and Information (IPCRI) (joint Israeli–Palestinian organization): www.ipcri.org

United Nations Relief and Works Agency (UNRWA): www. unrwa.org

Middle East Research and Information Project: www.merip. org

Foundation for Middle East Peace: www.fmep.org

MidEastWeb: www.mideastweb.org

Washington Institute for Near East Policy: www. washingtoninstitute.org

Israeli–Palestinian Conflict ProCon: http://israelipalestinian. procon.org

Middle East Media Research Institute: www.memri.org

References

Abbas, Mahmoud (Abu Mazen) (1995) Through Secret Channels, Garnet Publishing.
—— (2001) "Had Camp David Convened Again, We Would Take the Same Position," *Al-Ayyam* (Ramallah), July 28 (Arabic).
—— (2004) "Interview," *Al-Rai* (Amman), September 27.
—— (2011) "The Long Overdue Palestinian State," *New York Times*, May 16.
Al-Hasan, Hani (1993) "Interview," *Mideast Mirror*, October 9.
Al-Jazeera (Qatar) (2001) Middle East Media Research Institute, Special Dispatch no. 155, November 22, at http://www.memri.org.
—— (2011) The Palestine Papers, January 23, at www.aljazeera.com/palestinepapers
Al-Quds (Jerusalem) (2000) Editorial, September 1, World News Connection, FBIS-NES-2000–0901.
—— (2001) Editorial, February 14, World News Connection, FBIS-NES-2001–0215.
As-Safir (Beirut) (2001) "Faisal al-Husseini: Sharon Must Not Get a Chance," Middle East Media Research Institute, Special Dispatch no. 197, March 23, at http://www.memri.org.
Antonius, George (1946) *The Arab Awakening*, Capricorn Books.
Arian, Asher (1992) "Security and Political Attitudes in Israel: 1986–1991," *Public Opinion Quarterly* 56 (Spring): 116–28.
—— (1995) *Security Threatened: Surveying Israeli Opinion on Peace and War*, Cambridge University Press.
—— (2003) *Israeli Public Opinion on National Security*, annual, Jaffee Center for Strategic Studies.

Aronoff, Myron J. (1989) *Israeli Visions and Divisions: Cultural Change and Political Conflict*, Transaction.

—— and Yael Aronoff (1998) "Domestic Determinants of Israeli Foreign Policy: The Peace Process from the Declaration of Principles with the PLO to the Interim Agreement with the Palestinian Authority," in Robert O. Freedman, ed., *The Middle East and the Peace Process*, University Press of Florida, pp. 11–34.

Aversa, Jeannine (2006) "Levey: Iran 'Central Banker of Terror'," Associated Press, August 28, at http://www.iranfocus.com

Avishai, Bernard (2011) "A Separate Peace," *The New York Times Magazine*, February 13: 37–50.

Azouri, Negib (Najib Azuri) (1905) *Le Reveil de la Nation Arabe dans l'Asie Turque*, Paris: n.p.

Bachi, Roberto (1974) *The Population of Israel*, Institute for Contemporary Jewry, Hebrew University of Jerusalem.

Barel, Zvi (2001) "A 'Looking Glass' Kind of Fascism," *Ha'aretz*, January 22.

Barnavi, Eli (ed.) (1992) *A Historical Atlas of the Jewish People*, Schocken Books.

Barnea, Nahum (2003) "Olmert Parts from the Territories," *Yediot Aharonot*, December 5 (Hebrew).

Beilin, Yossi (1999) *Touching Peace: From the Oslo Accord to a Final Agreement*, Weidenfeld and Nicolson.

Ben-Ami, Shlomo (2001) "Camp David Diaries," Parts I and II, Ma'ariv, April 6 and 13, in Middle East Media Research Institute, *Special Dispatch* no. 207, April 20, and *Special Dispatch* no. 209, April 24, at http://www.memri.org.

Ben-Aryeh, Yehoshua (1989–90) "The Residential Pattern in Eretz-Israel on the Eve of Zionist Settlement," in Y. Kolat (ed.), *History of the Jewish Community in Eretz-Yisrael since the First Aliyah: The Ottoman Period*, First Part, The Israel National Academy of Sciences and the Bialik Institute (Hebrew).

Ben-Gurion, David (1939) at the Mapai Central Committee, 12 September 1939, Labor Party Archive, 23/39, cited in Segev 2000:450.

Bentsur, Eytan (2001) *Making Peace: A First-Hand Account of the Arab–Israeli Peace Process*, Praeger.

Ben-Yehuda, Eliezer (1941) *Complete Writings of Eliezer Ben-Yehuda*, Ben-Yehuda Publishers (Hebrew).

Birnbaum, Ben, and Amir Tibon (2014), "How Close They Came," *The New Republic*, August 4, 31–43.

Black, Ian, and Benny Morris (1991) *Israel's Secret Wars: A History of Israel's Intelligence Services*, Grove Weidenfeld.

Brom, Shlomo (2006) "Possible Resolutions to the Conflict in the North," *Strategic Assessment* 9, 2 (August) 19–21.

Cahill, Thomas (1998) *The Gifts of the Jews: How a Tribe of Desert Nomads Changed the Way Everyone Thinks and Feels*, Doubleday.

Carmi, T. (ed.) (1981) *The Penguin Book of Hebrew Verse*, Penguin Books.

Cohen, Avner (1998) *Israel and the Bomb*, Columbia University Press.

—— (2010) *The Worst-Kept Secret: Israel's Bargain with the Bomb*, Columbia University Press.

Congressional Research Service (2010) *US Foreign Aid to Israel*, RL33222, at www.crs.gov.

Della Pergola, Sergio (1998) "Will There be More Mass Immigration?," in Alouph Hareven (ed.), *On the Way to Year 2000: More War or Progress to Peace*, Van Leer Institute (Hebrew).

—— (2007) "Sergio DellaPergola vs. the authors of 'Voodoo Demographics'," *Azure*, Winter, at www.azure.org.

—— (2010) "Israel's Existential Predicament: Population, Territory, and Identity," *Current History* 109 (December): 383–9.

Divine, Donna Robinson (1994) *Politics and Society in Ottoman Palestine: The Arab Struggle for Survival and Power*, Lynne Rienner.

Dowty, Alan (1971) *The Limits of American Isolation: The United States and the Crimean War*, New York University Press.

—— (1984) *Middle East Crisis: US Decision-Making in 1958, 1970, and 1973*, University of California Press.

—— (1998, 2001a) *The Jewish State: A Century Later*, University of California Press.

—— (2000) "Much Ado About Little: Ahad Ha'am's 'Truth from Eretz Yisrael', Zionism, and the Arabs," *Israel Studies* 5, 2: 154–81.

—— (2001b) " 'A Question That Outweighs All Others': Yitzhak Epstein and Zionist Recognition of Arab Issue," *Israel Studies* 6, 1: 34–54.

—— (2006) "Despair is Not Enough: Violence, Attitudinal Change, and 'Ripeness' in the Israeli–Palestinian Conflict," *Cooperation and Conflict* 41, 1: 5–29.

Druyanov, A. (1933) "From My Archive – From the Notes of One of the Biluim," *Doar Hayom*, October 27 (Hebrew).'

Eban, Abba (1977) *An Autobiography*, Random House.

Eldar, Akiva (2002) "Moratinos Document – The Peace that Nearly Was at Taba," *Ha'aretz*, February 14.

El-Serraj, Eyad (1995) "Torture and Mental Health: A Survey of the Experience of Palestinians in Israeli Prisons," in Neve Gordon and Ruchama Marton (eds), *Torture: Human Rights, Medical Ethics, and the Case of Israel*, Zed Books for the Association of Israeli–Palestinian Physicians for Human Rights.

Epstein, Yitzhak (1907) "A Hidden Question," *Hashiloah* 17: 193–206, in Dowty 2001b.

Erlanger, Steven (2007) "Aid to Palestinians Rose Despite an Embargo," *New York Times*, March 21.

Ettinger, Shmuel (1976) "The Modern Period," in H. H. Ben-Sasson (ed.), *A History of the Jewish People*, Harvard University Press.

Farid, Abdel Magid (1991) *Nasser: The Final Years*, Ithaca Press.

Fattah, Hassan M. (2007) "For Many Palestinians, 'Return' Is Not a Goal," *New York Times*, March 26.

Foreign Relations of the Palestinian National Authority (2011), at http://en.wikipedia.org/wiki/Foreign_relations_of_the_Palestinian_National_Authority#Chronological__table_of_recognition_and_relations.

Friedman, Isaiah (1986) "The System of Capitulations and its Effects on Turco-Jewish Relations in Palestine, 1856–1897," in David Kushner (ed.), *Palestine in the Late Ottoman Period: Political, Social, and Economic Transformation*, Yad Yitzhak Ben Zvi and E. J. Brill.

Furlonge, Geoffrey (1969) *Palestine is My Country: The Story of Musa Alami*, Praeger.

Garfinkle, Adam M. (1991) "On the Origin, Meaning, Use, and Abuse of a Phrase," *Middle East Studies*, 27 (October): 539–50.

Ginzberg, Asher (Ahad Ha'am) (1891) "Truth from Eretz Yisrael," *Hamelitz*, June 19–30, in Dowty 2000.

Goldstone, Richard (2011) "Reconsidering the Goldstone Report on Israel and War Crimes," *Washington Post*, April 1.

Gordon, Aaron David (1938) *Selected Essays*, League for Labor Palestine.

Gorny, Yosef (1987) *Zionism and the Arabs, 1882–1948: A Study of Ideology*, Clarendon Press.

Ha'aretz (2003) "New Year Supplement: The Price of the Settlements," October 7.

Ha'aretz (2006) "Policy guidelines of the new government," May 4.

Halkin, Hillel (2002) "Why the Settlements Should Stay," *Commentary* 113, 6: 21–7.

Hamas (1988) Charter, at http://mideastweb.org/hamas.htm.

Hanieh, Akram (2001) "The Camp David Papers," *Journal of Palestine Studies* 30, 2: 75–97.

Harkabi, Yehoshafat (1972) *Arab Attitudes to Israel*, Keter Publishing House.

Herzl, Theodor (1997) *The Jews' State: A Critical English Translation*, Jason Aronson.

Hitti, Philip (1970a) *History of the Arabs from the Earliest Time to the Present*, 10th edn, Macmillan and St Martin's Press.

—— (1970b) *Islam: A Way of Life*, Gateway Editions.

Hizballah (1985) The Hizballah Program: An Open Letter at https://www.ict.org.il

Horowitz, Donald (1985) *Ethnic Groups in Conflict*, University of California Press.

Hourani, Albert (1991) *A History of the Arab Peoples*, Harvard University Press.

Inbar, Efraim (2000) "Arab–Israeli Coexistence: The Causes, Achievements and Limitations," *Israel Affairs*, 6 (Summer): 3–4.

—— and Giora Goldberg (1992) "The Likud: Moving Toward the Center," in Daniel J. Elazar and Shmuel Sandler (eds), *Israel at the Polls, 1988–1989*, Wayne State University Press.

Inside Israel (2016), "The Precise Number of Jews in the 'West Bank'," at http://www.israelnationalnews.com/News/News.aspx/213234.

International Atomic Energy Agency (2011) *Implementation of the NPT Safeguards Agreement and Relevant Provisions of Security Council Resolutions in the Islamic Republic of Iran*, May 24, at http://www.iaea.org.

Israel Central Bureau of Statistics (2011) Press Release, May 8, at http://www1.cbs.gov.il.

Israel Ministry of Defense, Office of the Co-ordinator of Government Operations in Judea, Samaria, and the Gaza District (1987) *Judea, Samaria, and the Gaza District, 1967–87: Twenty Years of Civil Administration*, Carta.

Israel Palestine Center for Research and Information (2001) – *Democratizing the Refugee Issue – Survey Results*, August, at http://www.ipcri.org/Publications/Research and Information.

Israel Radio (2005) "Another Matter," February 10, at http://www.jewishvirtuallibrary.org.

Jerusalem Media and Communications Center (1999–2011) Public Opinion Polls: no. 31, March 1999; no. 37, June 2000a; no. 39, December 2000b; no. 43, December 2001; no. 45, May 2002a; no. 47, December 2002b; no. 49, October 2003; no. 51, June 2004; no. 60, September 2006; at http://www.jmcc.org/polls.

—— (2000b) in cooperation with the Steinmetz Center for Peace Research, Tel Aviv University, December, Public Opinion Poll no. 39, Part Two, *Four Months after the Beginning of the Palestinian Intifada: Attitudes of the Israeli and Palestinian Publics Towards the Peace Process*, at http://www.jmcc.org/polls.aspx.

—— (2011b) Survey Question: Is a Two-State Solution or a Bi-National State the Preferred Solution for the Palestinian–Israeli Conflict? (Trend since January 2011), at http://www.jmcc.org/polls.aspx.

Johnson, Lyndon (1971) *The Vantage Point: Perspectives of the Presidency, 1963–1969*, Holt, Rinehart, and Winston.

Kahan Commission (1983), Israel Ministry of Foreign Affairs, *Report of the Commission of Inquiry into the events at the refugee camps in Beirut*, www.jewishvirtuallibrary.org/jsource/History/**kahan**.

Karsh, Efraim (2003) "Revisiting Israel's 'Original Sin': The Strange Case of Benny Morris," *Commentary* 116, 2: 46–50.

—— (2005) "Resurrecting the Myth: Benny Morris, the Zionist Movement, and the 'Transfer' Idea," *Israel Affairs* 11, 3: 469–90.

Katz, Elihu (1988) *Jerusalem Post International Edition*, August 28.

—— (1989) "Majority Hawkish, but Dovish Trend Seen," *Jerusalem Post International Edition*, February 18.

—— and Hannah Levinsohn (1991) "Poll: 75% Support the Return of Territories for a Peace Agreement," *Yediot Ahronot*, June 21.

——, —— and Majid Al-Haj (1991) *Attitudes of Israelis (Jews and Arabs) towards Current Affairs*, Publication no. (S)EK/1129/E, January 10, Guttman Israel Institute of Applied Social Research.

Kerry, John (2016) "Remarks on Middle East Peace," December 28, https: www.state.gov.

Khalidi, Rashid (1997) Palestinian Identity: The Construction of Modern National Consciousness, Columbia University Press.

—— (2001) "The Centrality of Jerusalem to an End of Conflict Agreement," *Journal of Palestine Studies* 30, 3: 82–7.

—— (2002) "Toward a Clear Palestinian Strategy," *Journal of Palestine Studies* 31, 4: 5–12.

—— (2004) *Resurrecting Empire: Western Footprints and America's Perilous Path in the Middle East*, Beacon Press.

—— (2009) *Sowing Crisis: The Cold War and American Dominance in the Middle East*, Beacon Press.

Khalidi, Walid (ed.) (1987) *From Haven to Conquest: Readings in Zionism and the Palestine Problem until 1948*, Institute for Palestine Studies.

—— (2005) "Why did the Palestinians Leave, Revisited," *Journal of Palestine Studies* 34, 2: 42–54.

Kifner, John (2000) "Talks Stir Memories but Not Much Hope for Refugees in Lebanon," *New York Times*, July 12.

Kimmerling, Baruch, and Joel Migdal (1993) *Palestinians: The Making of a People*, Free Press.

Kirkbride, Sir Alec (1976) *From the Wings: Amman Memoirs 1947–1951*, Frank Cass.

Kleinberg, Aviad (2002) "Back to the Barracks," *Ha'aretz*, September 28, http://www.haaretzdaily.com.

Kornberg, Jacques (1993) *Theodor Herzl: From Assimilation to Zionism*, Indiana University Press.

Laqueur, Walter and Barry Rubin (eds) (1984) *The Israel–Arab Reader: A Documentary History of the Middle East Conflict*, 4th edn. Penguin Books.

—— (1995) *The Israel–Arab Reader: A Documentary History of the Middle East Conflict*, 5th edn. Penguin Books.

—— (2008) *The Israel–Arab Reader: A Documentary History of the Middle East Conflict*, 7th edn. Penguin Books.

Laqueur, Walter and Dan Schueftan (eds) (2016), *The Israel-Arab Reader: A Documentary History of the Middle East Conflict*, 8th edn. Penguin Books.

Laskov, Shulamit (1982) *Writings in the History of Hibat Tsion and the Settlement of the Land of Israel*, vol. 1, Hakibbutz Hameuchad (Hebrew).

Lehrs, Lior (2016) "Jerusalem on the Negotiating Table: Analyzing the Israeli-Palestinian Peace Talks on Jerusalem (1993–2015)," *Israel Studies* 21, 3: 179–205.

Lewis, Bernard (1963) *Istanbul and the Civilization of the Ottoman Empire*, University of Oklahoma Press.

—— (1968) *The Emergence of Modern Turkey*, 2nd edn, Oxford University Press.

—— (1984) *The Jews of Islam*, Princeton University Press.

—— (1993) *The Arabs in History*, new edn, Oxford University Press.

—— (2002) *What Went Wrong? Western Impact and Middle Eastern Response*, Oxford University Press.

Maalouf, Amin (1984) *The Crusades through Arab Eyes*, Schocken Books.

Makovsky, David and Eran Benedek (2003) "The 5 Percent Solution," *Foreign Policy* 82, 5: 26–7.

Makovsky, David, Sheli Chabon and Jennifer Logan (2011), Imagining the Border: Options for Resolving the Israeli–

Palestinian Territorial Issue, January, at http://www.washington institute.org

Malamat, Abraham (1976) "Origins and the Formative Period," in H. H. Ben-Sasson (ed.), *A History of the Jewish People*, Harvard University Press.

Malley, Robert, and Hussein Agha (2001) "Camp David: Tragedy of Errors," *New York Review of Books*, August 9.

Mandel, Neville (1976) *The Arabs and Zionism before World War I*, University of California Press.

Martin, Robert (1983) *Spiritual Semites: Catholics and Jews during World War II*, Catholic League for Religious and Civil Rights.

Masalha, Nur (1991) "A Critique of Benny Morris," *Journal of Palestine Studies* 21, 1: 90–7.

Mattar, Philip (1988) *The Mufti of Jerusalem: Al-Hajj Amin al Husayni and the Palestinian National Movement*, Columbia University Press.

McCarthy, Justin (1990) *The Population of Palestine*, Columbia University Press.

Meir, Golda (1962) Address to the United Nations General Assembly, October 9. Repr. in Laqueur and Rubin 1984: 164–7.

—— (1975) *My Life*, Putnam.

Meister, Robert (2002) "Human Rights and the Politics of Victimhood," *Ethics and International Affairs* 16, 2: 91–108.

Melman, Yossi (2011a), "Former Mossad Chief: Israel Air Strike on Iran 'Stupidest Thing I Have Ever Heard,' " *Ha'aretz*, May 7.

Merom, Gil (2003) "The Architecture and Soft Spots of Israeli Grand Strategy," in Bradford A. Lee and Karl F. Walling (eds), *Strategic Logic and Political Rationality*, Frank Cass.

Middle Eastern Affairs (1956) "Gamal Abdul Nasser's Speech of 31 August 1955," December.

Mitchell, Thomas (2000) *Native vs. Settler: Ethnic Conflict in Israel/ Palestine, Northern Ireland, and South Africa*, Greenwood Press.

Morris, Benny (1988) *The Birth of the Palestinian Refugee Problem, 1947–1949*, Cambridge University Press.

—— (2001) *Righteous Victims: A History of the Zionist–Arab Conflict 1881–2001*, Vintage Books.

—— (2002) "An Interview with Ehud Barak," *New York Review of Books*, June 13.

—— (2004) *The Birth of the Palestinian Refugee Problem Revisited*, Cambridge University Press.

Morse, Arthur D. (1968) *While Six Million Died*, Random House.

Musa, Na'il (2001) "Report," *Al-Hayat Al-Jedida* (Ramallah), February 20, World News Connection, FBIS-NES-2001–0220.

Muslih, Muhammad Y. (1988) *The Origins of Palestinian Nationalism*, Columbia University Press.

Nasrallah, Hassan (1999) "*Secretary General of Hizbullah Discusses the New Israeli Government and Hizbullah's Struggle Against Israel*," *Tishreen* (Damascus), June 21, at http://www.memri.org.

National Committee for the Heads of the Arab Local Authorities in Israel (2006) *The Future Vision of the Palestinian Arabs in Israel*, at http://www.adalah.org.

Oren, Michael B. (2002) *Six Days of War: June 1967 and the Making of the Modern Middle East*, Oxford University Press.

—— (2007) *Power, Faith, and Fantasy: America in the Middle East 1776 to the Present*, W. W. Norton.

Palestine Center for Policy and Survey Research (2003–16) Public Opinion Polls: no. 8, June 2003; no. 15, March 2005a; no. 17, September 2005b; no. 21, September 2006; no. 23, September 2007; no. 34, December 2009; Israeli–Palestinian opinion poll, March 20, 2010a; no. 38, December 2010b; no. 40, June 2011; special Gaza war poll, August 2014; no. 60, June 2016a; no. 61, September 2016b; at http://www.pcpsr.org.

Palestine Royal Commission, Great Britain (1937) *Report*, His Majesty's Stationery Office.

Palestinian Authority (2000) "The End of the Conflict," August 22, at minfo.ps/English.

Palestinian Central Bureau of Statistics (2004) Statistical Abstract of Palestine no. 4, at www.pcbs.gov.ps.

—— (2011) On the Eve of the International Population Day 11/7/2011, at http://www.pcbs.gov.ps.

Pape, Robert A. (2003) "The Strategic Logic of Suicide Terrorism," *American Political Science Review* 97, 3 (August): 343–61.

Parmenter, Barbara McKean (1994) *Giving Voice to Stones: Place and Identity in Palestinian Literature*, University of Texas Press.

Peleg, Ilan, and Dov Waxman (2011) *Israel's Palestinians: The Conflict Within*, Cambridge University Press.

Penslar, Derek (2003) "Zionism, Colonialism, and Postcolonialism," in Anita Shapira and Derek Penslar (eds), *Israeli Historical Revisionism: From Left to Right*, Frank Cass.

Pundak, Ron (2001) "From Oslo to Taba: What Went Wrong," *Survival* 43 (Autumn): 31–45.

Rabinovich, Itamar (1998) *The Brink of Peace*, Princeton University Press.

Ravid, Baruch (2016), "Kerry: Israel and Palestinians headed for binational state, world must act or shut up," *Ha'aretz*, September 26.

Reiter, Yitzhak (2010) "Religion as a Barrier to Peace in the Israeli–Palestinian Conflict," in Yaacov Bar-Siman-Tov, ed., *Barriers to Peace in the Israeli–Palestinian Conflict*, Jerusalem Institute for Israel Studies.

Remez, Didi (2000) *Facts on the Ground since the Oslo Agreements*, at http://www.peace-now.org.il/.

Remnick, David (2006) "The Democracy Game," *The New Yorker*, February 27: 58–69.

Riad, Mahmoud (1981) *The Struggle for Peace in the Middle East*, Quartet Books.

Ross, Dennis (2002) "Yasir Arafat," *Foreign Policy*, July–August: 18–26.

—— (2004) *The Missing Peace: The Inside Story of the Fight for Middle East Peace*, Farrar, Straus and Giroux.

Roth, Cecil (1961) *History of the Jews*, Schocken.

Sadat (el-Sadat), Anwar (1979) *In Search of Identity: An Autobiography*, Harper and Colophon Books.

Schiff, Ze'ev (2001) "Misreading History Risks Catastrophe," *Ha'aretz*, April 5.

—— and Ehud Ya'ari (1986) *Israel's Lebanon War*, Unwin.

Segal, Jerome M. (1997) *Is Jerusalem Negotiable?*, Final Status Publications Series no. 1, Israel/Palestine Center for Research and Information, July.

Sha'th, Nabil (2000) "Interview," ANN Channel (London) (October 7, 2000), Media Research Institute *Special Dispatch* no. 134, October 8, at http://www.memri.org.

Shallah, Ramadan (2001) "Interview," *BBC Summary of World Broadcasts*, November 3.

Shamir, Jacob and Khalil Shikaki (2002) "Determinants of Reconciliation and Compromise among Israelis and Palestinians," *Journal of Peace Research* 39, 2: 185–201.

—— and Michal Shamir (1993) *The Dynamics of Israeli Public Opinion on Peace and the Territories*, Research Report no. 1, Tami Steinmetz Center for Peace Research, Tel Aviv University, December.

Sharon, Ariel (2004) "PM Sharon's Speech at the Herzliya Conference," December 12, Israel Prime Minister's Office, at http:// www.pmo.gov.il/PMOEng/Archive/Speeches/2004/12/ Speech161204.htm.

Shavit, Ari (2000a) "My Right of Return," *Ha'aretz*, August 18 (Hebrew).

Sheleg, Yair (2002) "Demographic Balancing Acts," *Ha'aretz*, June 13 (Hebrew).

Sher, Gilead (2001) *Just Beyond Reach: The Israeli–Palestinian Negotiations 1999–2001*, Yediot Ahronot (Hebrew).

Shikaki, Khalil (2001) "The Next Step toward Peace," *Jerusalem Report*, March 12.

Shragai, Nadav (2002) "Peace Now Survey: Most Settlers Would Pack Up and Leave Quietly," *Ha'aretz*, July 25 (Hebrew).

Siegman, Henry (2001) "Israel: A Historic Statement," *New York Review of Books*, February 8.

Smith Research Center (1986–9), polls reported in *Jerusalem Post*, October 2, 1986; *Near East Report*, July 25, 1988; *New York Times*, April 2, 1989.

Smith, Rupert (2005) *The Utility of Force: The Art of War in the Modern World*, Allen Lane.

Sontag, Deborah (2001) "Quest for Middle East Peace: How and Why it Failed," *New York Times*, July 26.

Stavenhagen, Rodolfo (1996) *Ethnic Conflicts and the Nation-State*, Macmillan Press and St Martin's Press.

Stone, Russell (1982) *Social Change in Israel: Attitudes and Events, 1967–1979*, Praeger.

Tamari, Salim (2000) "The Dubious Lure of Binationalism," *Journal of Palestine Studies*, 30, 1: 83–7.

Tami Steinmetz Center for Peace Research (1995–2016) *Peace Index*, at http://spirit.tau.ac.il/socant/peace.

Telhami, Shibley (2010) *Annual Arab Public Opinion Survey*, Brookings Institution, August 5, at http://www.brookings.edu.

Tessler, Mark (2009) *A History of the Israeli–Palestinian Conflict*, 2nd edn, Indiana University Press.

Teveth, Shabtai (1985) *Ben-Gurion and the Palestinian Arabs, from Peace to War*, Oxford University Press.

Thomas, Troy S., Stephen D. Kiser, and William D. Casebeer (2005) *Warlords Rising: Confronting Violent Non-State Actors*, Lexington Books.

Toynbee, Arnold (1955) *A Study of History*, vol. 1, Oxford University Press.

—— (1961) *A Study of History*, vol. 12, Oxford University Press.

Truman, Harry S. (1965) *Memoirs*, vol. 2: *Years of Trial and Hope*, Signet Books.

Turki, Fawaz (1972) *The Disinherited: Journal of a Palestinian Exile*, Monthly Review Press.

Twain, Mark (1974) *The Innocents Abroad, or The New Pilgrims Progress*, American Publishing Company.

United Nations (2002) Security Council Resolution 1397, March 12, at http://www.un.org

United Nations (2009) *Five Years after the International Court of Justice Advisory Opinion: A Summary of the Humanitarian Impact of the Barrier*, Office for the Coordination of Humanitarian Affair, Occupied Palestinian Territory, July, http://www.ochaopt.org.

United Nations (2015) *Human Development Reports*, at http://hdr.undp.org.

United Nations General Assembly (2009) *Report of the United Nations Fact Finding Mission on the Gaza Conflict*, September 24, A/HRC/12/48.

United Nations Office of the Special Coordinator in the Occupied Territories (1999) "Special Focus: Donor Disbursements and Public Investment," at http://www.unsco.org.

United Nations Relief and Works Agency(UNRWA)(2015), Annual Operation Report, at www.unrwa.org/sites/default/files/content/resources/2015_annual_operation_report.pdf, p. 113.

United Nations Security Council (1956) Official Records S/3706, October 30.

United States Department of State (2002) "President Bush Calls for a New Palestinian Leadership," at http://www.state.gov.

—— (2001) *Sharm El-Sheikh Fact-Finding Committee Report*, April 30, at http://www.state.gov.

United States Department of State (2003) "A Performance-Based Roadmap to a Permanent Two-State Solution to the Israeli–Palestinian Conflict," Press Statement, Office of the Spokesman, April 30, at http://www.state.gov.

United States White House (2001) "President Bush Speaks to United Nations," November 10, at http://www.whitehouse.gov.

—— (2004) "President Bush Commends Israeli Prime Minister Sharon's Plan," April 14, at https://georgewbush-whitehouse.archives.gov.

Weber, Max (1968) "Ethnic Groups," in Guenther Ross and Claus Wittich (eds), *Max Weber, Economy, and Society: An Outline of Interpretive Sociology*, vol. 1, University of California Press.

Wiesel, Elie (1969) *Night*, Avon Books.

Wistrich, Robert (1991) *Antisemitism: The Longest Hatred*, Schocken.

Ya'ari, Ehud (2002) "The Israeli–Palestinian Confrontation: Toward a Divorce," *Jerusalem Issue Brief* 1, June 30, Jerusalem Center for Public Affairs.

—— (2006) "The *Muqawama* Doctrine," *Jerusalem Report* 17, 15 (November 13): 60.

Yaniv, Avner (1990) "Israel National Security in the 1980's: The Crisis of Overload," in Gregory S. Mahler (ed.), *Israel after Begin*, SUNY Press.

Yediot Ahronot (2004a) May 5; (2004b), October 25; (2005, August 19, Jewish Virtual Library, at http://www.jewishvirtual-library.org.

YNet News (2011) "I felt weight of Jewish history on my shoulders," January 28, at http://www.ynetnews.com.

Zimmerman, Bennett, Roberta Seid and Michael L. Wise (2006) *The Million Person Gap: The Arab Population in the West Bank and Gaza,* Mideast Security and Policy Studies No. 65, The Begin-Sadat Center for Strategic Studies, February.

Index